BELOMOR

*Criminality and Creativity
in Stalin's Gulag*

Myths and Taboos in Russian Culture

Series Editor:
Alyssa Dinega Gillespie—*University of Notre Dame, South Bend, Indiana*

Editorial Board:
Eliot Borenstein—*New York University, New York*
Julia Bekman Chadaga—*Macalester College, St. Paul, Minnesota*
Nancy Condee—*University of Pittsburgh, Pittsburgh*
Caryl Emerson—*Princeton University, Princeton*
Bernice Glatzer Rosenthal—*Fordham University, New York*
Marcus Levitt—*USC, Los Angeles*
Alex Martin—*University of Notre Dame, South Bend, Indiana*
Irene Masing-Delic—*Ohio State University, Columbus*
Joe Peschio—*University of Wisconsin-Milwaukee, Milwaukee*
Irina Reyfman—*Columbia University, New York*
Stephanie Sandler—*Harvard University, Cambridge*

BELOMOR

Criminality and Creativity in Stalin's Gulag

Julie Draskoczy

Boston 2018

Library of Congress Cataloging-in-Publication Data:
A bibliographic record for this title is available from the Library of Congress.

Copyright © 2014 Academic Studies Press
All rights reserved.

ISBN 978-1-618118-23-3 (paper)
ISBN 978-1-618112-88-0 (cloth)
ISBN 978-1-618112-89-7 (electronic)

Book design by Adell Medovoy
On the cover: illustration from the USSR in Construction (*SSSR na stroike*).
Reproduced with permission of Productive Arts.

Published by Academic Studies Press in 2018
28 Montfern Avenue
Brighton, MA 02135, USA
press@academicstudiespress.com
www.academicstudiespress.com

For my parents, with boundless gratitude

Table of Contents

Acknowledgments — 9

A Note on the Text — 10

Preface — 11

Introduction: Born Again: A New Model of Soviet Selfhood — 17

I: The Factory of Life — 41

II: The Art of Crime — 76

III: The Symphony of Labor — 110

IV: The Performance of Identity — 145

V: The Mapping of Utopia — 165

Epilogue — 197

List of Figures — 201

Notes — 205

Bibliography — 233

Index — 246

Acknowledgments

This project has benefited from the insights of numerous colleagues. I would first like to thank heartily my dissertation committee, in particular my inimitable and indefatigable advisor, Nancy Condee. I am especially grateful for the generous mentorship of Cynthia Ruder, without whose early assistance this work would not have been possible. I am deeply indebted to the wit and wisdom of those I met at the "Memorial" human rights center. While I am grateful to all of the staff at the St. Petersburg and Moscow locations, I would like especially to thank Viacheslav Dalinin and Boris Mirkin for sharing their stories with me. For their seemingly endless help with the Russian language, I must recognize the patient and benevolent teachers at St. Petersburg State University's philological department. Alyssa DeBlasio, Drew Chapman, and Olga Klimova provided emotional support during the long years of research that culminated in this book. I benefited greatly from the shrewd guidance of J. P. Daughton and R. Lanier Anderson, the directors of the Mellon Fellowship at Stanford University, while transforming my dissertation into a book manuscript. Members of the Slavic department at Stanford University read early pieces of this project, and I would like to acknowledge Gabriella Safran, Grisha Freidin, and Monika Greenleaf for their helpful edits. The manuscript also benefited from commentary and suggestions by Sasha Senderovich and Irina Erman and from the astute permissions advice of James Thomas. I extend my deep gratitude to the Jewish Community High School of the Bay for their generous support of this project. Last but most certainly not least, I offer my endless appreciation to Philip Zigoris for being my rock.

A note on the text

The Library of Congress system of transliteration has been used throughout the text for Cyrillic characters. A few exceptions occur with more notable and well-recognized names, such as Fedor Dostoevsky, Maxim Gorky, Vladimir Mayakovsky, and Leon Trotsky.

Unless otherwise cited, all translations from the Russian language are mine.

Preface

> I with the pen, you with the shovel—together we built the canal.[1]
> —Vladimir Kavshchyn, Belomor prisoner

Dmitry Likhachev, a preeminent Russian scholar and historian, served time in two of the most infamous Soviet prison camps—Solovki and Belomor. In his memoirs he describes the irony of incarceration in the Gulag:

> When you consider [it], our jailers did some strange things. Having arrested us for meeting at the most once a week to spend a few hours in discussion of philosophical, artistic, and religious questions that aroused our interests, first of all they put us together in a prison cell, and then in camps, and swelled our numbers with others from our city interested in the resolution of the same philosophical questions; while in the camps we were mixed with a wide and generous range of such people from Moscow, Rostov, the Caucasus, the Crimea, and Siberia. We passed through a gigantic school of mutual education before vanishing once more in[to] the limitless expanses of the Motherland.[2]

Likhachev's recollection gets to the heart of just one of the many inconsistencies structuring the Soviet prison system: in separating unwanted elements from socialist society, the regime facilitated their communication. Likhachev's depiction addresses this irrationality while also highlighting the pedagogical function of prison, which he calls "a gigantic school of mutual education." Likhachev here reverses the standard relationship between homeland and prison camp. Rather than vanishing within the limitless expanse of the Gulag, prisoners are first educated in the Gulag and disappear only *after* their release from the camps. Here the camps are not unlike a hardscrabble type of higher education, similar in some ways to Maxim Gorky's education on the streets through low-skill professions in *My Universities* (1923) and mirrored in criminal slang terms for prison, such as "academy," "big school," and "college."[3]

Yet to imply that a Gulag camp could be more educational, more self-imprinting, than society itself seems controversial, almost repugnant. How do you make sense of a didactic death camp? In working with cultural narratives from Belomor, one of the most notorious and deadly prisons in the decades-long history of the Gulag, I was repeatedly faced by this uncanny educational quality. On the one hand, prisoners at the camp were remarkably creative. They worked as journalists, composed academic research papers, debated philosophical issues, and staged costumed operas. On the other hand, they lived in a landscape of destruction. The prisoners broke apart solid rock in twelve-hour shifts, dug a 227-kilometer canal with no modern equipment, and died by the thousands. How could one make sense of this seemingly irresolvable contradiction? That is the question this book tries to answer by asserting that such a paradox is in fact not a contradiction at all: the prison camp embraces the life-affirming thrust within violence itself, the possibility of creation within destruction.

I first became fascinated by Belomor because I could not believe that a Gulag prison, a place I would have assumed to be top secret during the ideologically charged atmosphere of the 1930s, was instead so candidly and positively depicted by prominent Russian figures. These camp enthusiasts were not necessarily official political representatives or devout Communist Party members—many were authors and artists, some of whom I counted among my favorites: Mikhail Zoshchenko, Viktor Shklovskii, and Maxim Gorky. These well-known Soviet writers, along with many others, depicted Belomor as a "school" of socialist education as well as a prison camp. While scholars and historians often explain away such statements by claiming that these artists had no choice, that they were intimidated by the State to make them, this did not seem like a satisfactory or sufficient explanation to me.[4] In addition to winning the support of artistic luminaries, the Belomor project spurred a play, a film, and innumerable other cultural products. I was continually left with a perplexing question: how was it possible to evince so much creativity in the face of death?

I could not stop thinking about the topic, and it eventually became the subject of my doctoral thesis. Yet I wanted to look at the project from a different angle. While published sources regarding the White-Sea Baltic Canal had long been available—a "history" of its construction was published in Russian as well as English in 1934—I was more curious about the prisoners who built the canal than about the outsiders who wrote about it. And here again Belomor represented a fortuitous opportunity: precisely because of the unique cultural dynamics of the project, the State preserved scores of documents regarding its history. The administration collected autobiographies of "shock-workers," the most productive laborers, and the camp newspaper held literary competitions that selected the best of the short stories, poetry, and plays of the prisoners. Russian archives still house these documents.[5]

I often wondered why so few people had looked at these texts, let alone analyzed them.[6] I think part of the reason is that it is assumed that the Belomor documents were mere propaganda items, not worthy of further study. This seems to be true even in relation to the collectively-written "history" of Belomor written by the well-known Soviet authors I mentioned. Even with these famous contributors, it took some time and a few insightful scholars, such as Cynthia Ruder, to demonstrate that this was a complex text worth studying. Perhaps the same is also true of these prisoner texts, with the added difficulty that they were stored in Moscow archives and not on a library shelf. And while it is important to study propaganda, no matter how consistent it might be, I noticed that these texts were not necessarily homogeneous, which deepened their mystery and complexity. The more I worked with Belomor narratives of all types, the more I found a multiplicity of approaches. Rather than actors in masks, brainwashed automatons, or self-serving careerists, the prisoners at Belomor were a mix of all three and more. While some worked to gain special privileges or because of psychological shame and peer pressure, others worked because they believed in the socialist system of education through labor, re-forging.

While it may be controversial to claim that prisoners in a labor camp believed in the very system incarcerating them, the idea seems less absurd when one considers Belomor within the broader context of the Gulag, and even the Soviet Union. Not only did the camps house, clothe, and feed the prisoners—however terribly—during the massively traumatic periods of famine and collectivization, the inmates served as a surrogate family for many criminals orphaned by the violence of the Civil War. In addition, the notion of dedication in the face of oppression is not unusual in Russian history; many victims of Stalin's purges fervently believed in the Soviet project, even when faced with execution.

I must pause here and appreciate the academic and intellectual climate in which I currently write, since to make such claims during the Cold War would not have been possible. To even hint that the camps were anything other than death machines, or that prisoners could have been proud of their labor performed at Gulag sites, would have made one an apologist for one of the darkest legacies of the twentieth century. Yet to acknowledge the creative fecundity at Belomor is not to ignore or belittle the many lives that were destroyed there. Just the opposite: acknowledging the creativity at the camps in the face of annihilation, and asserting that some prisoners might have bought into the project, is precisely what will help us to understand the mechanisms of Stalinism. It is much more frightening to realize that some prisoners could have "believed" in the camps than to assume they were all dissidents, since this fact demonstrates just how powerful and pervasive Soviet propaganda truly was. Casting the Soviet Union as entirely evil, and all prisoner responses as monologic in their contestation of the regime is just as misguided as proclaiming that the Soviet Union was the fairest and best country in the world. Both viewpoints are equally one-dimensional.

Working with Belomor narratives gave me a far more nuanced point of view, showing me that prisoners understood their time in the camp in varied ways. With this backdrop in mind, we can more fully understand the complexity of Stalinism. And the more I studied Belomor, the more I came to see the prison camp as a microcosm of Stalinism, a distillation of the many paradoxes that framed the Soviet experience. The camp was a synecdoche for the Soviet Union, the representation of a whole with a part. It contained all the necessary elements: oppression, ideological indoctrination, utopianism, the New Man, the Cultural Revolution, achievement through labor, cultural richness, whisperers and liars, fudged work reports, and the desperation to "catch up" with the West technologically. If the "whole notion of transformation [...] was at the heart of the Soviet project,"[7] Belomor mirrored this desire for conversion with its penal philosophy of re-forging (*perekovka*). At Belomor, common criminals would be re-born as socialist subjects. The key motifs around which this book is organized all reverberate with features of the larger Soviet experience.

Finally, Belomor made me think about the implications of incarceration in the most general of senses. I could not help but notice commonalities between these prison narratives and others. Certain questions kept persisting. Why are prisons so often sites of intense creativity? What happens to the mind when the body is locked up? How does the physical restriction of space affect one's psychology? Should prisons be for rehabilitation or punishment? What is the allure of crime itself? These questions were brought to life in me in the most powerful of ways when I had the personal experience of teaching Soviet history, among other topics, in San Quentin State Prison while revising this book. My group of students—twelve male inmates of varying ages, races, and ethnicities—taught me just as much as I taught them. I was surprised by their tepid, nonplussed reactions to horrific portions of Gulag memoirs. I was also intrigued by the correspondences between a contemporary California prison and a 1930s Soviet labor camp, both of which were mired by paradoxes and framed with the languages of rehabilitation. My geographic location seemed extraordinarily appropriate for revising this manuscript and the ideas within it, since California, according to some government analysts, had undertaken the largest prison-building and prison-filling project "in the history of the world."[8] Some researchers even referred to the state's massive penal system as the "Golden Gulag."[9]

Nevertheless, Soviet incarceration was entirely unique, and part of my research was to ascertain just what made it different. In the end, it came down to one very simple, yet perhaps surprising, element: art. While many prisons seem to be sites of intense creativity, given their altered contexts of time and space, there was something uncanny about the Gulag's relationship to the aesthetic. Only in the Soviet context does art become so inextricably linked to labor and to the remaking of the human body. While creativity was certainly a mental escape from the prison walls, it was also a tool for the regime. With art, the authorities could not only motivate prisoners to work but could also commemorate and glorify their labor efforts. This phenomenon inevitably brings the body into any discussion of Russian culture. It is impossible to forget—and important not to underestimate—the role violence played in everyday life in the Soviet Union. Raw physicality invades every aspect of Soviet culture, a physicality only augmented by the viciousness of life in prison. The long arms of the State invaded not only the bodies of the prisoners at Belomor but also their minds, as the administration attempted to harness and control even the very mechanisms of creative expression.

Creativity and criminality were ubiquitous at Belomor, and each supported the other in the performance of identity. Stalinism itself, like the canal's construction, was paradoxical, convoluted, and messy in its wedding of the aesthetic with the corporeal. It was inspirational and devastating, creative and destructive in the most violent and physical of ways, in a way that blurred fact and fiction, just as so many Belomor authors did.

INTRODUCTION
Born Again: A New Model of Soviet Selfhood

> Ah, to be born again is as terrible as to die.[10]
> –Fedor Gladkov, *Cement* (1925)

In his autobiography the Belomor prisoner Andrei Kupriianov wrote, "No, I am not an alien element. I am united with the working class in soul, body, and blood. My father, mother, and I were all killed for the cause of the working class."[11] While his parents' deaths were literal, Kupriianov's own death was metaphorical—his former, criminal self had been killed to allow for the creation of a devoted Soviet citizen. Kupriianov immediately introduces physicality and violence into the understanding of his identity, directly placing creation alongside destruction in what is a mirror of the central thesis of this book.

Kupriianov was born in 1902 to a poor peasant family. After the death of his mother and father in 1918, he took the name Pavlov in an initial, symbolic transformation of identity. His parents were killed during the Russian Civil War, and he served in the Red Army for almost four years before returning home in 1921. After murdering a White Army bandit in a forest, he became more acquainted with the criminal world. He eventually planned to rob a wealthy businessman with a partner in crime, but it all went wrong: the intended robbery victim was killed in the tussle, and both criminals were sentenced to long prison terms. Kupriianov began reading avidly in the Kresty prison in Leningrad (St. Petersburg) and soon started writing short stories. The first time he saw his name in print— one of his stories was published in a newspaper—he rejoiced like a child. He was ultimately sent to Belomor, where he became "re-forged" into a laboring socialist citizen. Prison facilitated his artistic development; it was where he learned to love to read and where he began to write. The author declares his "old self" and family dead, and embraces his "new family": the USSR. He receives a distinct reward for his dedication: early release. Kupriianov receives the news that he is being freed while he is in the middle of writing his autobiography, and the timing hardly seems coincidental. He was a model worker and writer, and the canal administration needed his story to use as an exemplar for other prisoners. Art, in turn, facilitated not only an individual's re-forging—the ideological backbone of Stalin's White-Sea Baltic Canal, or Belomor—but also the re-forging of other prisoners who read about Kupriianov's path. Art here is not for entertainment purposes but has a specific and tangible function. It serves as evidence or proof of an individual prisoner's commitment to the socialist method of rehabilitation while also explaining the Soviet method of *perekovka* to other prisoners and, ultimately, the world.

Figure 1. An entrance to the prison camp at Stalin's White Sea-Baltic Canal. Stalin's portrait hangs at the top of the gate, above slogans concerning political re-education. Photograph reproduced with permission of Iurii Dmitriev.

Figure 2. A group of prisoners at the construction of the Stalin's White Sea-Baltic Canal. Photograph reproduced with permission of Iurii Dmitriev.

Convict laborers built Stalin's White-Sea Baltic Canal (*Belomorsko-Baltiiskii kanal im. Stalina*), or Belomor for short, in a mere twenty months from 1931-33. They were working with crude tools in unbelievably difficult working conditions. The connection between art and violence rendered the camp a site of both destruction and production. Thousands of prisoners lost their lives, while at the same time costumed plays were being staged; nature was permanently altered, while literary competitions were being organized. Yet rather than being a paradox, such anomalies exemplify Stalinist culture. In the industrializing push of Stalin's first Five-Year Plan (1928-32), the destruction of the old world facilitated the creation of the new, and art and culture were to be the handmaidens of a grand, material transformation. The prison, as a site of both intense creativity and physical violence, is an excellent example of this uncanny artistic-corporeal combination.

During the Soviet period, the Gulag became the principal site of formalized retribution. The Gulag, an acronym that referred to the central camp administration[12] but came to mean the Soviet prison system as a whole, was a complex institution. Far from being relegated to the Siberian tundra, it was urban and rural, with individual camps both large and small. The Gulag population included men, women, and children; the innocent and the guilty; political and criminal prisoners. Its function was both economic and social, it was a tool of both oppression and re-education. Scholarly debate continues regarding which of these purposes was more significant.[13]

Belomor: Criminality and Creativity in Stalin's Gulag explores prison narratives from the construction of Stalin's White Sea-Baltic Canal within the larger contexts of penal and Stalinist culture. From this analysis emerges a revised vision of the Soviet self, one that underscores the link between artistic expression and the physical body in the forging of socialist identity through performance. Belomor was touted as both a technological achievement of Stalin's first Five-Year Plan and a metaphorical "factory of life" (*fabrika zhizni*) for recalcitrant prisoners. Alongside the locks and dams, socialist subjects were made out of common criminals through the process of *perekovka*, or re-forging. According to this penal philosophy, the dual forces of physical labor and artistic expression had the power to, quite literally, re-create human beings. Yet the belief in the malleability of people did not begin with Belomor—it was an essential component of the Marxist understanding of human nature. The prison camp, as a zone both internal and external to the Soviet experience, simultaneously intrinsic and extrinsic, served as an ideal laboratory for the exploration of character transformation according to socialist ideals.

The Gulag: Aesthetically Productive, Physically Destructive

Prison in general—as a "total institution," in the parlance of Erving Goffman—is characterized by its separation from the outside world, a separation that is often visibly apparent in the physical setting of the establishment.[14] Total institutions render indistinguishable the boundaries between sleep, work, and play—activities that on the "outside" are normally conducted in different arenas with different people. This collapsing of barriers fosters an intense desire for the demarcation of space,[15] and the creation of numerous identities is a direct response to the forced homogenization that occurs behind bars. Members of total institutions undergo a "stripping" process upon entry, often losing their clothes, their hair, and even their names. As both a reaction to this theft and a survival mechanism, prisoners create stories.[16] Narratives of selfhood occur in numerous registers and various contexts within the Gulag, necessarily making it a site of active creativity, both of people and of texts.

Given the emphasis on the production of identity at Belomor in particular, selfhood becomes a central concept when one grapples with the camp's narratives. Research on this area, in turn, is indebted to the work of numerous scholars of Soviet subjectivity, most notably: Jochen Hellbeck's concept of creative selfhood, Irina Paperno's work on diaries and dreams, Thomas Lahusen's extended analysis of *perekovka* and re-writing of the self, and Igal Halfin's exploration of communist autobiographies as conversion narratives. Although it was released after I completed this book, Stephen Barnes' landmark *Death and Redemption* echoes my argument here, demonstrating that the Gulag camps went to great lengths to "reform" prisoners in a highly elaborate system of indoctrination in which *perekovka* remained a central philosophy. This cycle, as Barnes also notes, often occurred in repeating patterns of creation and destruction.[17]

In the prison's "production" of various selves, an individual prisoner may have multiple monikers: a prisoner number, a given name, and numerous nicknames. My notion of creative selfhood has much in common with Hellbeck's work on subjectivity and his assertion that the Stalinist period *produced* rather than destroyed individuals.[18] Yet my purpose here is not to use prisoner narratives to demonstrate that the prisoners truly believed in the regime or that they certainly did not. Some believed, others did not believe—the question is a spurious one. We do not have access to the prisoners' psyches to ascertain their "real" beliefs, beliefs that were uncertain, fluctuating, and difficult to express in the first place. Faith in and uncertainty about the Soviet project, I would argue, co-existed on an individual level.

Instead, this work analyzes prisoner narratives as a type of discourse, accentuating the complexity of life and death within the camp and, by extension, within the larger Soviet context. Each chapter takes up a central metaphor related to the canal's construction—the factory of life; the art of crime; the symphony of labor; the performance of identity; and the mapping of utopia—and demonstrates how these framing concepts relate to broader cultural trends within the Soviet Union. I often focus on the criminal realm, a subset of prisoners who not only represented the majority of the population throughout the camps' history, but whose way of life—language, mores, and music—had a significant impact on culture beyond the barbed wire. Since only criminal prisoners were eligible to take part in the process of re-forging at Belomor, the regime encouraged them to participate in literacy programs and writing competitions, which allowed for the production of a large body of criminal-written texts preserved in the Russian State Archive for Literature and Art (RGALI) and the State Archive of the Russian Federation (GARF). By analyzing these never-before-published materials, *Belomor* not only sheds light on this criminal population but also offers a new understanding of the group's relationship to political prisoners. Criminal-written autobiographies, poetry, and short stories lie at the heart of this trove of artistic texts, and they are interpreted alongside the political prisoners' conceptions of the criminal realm.

In the extension of Belomor tropes to the larger Soviet experience, two key characteristics become evident: the import of the physical body and the ubiquity of creative activity. The physical culture, or *fizkul'tura* movement, attested to the centrality of the physical body in the Soviet Union. In 1929 the holiday "Physical Culture Day" was created, with grand parades through Red Square highlighting the strapping physiques of young Soviet men and women. The emphasis on training the physical body that began in late 1920s and early 1930s continued into the 1940s and beyond, with fitness promoted as a vital feature of a good Soviet citizen.

Figure 3. A 1945 photo exhibit in Moscow that emphasized the importance of promoting physical fitness among youth. Russian Pictorial Collection, Box 29, Hoover Institution Archives.

Yet despite the athletic connotations, these parades were artistic productions rather than sporting events. The facts that they were carefully scripted and choreographed and that theater personnel were in charge of orchestrating them, demonstrate the inextricability of art and physicality.[19] Art, as a fiction-producing mechanism, was precisely what was needed to disguise broken bodies as healthy ones.[20] Art and physicality, as this monograph will demonstrate, reimagine themselves as creativity and destruction. The physicality that I am describing here is not limited to the boundaries of the human body; it is a capacious category that includes the tangibility of landscape, the materiality of text, and the corporeality of labor. Nature, text, and body are all violently destroyed and dramatically reimagined. Art is part and parcel of the physical—it serves as the vehicle by which the physical components of reality can be drastically refashioned.

Given that art and physicality are fundamental components of the Gulag experience, Belomor serves as an especially productive case study for understanding the mechanics of Stalinist culture. In response to the regime's demand for a multiplicity of cultural narratives within the face of destruction, Belomor produced selves as both re-forged beings (physical) and paper texts of autobiography (art). As Igal Halfin notes, "autobiography does not only express the self; it creates it."[21] Given that autobiography stems from the confessional mode, it is particularly conducive to re-forging narratives. For both, the destruction of the former, sinning self must occur before the new, textual self can be created.[22] In the highly industrialized atmosphere of Stalin's first Five-Year Plan (1928-32), the self becomes a ware. It is both metaphorical and material; it can be produced like a good on a factory line and altered according to the State's requirements. Although intended to follow strict ideological demands, these selves were anything but stable. Some might give voice to a newly forged self to disguise actual feelings of disloyalty, others might wholeheartedly believe in the Soviet project, and still others might be struggling with how to express themselves properly in what Stephen Kotkin would call "speaking Bolshevik." This multiplicity of self-narratives within the Gulag is mirrored in outside society by the requirement that all Communist Party members have an autobiography in their file, a text that could be re-written numerous times over the course of one's life, thus implying that the past could be edited and crafted.[23] Despite prison seeming to be "the least intellectual of places," there "concern about words and verbalized perspectives [...] plays a central and feverish role."[24] The highly charged atmosphere of incarceration demands that discourse matter. The production of self-narratives is accompanied by the destruction of the physical body, creating a contradiction endemic to total institutions. The paradox is self-sustaining—the physical duress endured in prison is both a response to the environmental conditions and an impetus for escape by intellectual, spiritual means. In the Soviet Union, the body, especially in its relationship to labor, had a unique function that the prison setting only accentuated.[25]

While the regime intended artistic productions to inspire labor at Belomor, many Russian artists—including well-known authors such as Vladimir Mayakovsky and Maxim Gorky—understood art itself as a type of labor. This collapsing of creativity into labor is precisely what distinguishes the Russian experience: even beyond the Soviet period, writers acknowledge the transformative potential of both prison and labor. Nikolai Chernyshevskii penned his influential *What Is to Be Done?* (1863) while confined in Peter and Paul fortress in St. Petersburg; Fedor Dostoevsky wrote of the re-birth (*pererozhdenie*) of his convictions after time spent in prison.[26] Mayakovsky decided to become a poet only after spending time in prison, where he devoured books. Numerous Russian authors upheld labor as a physical activity that is both transformative and redemptive. Even while warning about the dangers of routinized labor, Dostoevsky singled out work as the single most important activity in prison, as it was the only way to survive such an oppressive environment. Mayakovsky, not unlike Gorky, equated his writing with labor and underlined its transformative potential: "My verse / by labor / will break the mountain chain of years, / and will present itself / ponderous, / crude, / tangible, / as an aqueduct / by slaves of Rome / constructed, / enters into our days."

Although it shared many qualities with total institutions, the Gulag also differed in many respects from the average prison. The fusion of socialist ideology with corrective labor was perhaps the most significant distinction, as Soviet prisons were intended not simply for punishment but for reformation, not simply for retribution but for conversion. This was particularly true in the example of the White Sea-Baltic Canal, where the penal philosophy of *perekovka* (re-forging) held sway. This concept asserted that criminals could be crafted into socialist citizens through the moralizing power of hard labor and socialist education. Another characteristic feature of the Gulag was the strategic function of creativity, particularly at Belomor—it was not just labor that would set the prisoners free, but also the artistic articulation of their new selves. This adeptly encapsulated the creative/physical duality endemic not only to Belomor but also to Stalinist culture. While social mobility in most total institutions is severely restricted between inmates and staff,[28] barriers among ranks were often porous in Soviet prisons. Sergei Alymov, a Belomor prisoner, participated in the publication of the official history of the construction effort with an editorial collective composed entirely of non-prisoners. Naftalii Frenkel', the purported originator of the inhumane work-for-food system,[29] was himself a prisoner at Solovki, one of the first camps in Gulag history, before he rose in the ranks of the regime's administration and eventually achieved the title "Hero of Socialist Labor." The reverse path was also possible: many of the most prominent figures in the canal's administration were later purged from the Communist Party altogether.[30]

The inherent industrial connotation of re-forging played a significant role in the creation of selfhood at the White Sea-Baltic Canal, and the close connection between industry and culture was ubiquitous in the Soviet Union in the 1920s and 1930s. "Forge" serves as both a noun and a verb: it is both the fire in which metal is melted and the process of melting itself. The term *perekovka*, therefore, succinctly captures the *perpetuum mobile* of transformation at Belomor: the prisoners themselves produce the furnace in which they are to be smelted. The fiery heat of industrialization renders self-molding permanent, physical, and transformative. This identity conversion, like a metallurgical process, would be violent, and the Soviet labor camp was an ideal site for building the New Man.

The recasting of industrial processes as cultural constructs began long before the construction of the White Sea-Baltic Canal; it was a favorite rhetorical device of the Bolsheviks. In a 1924 speech by Leon Trotsky, workers' clubs are cited as a "smithy" where proletarian culture is "forged."[31] In the violent and heady years following the Russian Revolution, a massive restructuring of culture and society occurred, one that was very often portrayed in metallurgical terms.[32] The concept of smelting is apparent in other utopian visions as well. In Book Three of Plato's *Republic*, the "myth of the metals," a fiction assuring citizens that they all have a bit of metal from the earth in their souls—gold, silver, or iron/bronze, depending on their level in society's hierarchy—is discussed in detail. This "noble lie" is intended to foster patriotism, as one who believes they literally come from the land will most likely be loyal to it. The prisoners at Belomor were encouraged to take pride in the canal project in a similar, fabricated fashion; since they are part and parcel of the industrialization plan—both metaphorically and literally—they must swear allegiance to the Soviet project.[33] Many prisoner narratives, in turn, imagine the project as a homeland, as more dear to them than their families, or even as a romantic lover.[34]

The violence inherent in the molding of prisoners' consciousnesses— as well as the ferocity that characterized the Gulag more generally—cannot be underestimated. This was a characteristic feature of Soviet ideology. The recent scholarly debate surrounding Soviet subjectivity too often miscalculates the role of violence. By applying Michel Foucault to the creation of selfhood, scholars like Igal Halfin, Jochen Hellbeck, and Oleg Kharkhordin understand Stalinist Russia as a largely successful project in the forging of modern subjectivity.[35] Even though these scholars' groundbreaking research is essential to my project, I believe something vital is lost in the appropriation of subjectivity and the widespread application of Foucault.[36] This view does not truly capture the collective violence endemic to the Soviet creation of selfhood, violence overwhelmingly apparent in the Belomor context. In addition, the use of Foucault does not allow the multiplicity of self-narratives to emerge in all of their complexity. As Jerrold Seigel notes of Foucauldian models of selfhood, "both bodies and selves are imprisoned inside the discourses or structures where their formation took place."[37] I instead posit Nietzsche— and by extension Maxim Gorky—as alternatives in the discussion of Stalinist selfhood. For Nietzsche, as for Gorky, selfhood becomes a task or achievement, with the distant, at times seemingly unrealizable, goal of the Übermensch as something that must be actively fashioned, often by way of a violent process. The self is not a stable concept, which makes it impossible to determine if a person "believed" in an ideology or not; it is, rather, the sum of an individual's drives and will that forces them to act, and the only conception of self can be one's construction of it.[38] While some might claim that my substitution of Nietzsche for Foucault is spurious given the former's significant influence on the latter, I would like to underscore here that I choose to emphasize Nietzsche through *his relationship* to Gorky. Gorky is the philosopher truly at the heart of this project, and it is by examining Gorky's affinity for Nietzsche that I hope to argue my claim that these two thinkers offer a much more appropriate blueprint for Soviet selfhood than does Foucault. Gorky was deeply influenced by Nietzsche's writing. Many noted the philosopher's wild popularity in the country, as the writer Vasilii Rozanov explained:

> Did we ever devote so much strength and enthusiasm, so much reading and so many sleepless nights to a Russian [...] as we have to Nietzsche in recent years? Nietzsche's "Zarathustra" has been quoted here like our most favorite Russian verses, like a cherished ... fairytale; Pushkin never knew a period of popularity comparable to our "Nietzschean period" at its height.[39]

In an alternative Nietzschean/Gorkyan model of selfhood, a framework emerges that allows for the inclusion of physical violence and a multiplicity of aestheticized selves. Rather than assuming a "successful," or total, construction of self, Nietzsche fosters an understanding of selfhood as perennial striving, as task or achievement that would closely follow the rhetoric of *perekovka*. The violence of the prison camp and the forging of individuals demonstrate the necessity of overtly introducing the body into the discussion of Soviet selfhood. Nietzsche imagines the body as a kind of political structure that is both complex and contradictory.[40] His Zarathustra claims, "The awakened and knowing say: body am I entirely, and nothing else; and soul is only a word for something about the body. The body is a great reason, a plurality with one sense, a war and a peace, a herd and a shepherd."[41] At Belomor the self was profoundly physical: not just created by autobiographies and other written texts, it was inscribed in flesh. The prisoners' aching muscles and sore limbs after a twelve-hour workday reminded them that they were being transformed not only mentally but physically, and their refusal to submit would be met with even more severe bodily consequences.

The well-known Gulag author Varlam Shalamov writes how the Gulag experience literally imprints itself on the prisoner: "On every face Kolyma wrote its words, left its mark, carved excess wrinkles, fixed eternally frostbite's stain, that indelible stamp, ineffaceable brand!"[42] Such evidence is *written* (*napisala*) on the face like a literary text; the physical and creative are combined in a paradoxically destructive way.[43] The body of the prisoner, in turn, can be understood as the sole reliable document of the camp experience.[44] The act of glimpsing a mirror in the Gulag captures the changing body as a textual testament to the horrific experience of the camps. Since mirrors were virtually nonexistent in the Gulag, many prisoners remember their first glimpse of their reflections as a painfully intense moment of *non-recognition*, a non-recognition that occurred because the faces' owners had changed so drastically that they no longer recognized their own features. Upon seeing a mirror for the first time in three years, the Gulag prisoner Ol'ga Adamova-Sliozberg searches for her face everywhere but is unable to find it. Finally she realizes that the worn and tired face of her mother is actually *her* reflection; the camps have aged her so greatly that she is unrecognizable to herself.[45] The camp memoirist and poet Irina Ratushinskaia also recalls her reflection as a painful (and male) one.[46] This inability to identify oneself actually reproduces the self—the healthy, pre-Gulag self along with the new, unfamiliar visage. This ability to see oneself outside of oneself is an odd and peculiar privilege, one that creates an additional text of corporeality almost akin to W. E. B. DuBois' concept of "double-consciousness."[47] As a corporeal existence is being destroyed, a new and unrecognizable textual body is being created.

According to Nietzsche, violence is inherent in the formation of society, a process he describes in terms uncannily similar to those of the Soviet project of re-forging:

> The welding of a hitherto unchecked and shapeless populace into a firm form was not only instituted by an act of violence but also carried to its conclusion by nothing but acts of violence—that the oldest "state" thus appeared as a fearful tyranny, as an oppressive and remorseless machine, and went on working until this raw material of people and semi-animals was at last not only thoroughly kneaded and pliant but also *formed*.[48]

Coupled with physical force (thousands of prisoners died in building a waterway that came to be known as the "road of bones") was ideological force. As prisoners toiled at Belomor, the regime transmogrified their minds as well as their bodies. Imbedded in the ideals of the Russian Revolution was a sense of aggressive transformation, and the Bolsheviks sought to re-mold forcefully those not willing to submit to their worldview. According to Lenin, Marxism had "assimilated and refashioned everything of value in the more than two thousand years of the development of human thought and culture."[49] The Communist Party, in turn, served as the vanguard of the proletariat. Their task was to actively lead the workers and peasants to consciousness, to help them make the pilgrimage from darkness to light. Not only Belomor but the entire Soviet project is modeled off of the assumption that *perekovka*—the potential for human self-transformation—is possible. Marxism-Leninism particularly embraced this possibility, since peasants and workers had to become enlightened, class-conscious citizens in the absence of the full development of capitalism.

A New Soviet Religion:
God-Building as Precursor to Perekovka

God-building (*bogostroitel'stvo*), a type of socialist religion that locates the divine within humankind rather than in the heavens, adeptly addresses the close link between religiosity and socialist idealism. Popular in the early years of the twentieth century but later deemed heretical in the Soviet Union,[50] god-building relates directly to Nietzschean philosophy, demonstrating that the thinker is relevant to Belomor as both a historical and a theoretical touchstone. Nietzsche recognized the societal function that Christianity fulfilled,[51] and in *The Gay Science* he acknowledges humanity's need to fill the void that the death of God has created.[52] So did the Bolsheviks, and the revolutionaries thought that god-building could serve as a substitute for deeply entrenched Orthodox tradition. The notion of god-building claimed that through communism men would become like God—imagining Bolshevism as a *literal*, not just *functional*, substitute for religion.[53] This positing of humankind above God echoed the Nietzschean Übermensch and created a quasi-religion, a phenomenon made evident by the ubiquitous spiritual terminology in *Thus Spake Zarathustra*. The idea of god-building gained credence among key thinkers in the early days after the revolution, including Anatolii Lunacharskii, Aleksei Bogdanov, and Maxim Gorky. Although the alleged "father of Socialist Realism" was forced to abandon his interest in the concept due to its "bourgeois" connotations, evidence of a Nietzschean influence is ubiquitous in Gorky's work and reconfigures itself as re-forging. Traces of god-building are apparent even in Gorky's most politically correct works; in Gorky's novel *Mother* (*Mat'*, 1907), heralded as a classic of socialist realism, the mother's evolving relationship to spirituality demonstrates clearly how revolutionary fervor can fill the vacuum created by the death of God.[54] Gorky's essential role in the cultural project of Belomor requires further elaboration on his proclivity for god-building, and his novel *Mother* is a useful starting point.

The mother in *Mother* is a symbolic, metaphorical mother to all. A universal mother figure can be used as a political tool; in the novel one of the protagonists insists, "We are all children of one mother—the great, invincible idea of the brotherhood of the workers of all the countries over all the earth."[55] This passage in *Mother* is later echoed in Gorky's 1934 speech to the All-Union Congress of Soviet Writers: "speaking figuratively and despite our age differences, we here are all children of one and the same mother—all-Union Soviet literature."[56] Casting ideological pronouncements in familial terms allows Gorky to naturalize them, adding both continuity and inclusivity. Similarly, Belomor prisoners were encouraged to think of themselves as members in the "workers' family," and they often described the educators in charge of their reformation as substitute parents. Given that many of the criminal prisoners were homeless or orphaned, the idea of belonging to a family—even if it was a metaphorical, oppressive one—likely had some appeal.

The idea of mothering and procreation morphed into Gorky's fascination with prisoner transformation and *perekovka*. The labor camp would be the mother of a new working class. Both god-building and the maternal impulse dovetailed with the author's largest philosophical and intellectual preoccupation: human fashioning. Whether it was the literal, biological creation of the human by the maternal womb or the transformation afforded by a personal journey or individual greatness, Gorky remained intrigued by the individual's ability for creation, journey, and self-discovery. Maintaining that humans were inherently malleable and eternally improvable, he believed in the potential for endless refinement through diligent effort.

Gorky's special relationship to the Belomor project allows for an understanding of his career as a symbolic representation of the ideals promoted at the camp.[57] Gorky was a staunch enthusiast of prisoner labor and even predicted the possibility of a waterway similar to Belomor in his early works; in the April 1917 issue of his journal *New Life* (*Novaia zhizn'*) he writes, "Imagine, for example, that in the interest of the development of industry, we build the Riga-Kherson canal to connect the Baltic Sea with the Black Sea [...] and so instead of sending a million people to their deaths, we send a part of them to work on what is necessary for the country and its people."[58] Gorky's condoning of Gulag camps such as Solovki and Belomor seems paradoxical to many scholars in light of his humanitarian endeavors, and some speculate either that Gorky was ignorant of the full extent of Stalin's butchery or that he was aware, but was in a position that necessitated acquiescence to safeguard his well-being.[59] When viewed in the context of his philosophical outlook on literature and labor, however, his support of prison camps seems not like an aberration but rather a natural extension of his belief in violent re-birth, a belief related to Marxist-Leninist ideology and the concept of god-building. Gorky sees people and language alike in the framework of craftsmanship. Perhaps his mistake was not so much his general support of Gulag projects, but his belief that human flesh can be formed like words on a page or cement in a factory. Gorky, after all, cared more about the craft than people themselves; in his 1928 essay "On How I Learned to Write" (*O tom, kak ia uchilsia pisat'*), he claimed that "the history of human labor and creation is far more interesting and meaningful than the history of mankind."[60] Gorky was key to the canal project because his philosophical interests exemplify the very core of Belomor: the violent transformation of people through creative acts.

Technology's magic demonstrated humans' usurpation of God in a tangible way, with the ever-widening capacity to harness and transform the natural environment showcasing the potential of man-made machines. Soviet pilots were imagined as literal incarnations of the New Man,[61] and the massive expansion of the Soviet aviation industry in the mid 1920s provided some of the most concrete evidence of human superiority over the divine. Short voyages known as "air baptisms" (*vozdushnye kreshcheniia*) supposedly eradicated peasants' belief in God while highlighting the majesty of Red aviation. In such "agit-flights," pilots would take Orthodox believers into the skies and show them that they held no celestial beings.[62] Those who participated in the flights would narrate their experiences to neighboring villagers, describing "what lies beyond the darkened clouds." This phrase served as the title of a 1925 essay by Viktor Shklovskii in which a village elder embarks upon a conversional agit-flight that he later recounts to his fellow peasants. Six years later, Shklovskii participated in the writers' collective that co-authored the now infamous monograph *History of the Construction of the White Sea-Baltic Canal*,[63] in which a different, often deadly, type of technological program offered the promise of conversion. In both instances, darkness will be overcome by the enlightening potential of socialist rationalism: aviation will liberate the peasants from their ignorant beliefs, just as labor will supposedly bring the Belomor prisoners to the light of Soviet ideology. Such endeavors occurred before the backdrop of a larger civilizing project, since both the rural reaches of peasant villages and the wild expanses of untouched Karelia necessitated modernization.

Yet could such projects ever be completed? Did the New Man really exist, and could his creation ever be achieved? The messianic vision of Soviet socialism necessitated that paradise lie always just out of reach. Similarly, Nietzsche posits the development into the Übermensch as a perennially elusive goal; like the Faustian concept of striving, the individual is forever trying to perfect oneself without necessarily ever achieving perfection. This constant yearning renders the present as the future, as the purpose of today is necessarily the reward of tomorrow. In the Soviet Union, the regime assured people that the difficulties they endured were required in order to reach the *svetloe budushchee* (radiant future), a utopia found at the end of an interminable road.[64] In the absence of an end result or final destination, the voyage itself becomes the site of cultural exploration.

Prisoners at Belomor used skills they had developed in the criminal world to manage and manipulate the prison system, and although they were encouraged to drown their past lives in the depths of the canal, they nevertheless used their life experiences as springboards for the articulation of their "new" lives. The regime encouraged prisoners to reinterpret their pasts in order to move beyond them, to craft a new, creative version of the self that was highly dependent on the power structures surrounding them. While Nietzsche would not have condoned this restraint of individuality, he certainly would have acknowledged the power of the State to undertake such a project—this is precisely why he found political regimes to be so dangerous and restrictive.[65] Yet the creative, aesthetic aspect of selfhood is apparent both at Belomor and within Nietzsche's work; the philosopher created an artwork of himself. He produced a literary narrative of his life as his ultimate statement of self,[66] just as the Belomor prisoners—and many others in the Soviet Union—had to cobble together coherent, fictional narratives about their own histories.[67]

While total institutions can be generally configured as creative locales, the Soviet context adds another dimension to such production. Unlike in the average prison, creative acts were not only supposed to serve as a coping mechanism or means of escape for the prisoner; instead, they were to facilitate his or her re-forging. Such a move places a convict in a double bind, as he or she is denied even the possibility of artistic freedom of expression, a realm that is theoretically characterized by individual inspiration. The forceful aestheticization that occurred at Belomor, in turn, is one of its most unusual and characteristic features. Perhaps the most well known image from the project is Aleksandr Rodchenko's photograph of a full orchestra playing before convict laborers in one of the newly completed locks. The viewer is not only struck by the seeming absurdity of such an incongruent combination (high culture + prison) but must also recognize the photograph as a beautifully composed art object unto itself. Despite the penal context, art abounded at Belomor. Some of the country's most recognized photographers documented the project, some of its most famous authors wrote about it, and some of its most important cultural icons served time at it. Criminal prisoners were expected, in turn, to craft laudatory allegiances to labor and socialism. This bizarre artistic richness renders the Gulag different from other prisons and speaks to its normative, totalizing atmosphere.

Art certainly appears in other unexpected punitive contexts—most significantly in the Nazi concentration camps of the Holocaust. Terezin stands out as a camp known for its production of both art and propaganda; art in the form of extensive children's drawings, propaganda in the form of sanitized documentary films that demonstrate the supposed humane conditions at the camp. While the connection between Nazism and Stalinism will be explored further later in the book, it suffices to note here that at Terezin the prisoners' art and the State's propaganda were more or less independent of each other; one did not facilitate the existence of the other. Yet in the Soviet example, the categories are collapsed. Prisoner art could be used as State propaganda, and State propaganda at times mimicked prisoner art. Such distinctions are less clear, and the end result, in some respects, is more nefarious.

Thomas Lahusen writes, "People, their deeds and works, are remembered by History only if they succeed as story."[68] Although focusing on criminal-written texts, the present volume attempts to preserve the Belomor story from multiple perspectives: the stories prisoners told themselves and each other as well as the story the regime foisted upon the incarcerated and the outside world. Grasping both the individual stories and the larger narrative of the project is the key to understanding Belomor. Yet while we acknowledge this fictional fecundity, it is necessary to remember that the Gulag was also a destructive entity. This seemingly paradoxical arrangement—life-creation in the face of death, religiosity in the wake of atheism—was endemic to the Stalinist worldview. Rather than remaining a contradiction, the dialectic of opposing forces sustained the socialist vision: in order to be born again, it was necessary first to die.

― INTRODUCTION ―

The Construction of Stalin's White Sea-Baltic Canal: A Brief History

The White Sea-Baltic Canal was built in a mere twenty months, a brief episode in the decades-long history of the Gulag. Yet this Soviet prison project is, perhaps more than any other, immortalized in the popular imagination of scholars and citizens. Pictures of Belomor wheelbarrows accompany nearly every overview article on Gulag history, and the project is cited in innumerable sources as the foundation of Soviet forced labor.

Figure 4. Prisoners work with wheelbarrows during the construction of Stalin's White Sea-Baltic Canal. Photograph reproduced with permission of Iurii Dmitriev.

Just one small section of the collectively written "history" of Belomor, "The Story of a Man's Re-forging," has been the subject of numerous analyses. In her recent monograph, Miriam Dobson repeatedly cites the Belomor model of prisoner narratives as a touchstone for her exploration of Khrushchev-era penal texts.[69] The project is perhaps the only Gulag experience to be preserved in material culture (the brand of Belomorkanal *papirosy*, or cigarettes, has now expanded to include a cheap vodka) and musical production (Belomorkanal is a *shanson* group that uses the cigarette label on their album covers). Kitschy items referencing the project are hawked at nostalgic tourist shops in the center of Moscow—you can purchase a "Belomorkanal" notebook for 200 rubles or a "Belomorkanal" ashtray for 380—and the camp serves as the inspiration for visual art and poetry in contemporary Russia. In the face of its rapid completion and ultimate failure as a technological achievement (the canal is barely used today), how can we explain the ubiquity of its cultural references and its continued importance in historical debates? It is the purpose of this book to explore this question, demonstrating how Belomor—with its uncanny blend of the physical and the aesthetic in the ultimate goal of performative self-transformation—exemplifies Stalinist cultural values. Belomor's aesthetic imagination distills key cultural tropes around which the structure of this book is organized.

Narrating the history of the desire to build a White Sea waterway will demonstrate how Belomor not only reaches forward in time by influencing Soviet history that is to come, but also maintains close connections to Tsarist-era desires, perhaps speaking to a broader imperialist-socialist continuum. The drive to build such a waterway has a long history. In the second half of the sixteenth century, mercantile ties were established between Western Europe and Russia, and in 1584 the Karelian city of Arkhangel'sk was founded as a trading port. English explorers were the first to propose a canal in order to open Moscow to northern trading routes.[70] The Russia Company, the major English shipping company that traded with Russia, understood the need for an uninterrupted waterway in northern Russia to shorten their trade route and make it less dangerous.[71] It was not until Peter the Great, however, that the idea gained more credence; in July of 1693, Peter made an arduous voyage by land and sea to Arkhangel'sk and realized the necessity of establishing an independent Russian fleet given the vast number of foreigners in northern Russia. He traveled on what became known as the *Osudareva doroga*, or the Tsar's Road, dragging his newly built fleet of ships overland from the White Sea to the Baltic Sea, for there was as yet no waterway.[72] The Tsar's Road would eventually become the pathway of the White Sea-Baltic Canal. Mikhail Prishvin's 1957 novel *The Tsar's Road* (*Osudareva doroga*), while focusing on the era of Peter the Great, also implies the egregious power, suffering, and loss of human life at the White Sea-Baltic Canal as a parallel example. Even before the actual construction of the canal, physical hardship and injustice had marred the natural landscape. Thousands of people traveled the Tsar's Road in August 1702 during the Great Northern War in the horrible conditions of penal servitude; as one laborer recalls, "There were three doctors on the entire expedition. The first—Vodka. The second—the Lash. The third—Death, that good aunt."[73] These extreme conditions were not so different from what would become life at BelBaltLag, the prison camp for the construction of the White Sea-Baltic Canal.

The first quarter of the nineteenth century began with a genuine battle for the construction of the White Sea-Baltic Canal, and in February 1827 the fisherman and supplier Fedor Antonov delivered a letter to the Karelian minister asking for a canal to be built. Local residents saw promise in the potential construction project, hoping that a waterway connecting the Karelian region with central Russia would end their economic and social isolation. Various parties submitted no fewer than fifteen proposals for such a project, but the government cited lack of funds and inappropriate timing as reasons for rejecting them. In 1868-69 private companies put together their own funding in light of the regime's inaction, but they were not able to raise enough money for the completion of a waterway. Finally, on 8 March 1886, the government reacted positively to the idea of the waterway, and began expeditions to explore the economic impact and feasibility of developing a canal, eventually publishing the results of the survey.[74] Despite the growing discussion of a White Sea-Baltic Canal in 1900-01,[75] due to the outbreak of World War I and the building of the Murmansk railroad in 1915 (which underscored the strategic and technical advantages of such a venture), the canal was never begun in Tsarist Russia.[76]

The project gained popularity after the 1917 revolution, as it represented an avenue for Soviet Russia to highlight its technological progress as a newly industrialized country. On 5 May 1930, the Politburo approved a resolution that would finally allow work to begin on the construction; in the initial plan, the canal was divided into two sections: southern and northern. The southern section was to be built to a depth of eighteen feet and completed in two years, with work beginning in 1931; the northern section, between Lake Onega and the White Sea, was to be handled by the OGPU, with costs minimized in light of the proposed exploitation of prison labor.[77] Stalin himself, in a message to Viacheslav Molotov, suggested the use of prisoner labor in order to cut costs after the 5 May presentation of the project.[78] After several further decrees, with additional revisions to the plan and the organization of operating and administrative committees for Belomorstroi (the Belomor Construction), authorities approved the work plan in its final form on 18 February 1931. The new plan relied exclusively on prisoner labor, reduced the depth of the canal to 10-12 feet in order to minimize costs,[79] set the completion date as no later than the end of 1932, and estimated a total cost of 60-70 million rubles for the project.[80] In November 1931 work officially began on the canal, and Genrikh Iagoda, head of the OGPU, took control of the project, signing the formal decree in which the other heads of the project are enumerated: Lazar' Kogan (director of the Belomor construction project), Iakov Rapoport (assistant director of the Belomor project), and Naftalii Frenkel' (director of labor) were among the most visible supervisors on the canal. While estimates of the number of prisoners passing through the canal project have ranged from 100,000 to 500,000, new research demonstrates that about 65,000 hands worked on it daily, with a total number of 143,000 prisoners working over the construction period. If we accept the Russian historian V. N. Zemskov's estimated mortality rate of 10% of the workers annually, approximately 25,025 prisoners died during the 21 months of constructing the canal. Yet this number would account only for immediate deaths and would not include the great number of prisoners who likely perished later as a consequence of the debilitating work of canal-digging.[81]

On 28 May 1933 the ship *The Chekist* sailed through the waterway, marking the first navigation of the canal, even as work on the project was still being finished.[82] On 2 August 1933, Viacheslav Molotov signed a decree announcing the official opening of the canal, and on 4 August 1933 the Soviet Union awarded various prizes and honors to the best officials, engineers, and workers on the canal.[83] The goal was achieved: what Tsarist Russia had aspired to for hundreds of years, the Soviet Union realized in just twenty months.

A historical survey of the interest in building a White Sea-Baltic waterway makes it possible to draw parallels between Tsarist and Soviet-era ambitions. The documented suggestions for the project in the 1800s include the notion of "civilizing" the wild reaches of Karelia, and argue that the connection of northern Russia to its central portion would allow money and people to flood into the region, introducing "culture" into the remote area.[84] This remained one of the key ideological motivators during the construction of the canal in the 1930s; in an August 1933 memo signed by Viacheslav Molotov, he notes the importance of the "colonization of the area" (*kolonizatsiia kraia*) and the increase of the population that would occur with the influx of workers.[85] Both the rehabilitation of prisoners and the stimulation of economic activity in the far North "would serve to transmit Soviet civilisation to the frontier."[86] The importation of a massive workforce to a sparsely inhabited area allowed for freed prisoners to remain in the region and build the population base. The Soviet goal was unequivocal—the waterway was intended to have a colonizing function by transmogrifying both landscape and people.

The harsh physical conditions and subsequent high fatality rate also link the construction of the White Sea-Baltic Canal with the Tsarist-era project of a boat conduit. Both the Tsar's Road and the pathway of the White Sea-Baltic Canal come to be known colloquially as the *doroga na kostiakh*, or the "road of bones," underscoring the interconnectedness of these two historical experiences and the brutality imbedded in the landscape. As with any colonizing project, violence cannot be subtracted from the equation. Interestingly, the *doroga na kostiakh* is mentioned in the Belomor volume *History of the Construction*, but only in order to contrast the supposedly humane, Soviet approach to the project with the deadly road-building done by prisoners during the Tsarist era, "The road of bones! says Deli. Karelians say that war captives, working on the building of the road, were dropping by the hundreds. Every meter there is a grave. But we have ten thousand without a single death, only stomach aches."[87] Despite the fact that the Tsarist and Soviet-era ambitions to build a waterway share clear commonalities in terms of motivation and implementation, they are contrasted in the *History of the Construction* in order to distinguish Soviet ideology from its Tsarist precedent. In reality, the two approaches appear more alike than dissimilar. While in Tsarist Russian inefficiency stemmed from continuous stalling and lack of funds for the project, in the Soviet Union the fast-paced construction and use of penal labor as solutions created an even greater inefficiency—a canal that was too shallow to be used, but for which thousands of prisoners had sacrificed their lives.

In contrast to the imperial interest in building a canal, the Soviet Union used Belomor for its own propaganda purposes, claiming that what had been impossible to complete in the Tsarist era was achievable only with the organization and determination of the socialist labor force. Although in a literal sense this was indeed true, it is necessary to once again take into account that the Soviet Union exploited the free manual labor of prisoners, thereby drastically cutting costs. They also built the canal to such a shallow depth—another cost-saving measure—that it is barely navigable.[88] Nevertheless, the canal was completed—on budget and on time—and hydro-technical engineers continue to marvel at its construction even today.[89] The engineering feat of the canal's construction exemplifies the notion of Gulag as laboratory, where new techniques, such as the all-wooden locks developed by the engineer V. N. Maslov, could be attempted.[90] The lack of equipment led to innovation, and the prisoners accomplished numerous other technological feats, including the development of wooden trucks (ironically called "Fords"), the construction of primitive derrick furnaces, and the on-site production of iron.[91] The successful completion of the canal project, in turn, encouraged the continuation of other construction projects awarded to the OGPU, spreading the influence of the Belomor model.[92]

Figure 5. An example of the wooden construction at Stalin's White Sea-Baltic Canal. Photograph reproduced with permission of Iurii Dmitriev.

Despite the Soviet Union's purported break from the imperialist ambitions of pre-Revolutionary Russia, colonial rhetoric was ubiquitous. Some even argue that the Soviet project was actually an extension of Tsarist, imperial, aims.[93] Significantly, parallels were often drawn—whether visually or textually—between Belomor and imperialist Egypt, with images of pyramids alongside the banks of the canal.[94] Just as religious proselytizing often accompanied imperial colonization, the Soviet experiment—and *perekovka* in particular—offered citizens the chance to be born again as socialist subjects. The Tsarist-Soviet connections illuminate important elements of the Belomor story: that its ambitions reached far beyond the waterway's banks, and that the project's religious, colonial, and imperial subtexts were always just below the surface. These broad narratives served as the backdrop for the will to mold a New Man in the New World, a project that addressed both body and mind.

It is challenging to assess the "success" of re-forging as a penal strategy. While many prisoners were indeed released early for their stunning labor output and allegiance to the Soviet state, it is very difficult to follow their paths after they left prison. While some may have effectively used skills they acquired in prison to create new selves, others surely ended up in the camps again. After his release from Belomor, Igor' Terent'ev (discussed at length in Chapter Two) willingly submitted himself back into the "meat-grinder," only to suffer extreme consequences. While tracing individual criminal prisoners and their relative successes is difficult, it is much easier to follow the popularity of re-forging as an ideological device. Not only does it have an antecedent in the concept of god-building and the self-improvement doctrines of the 1860s, but the idea continued to resonate in the Gulag and beyond, even if the official project was eventually abandoned. In contemporary Russia, we now have not the New Man but the New Russian, yet another metamorphosis in the understanding of selfhood. Yet no other version of self-fashioning more productively summarizes Stalinism than re-forging, a violent and aesthetic process in which one had to die in order to be born again.

I
The Factory of Life

> As a factory, the factory is right. As life, the factory is a flop.[95]
> –Viktor Shklovskii, *Third Factory*

Kostia, the main criminal character in Nikolai Pogodin's Belomor-based play *The Aristocrats* (*Aristokraty*, 1934), acts out numerous identities in both the thieving and the laboring worlds. Upon his arrival at the prison camp, Kostia makes apparent these many personalities: "About this registration—let's see, what name was I tried under? Blium? Ovchinikov? My biography has gotten all mixed up. What kind of questions are these? I'll register myself under my father's name. Kostia Dorokhov."[96] Similar to how he assumed various identities in the criminal world, Kostia (who actually goes by the *klichka*, or nickname, "Captain") also adopts different personalities at the labor camp. He pretends to be an engineer, an aviator, and even an electrician in his humorous efforts to dupe fellow prisoners and officials into procuring illegal goods for him. When Kostia is eventually "re-forged" into an upstanding Soviet citizen at the end of the play, he dramatically drops all assumed names and criminal sobriquets: "I ask you to remember—my surname is Dorokhov, my name is Konstantin Konstantinovich. Criminal nicknames are not to be used from this day on. Konstantin Konstantinovich."[97] Real-life criminals also depend on theatricality for material advantages, convincing ruses, and the evasion of authorities. Beggars in particular need to have dramatic yet believable performances while plying their trade.[98] Performance, therefore, has a strong link to the criminal realm, blurring the line between reality and theatricality. At Belomor, the most grandiose performance was that of *perekovka*—the re-forging of common criminal to New Soviet Man.

The penal philosophy of *perekova* promoted at the construction of Stalin's White Sea-Baltic Canal (*Belomorkso-Baltiiskii kanal im. Stalina*) sought to remake lives against a backdrop of destruction. This teleology was rooted in the OGPU's[99] desire to mold criminal prisoners into dedicated believers of Soviet ideology, and thus rendered Belomor one of the most infamous forced-labor projects. *Perekovka* was ubiquitous at the camp: criminal prisoners wrote of their transformations in autobiographical sketches; the camp newspaper was named in its honor; and poetry and plays were dedicated to its grandiose potential. By invoking the smelting of metal, the term *perekovka* adeptly highlighted the industrial atmosphere of Stalin's first Five-Year Plan and asserted that people—along with factories, plants, and waterways—could be built according to a master design. While it is possible to question the legitimacy of the process as a whole and the veracity of the declarations of allegiance to it, the phenomenon plays an essential role in cultural narratives emerging from the project and must be examined as such.[100]

Criminal autobiographies housed in Moscow archives narrativize the process of *perekovka* and document the path, or *put'*, of their authors' transformations.[101] The notion of pathway is essential in these tales, and calls to attention the religiosity inherent in Marxist-Leninist doctrine. In both Western and non-Western religions, to find God one must follow a path. The ritual of pilgrimage analogizes the metaphorical journey to enlightenment with an actual, physical journey. Prisoners laboring at Belomor experienced both literal and metaphorical pilgrimage: first the prisoners had to travel the difficult road to the camp site—a horrific voyage often described in prisoner memoirs as more arduous than the experience of prison life itself[102]—and then they were forced to experience the metaphorical voyage of re-forging, a trip intended to transport them from the darkness of the criminal world to the light of socialist labor.

Yet several elements render the Soviet brand of conversion unique, distinct from its religious counterparts. While finding God in Christian and other traditions can be a lifelong process, re-forging at the White Sea-Baltic Canal—as described by prisoners and camp officials—often happened literally overnight. The immediacy of transformation alludes to the industrial component inherent in the Soviet re-fashioning of religion (the spontaneity of a metallurgical process) and also brings into question the conversions' legitimacy. In addition, the trope of the pathway is apparent not only in socialist conversion narratives: prisoners' fall into the criminal world often serves as a counterpoint to their ascent into socialist society. Despite their very different destinations, the two routes share important qualities: the substitution of an artificial family for its biological counterpart and the role of collective identity in forming individual consciousness. The transformative journey of *perekovka* echoes elements of the socialist realist master plot, itself laden with ritualistic attributes. As Katerina Clark has outlined in her classic work *The Soviet Novel: History as Ritual*, the production novel, which charts how a plan is fulfilled or a project is constructed, exemplifies the master plot.[103] In this highly ritualistic plot construction, the hero arrives at the worksite and is presented with a specific, challenging task to fulfill. While there are trials or mishaps along the way, the hero eventually fulfills the task and completes the journey to consciousness, often with the help of a mentor to guide them along the path. At Belomor, the hero is the criminal who arrives at the separate, enclosed world of the Gulag camp. The task is the construction of the canal, a building process echoed metaphorically by the reconstruction of the criminal's personality. The mentor developed in classic socialist realist texts is mirrored by the *vospitatel'*, or educator-reformer, a figure who is paramount in facilitating the re-forging of the criminal. The *vospitatel'* helps the criminal journey along the path towards *perekovka* and ultimately allows the convict to achieve the task. Such a mentor figure is also present in the criminals' stories about their past lives—having a "mentor" to inaugurate one into a life of crime is just as important as having an educator for socialist conversion. Historically, fictional Russian bandits were "condemned to an orphan's life, with comrades in crime serving as a poor substitute for true kin."[104] While communist autobiographies have previously been interpreted as conversion narratives,[105] it is significant here that the conversion goes both ways utilizing the same tropes—a criminal falls into a life of crime with an "educator" just as he or she transforms into a conscious citizen with the help of one.[106]

The Mechanics of Perekovka

The KVO (*kul'turno-vospitatel'nyi otdel*) at the White Sea-Baltic Canal was in charge of re-forging prisoners as well as all other aspects of the re-educational process: it helped to abolish illiteracy among the convicts, organized professional-technical courses for the re-training of the incarcerated, maintained the "red corners" (areas in a room used for focusing attention on Soviet leaders and ideology in the barracks), and established social and recreational groups for the prisoners.[107] The department was divided into sub-divisions, or *chasti*, each of which was headed by a different *vospitatel'*. The *vospitateli* were key figures on the canal and were frequently mentioned in prisoner autobiographies and stories. They were directly in charge of remaking criminals' consciences, serving as true "engineers of the human soul,"[108] to echo Stalin's famous statement on the role of writers in the Soviet Union. The authorities, in turn, encouraged *vospitateli* to pen their own autobiographies, which were intended to serve as inspiration for recalcitrant prisoners. Part of the reason behind the apparent success of this method was due to the fact that the call to work and evidence of transformation came directly from former criminals rather than members of the administration.[109] Nevertheless, such successes must be qualified, as a thief-turned-reformer often could take advantage of his or her "privileged" position to indulge more readily in drunkenness and card-playing; as the political prisoner Dmitrii Vitkovskii recalls, "Usually the educators (*vospitateli*) withdraw into an attic in some or another barrack, play cards, eventually manage to get drunk and enjoy various thieves' amusements."[110] This observation makes apparent a certain inability to control the thieves-turned-reformers who, in the rearranged realm of Belomor, actually enjoyed a certain level of freedom in a prison camp. It is important to remember that the *vospitateli* are prisoners themselves, and the camp officials clearly could not control them nor prevent them from getting drunk.

The volume *From Crime to Labor* (*Ot prestupleniia k trudu*, 1936), a sort of bible of Soviet penal philosophy, offers insight into the process of *perekovka* as a specifically pedagogical phenomenon. The prisoners go through the "school of the Belomor construction" and have an important influence on the workers at the Moscow-Volga Canal, a subsequent Gulag project run by the OGPU.[111] Chapters focus on remaking prisoners' attitudes, the organization of cultural-educational work, the importance of collectivity as a work principle, and *udarnichestvo* (shock-worker labor) as a method of work stimulation—all of which were key components of the Belomor program. Most importantly, as the volume argues, *perekovka* concerns the transformation of human consciousness, and prison is not simply a tool for punishment or economic gain.[112] This idea did not make a sudden appearance in the 1930s; the Bolsheviks believed that crime was solely a byproduct of an unjust social system,[113] and that the reformation of all prisoners was possible, which is why a maximum sentence of five years was originally sought for all criminal offenses.[114] Some scholars argue that "years of Gulag propaganda" stressed that "prisoners were temporarily isolated from society but could be reeducated and reintegrated into that society"[115] and that the potential for prisoner reeducation persisted long past the construction of the Belomor Canal. The malleability of human nature, so central in Marxist philosophy and Lenin's subsequent adaptation of it, lends credence to the argument that belief in the possibility of human transformation existed throughout the Soviet Union.

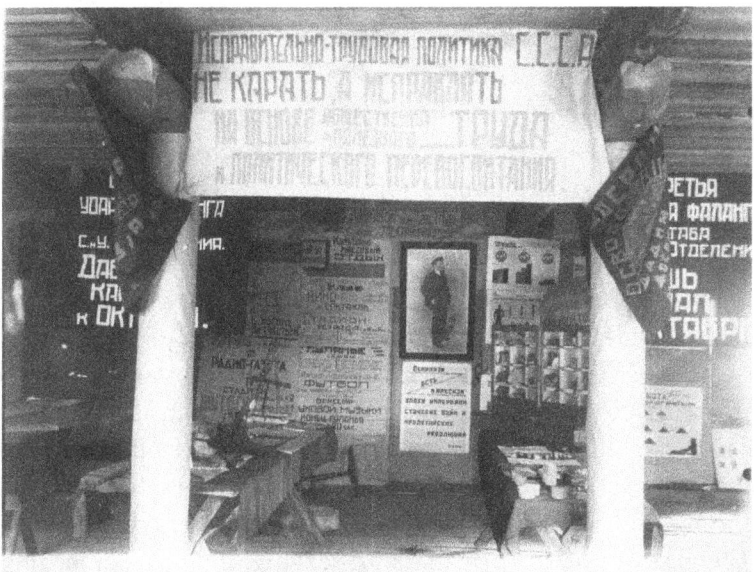

Figure 6. Slogans and banners at the White Sea-Baltic Canal. The banner across the top reads, "The USSR's corrective-labor politics does not punish, but rather corrects on the basis of socially beneficial labor and political re-education." Note also the portrait of Lenin. Photograph reproduced with permission of Iurii Dmitriev.

Lenin, therefore, actively supported research on the criminal realm in the 1920s and sought to create Soviet specialists in criminology. The Moscow Soviet created the Moscow Bureau for the Study of the Criminal Personality and Crime (*Moskovskii kabinet po izucheniiu lichnosti prestupnika i prestupnosti*) in 1923 in an attempt to understand and prevent crime in the turbid world of post-revolutionary chaos. While such Soviet organizations tried to understand crime as a scientific phenomenon, historically the Russian people had a long tradition of sympathy to thieves. Given the weak sense of private property in the countryside, nineteenth-century Russian peasants might actually applaud theft, particularly if the victims were outsiders. The large-scale thieving by the Bolsheviks in the name of the revolution, in turn, continued the tradition of sanctioned crime.[116] Yet with the growing menace of criminals under Stalin, and the potential for even common criminals to be understood as hooligans disrupting the political order, any soft approach to crime largely dissipated in the mid-1930s.[117]

In the flattering portrayal of the Soviet system in the 1936 volume *From Crime to Labor*, the penal methods of the USSR are compared to those of capitalist countries. While Fascist Germany presents crime as something inborn and thus impossible to change, the Soviet Union, the book claims, believes in the possibility of reforming even the most difficult portions of the population.[118] The Soviet penal system is also contrasted to its Tsarist precedent, with images of whips and bodily punishment meant to drive home for the reader the high degree of cruelty in pre-revolutionary Russia.[119] According to the volume, and as the title makes evident, the key to reformation was hard physical labor. That labor was most effective when it could be done on large construction projects with a concentrated group of prisoners, such as with the White Sea-Baltic Canal or Moscow-Volga Canal.[120] The prison site, therefore, becomes a *perpetuum mobile* of *perekovka*: the criminals' labor fires the forge in which they are re-forged. The physicality of convict labor mirrors the violence of the prisoners' re-forging; in both, something new must be hammered into shape, using heat, fire, and sweat. The stress on a strict work ethic—and its supposed benefits—has a chilling resonance with the infamous German slogan "Arbeit macht frei" ("work makes you free") of the Nazi era, and is echoed in the Soviet labor slogan published on the front page of every camp newspaper: "Labor in the USSR is a matter of honesty, glory, valor, and heroism."[121] While the sentiments of the two slogans are similar, their application is vastly different. Very little labor occurred in Nazi concentration camps, and the idea of a factory was a poor disguise for the Germans' ultimate goal—total annihilation. Given the horrific and inescapable fate of Nazi camp victims, there was little effort made to maintain the prisoners' health and cultural education. Yet in the Soviet context, camp administrations often relied on the inmates as a vital supply of inexpensive labor during a time of rapid industrialization. Keeping convicts at least moderately well-fed and well-clothed was of importance to those who ran the camps, although the definitions of well-fed and well-clothed could vary dramatically. The emphasis on labor and its transformative potential was a very real phenomenon in the Soviet Union.

While there are limitations to comparing Hitler's concentration camps with Stalin's Gulag,[122] it is also important to examine the potential connections between the Nazi and Soviet camps, especially given the present monograph's focus on creativity in the wake of destruction. If one emphasizes the role of the Gulag as a machine of political repression—not its only characteristic, since the camps have an economic function (however faulty), whereas Nazi concentration camps had virtually no profitable component—the comparison has some weight. There has been a revival in this debate in recent years, and current scholarship focuses not on the idea of totalitarianism as shared ideology but rather on numerous other common characteristics of the two regimes—violence, propaganda techniques, surveillance politics, antisemitism—and their critical impacts on twentieth-century history. The violent acceleration endemic to both systems has been interpreted as a dynamic between heroic reconstruction and aggressive self-destruction, a reading that mirrors the core thesis of this book. Both regimes create a tangible sense of belonging for approved citizens while revealing the prevalence of violence endemic to the larger social sphere.[123] The Gulag's existence augmented—or at least revealed—the already extant social violence in the country.

The connection between art and incarceration in the two penal systems must also be noted; while aesthetics are important to both, the roles are often different. It is more common to appreciate art from concentration camps in a purely heroic manner—in seemingly unimaginable conditions, art, poetry, and plays were produced.[124] Freidl Dicker-Brandeis, a prominent Jewish artist ensnared in the fatal abyss of Terezin, writes, "Aesthetics are the ultimate authority, the moving force, the motor capable of creating production, while defending man from forces over which he has no control."[125] In the Belomor context, such a noble and pure role for the artistic is not possible. Given that Stalin wanted to control the very levers of inspiration and that Belomor officials thought to dictate the content and tone of poetry, plays, and stories, such a sacrosanct role for expression seems impossible. The vagaries of aesthetic expression are complicated by the facts that prisoners *did* comply with the directives they were given and that Soviet artists *did* become excited about the prospect of such novel literary endeavors. It is too simplistic to negate the artistic value of pieces created at Belomor—or other Gulag camps—merely because they are propagandistic.

Scholars of the Holocaust have noted art's essential role as survival technique,[126] a role that art certainly played in the Gulag camps as well. Yet given the wide array of expression, uses for art, and types of camps, understanding art solely as a mechanism of resilience even in the Nazi context would be an overly romanticized and simplified view. Such an interpretation presumes solidarity among the victims of the Holocaust and attempts to fill the black, gaping hole of horrific—and potentially meaningless—violence with a heroic grand narrative.[127] In both of these most improbable carceral settings, artistic expression continued and, in some instances, flourished. This is a phenomenon I have also observed while working in the American prison. Creative activity, it seems, is an inevitable product of incarceration.

Crime and the Violent Application of Perekovka

In the disorienting shift from an old world to a new society, the crime rate in Russia rose nearly four hundred percent after the 1917 revolutions.[128] The Bolshevik government took an increased interest in the causes of such transgressions, setting up the Moscow Bureau for the Study of the Criminal Personality and Crime in 1923 and releasing the institute's research.[129] One of the first projects to emerge from this institution, the volume *Moscow's Criminal World* (*Prestupnyi mir Moskvy*, 1924), highlighted the difference between the Russian approach and those of more traditional criminologists. "If Professor Lombroso [the famous Italian criminologist] created the theory of the born criminal, then we wanted to put the words criminal world in quotation marks while underlining the conditions of understanding criminality, its changeability and dependence on the conditions of time and place."[130] Popular taste reacted to the burgeoning crime rate with an increased fascination with the thieves' underworld.[131] Historically, the art of crime in the Soviet Union was both a collective and an individual matter. On the one hand, Bolshevism understood crime as a social ill caused by an unfair class structure and criminals as representative of the masses who suffered such injustice. On the other hand, the prison regime recognized the individual needs of specific criminals in order to tailor rehabilitation to personal background.[132] Similarly, the ubiquitous bandit character in Russian popular literature had to choose between individuality's freedom and membership in the collective.

Although political conditions in the 1920s particularly favored the study of crime, by the early 1930s the tide was already changing. Even if the regime promoted crime as something changeable, and criminals as people capable of reformation, the burgeoning rate of crime—growing ever higher against the State and declining against private citizens—threatened the Stalinist social order. Distinctions were made between infractions of disobedience (*stikhiinost*), resistance (*soprotivlenie*), and opposition (*oppozitsiia*), and the regime came to understand crime in general as the social equivalent to opposition to the Stalinist State.[133] The growing issue of crime, therefore, needed an immediate and severe response. The high number of prisoners indicted on charges of "disrupting camp life and wrecking" at Belomor demonstrated this phenomenon of social disorder, and indicated that the camp contained a particularly unruly population.[134] Official approaches to crime, in turn, included the carrot as well as the stick.

While attempting to underscore the inherent humaneness of the socialist method as opposed to the penal techniques employed in "bourgeois" (capitalist) countries, the volume *From Crime to Labor* does not refrain from acknowledging the strict discipline and physical duress in the Gulag:

> Labor in the camps is hard work, the discipline is most strict and demanding. The shock-worker labor, the conscious relationship to responsibility, and the genuine striving towards re-forging find absolute encouragement; the breaking of camp discipline, the refusal to work or a lackadaisical approach to work, and even more importantly, the attempts to undermine the realization of corrective-labor politics and the sortie by the class enemy meet a decisive opposition in various forms—from measures of coercion by the camp elite to strict disciplinary measures.[135]

Following this ominous warning, the volume notes that the remaking of prisoners' consciousness cannot be considered a philanthropic or sentimental endeavor; instead, the path to reformation is a "strict and harsh route" (once again, the notion of *put'*) where the "iron discipline" of the camp holds sway.¹³⁶ As the above passage suggests, the class enemy plays a particular role, demonstrating how a type of Soviet ideological school is "in session" at the White Sea-Baltic Canal and other Gulag construction projects. In addition to building a canal and re-building themselves, the prisoners were also being indoctrinated in "Soviet speak"¹³⁷ while in a secluded, collective laboratory where propaganda could easily be disseminated and carefully controlled. The Marxist conception of class struggle assumed primary importance at the camp, and the prison's cultural-educational division had to address political questions closely.¹³⁸

Figure 7. A graphic representation of shock-worker output at the canal's construction. Note that even 100% is not ideal—all prisoners should be producing at 130% or higher. Photograph reproduced with permission of Iurii Dmitriev.

Several components comprised the cultural-educational work intended to assist in the goal of reformation of inmate consciousness through physical labor. The elements of competition (*sorevnovanie*) and shock-worker mentality (*udarnichestvo*) were essential in the implementation of *perekovka*.[139] The notion of socialist competition became a key driving force behind the prisoners' labor output. Since prisoners worked together in brigades and phalanxes, success was a collective matter. Gulag officials commented upon this phenomenon, encouraging group, rather than individual, measurements of work so as to facilitate a "collective psychology" that was in line with Soviet ideology.[140] This emphasis on group responsibility also had a secondary, pragmatic function: it made it virtually impossible for prisoners to refuse to work. If a prisoner shirked his work duty and held up the brigade, he would theoretically become ashamed of his behavior, since others were working diligently alongside him. Eventually, this guilt would coerce even the laziest of prisoners into adopting a work ethic.[141] Aleksandr Solzhenitsyn discusses the system in his landmark Gulag novella, *One Day in the Life of Ivan Denisovich* (*Odin den' Ivana Denisovicha*, 1959):

> To outsmart you they thought up the work squad—but not a work squad like in freedom, where Ivan Ivanych receives his separate pay and Petr Petrovich receives his separate pay. In the camps the brigade was arranged such that it was not the administration that hurried along prisoners, but rather the prisoners hurried along each other. It was like this: either you all got a bit extra or you all croaked. You're not working, you bastard—because of you I will be hungry? Put your guts into it, slob.[142]

The work-for-food system institutionalized cruelty in the Gulag, making survival nearly impossible for the malnourished or feeble.

Records of work-fulfillment percentages were documented publicly on chalkboards, on either the *chernaia doska* (black board) or the *krasnaia doska* (red board), and graphic diagrams around the canal served as a constant reminder of the inherent shame in sub-par labor output. This tradition continued for years in the Soviet Union, in camps as well as in non-carceral work environments (see Figures 28, 29). If prisoners were complaining about the difficulty of achieving the norm or about working in general, other "model" convicts would work alongside them to teach them a lesson—out of shame or embarrassment, the other prisoners were coerced to work by example.[143] Prisoners formed work brigades (or *brigady*, smaller groups with 25-30 members) and phalanxes (or *falangi*, larger groups consisting of 250-300 prisoners), and these teams competed actively, trying to outdo one another's norm-fulfillment percentages, with the standard norm unearthing 2.5 cubic meters of rock per day.[144] The creation of work collectives was encouraged strongly by the authorities; however, prisoners sentenced under article 58 (counter-revolutionary crimes) were in theory not allowed to participate in these groups. This demonstrates the predilection for criminal prisoners and most likely augmented the animosity between the two groups.[145] The importance of collective work and its supposed positive effects set an example for future projects, influencing the work system developed at the Moscow-Volga Canal.[146] Workers, therefore, had multiple incentives for over-fulfilling their norms: increased food rations, monetary bonuses, and shortened prison terms (the most powerful of all motivations).[147] Records indicate that 59,516 prisoners' terms were reduced upon the completion of the canal, and 12,484 prisoners were released entirely. Many of the remaining prisoners who survived were transferred to work on the Moscow-Volga Canal, another Gulag construction project.[148]

Perekovka was not a peaceful process. It was a violent, aggressive experiment in human transformation wherein a past life was annihilated to accommodate a new one. Mikhail Zoshchenko narrates the re-forging story of the prisoner Rottenberg in the Belomor volume *History of the Construction* in medical terms: "Now we will try a new surgery with the knife, that is, to cut the tissue of the surface."[149] In Maxim Gorky's introduction to this all-important monograph regarding the canal's construction, he claims that he fights "not to kill as the bourgeoisie does, but rather to resurrect laboring humankind into a new life, and I will kill only when there is no longer the possibility to blot out man's former habits of feeding on the flesh and blood of people."[150] Not only is violence an inherent component of the re-forging process, but prisoners may be met with violence if they do not subject themselves to the demands of *perekovka*. A human being is physical matter that can be melded and shaped or otherwise tossed away: "It is immeasurably more difficult to refine human raw material than wood, stone, or metal."[151] Yet Lenin himself insisted that the New Man must be built not with imaginary material but with the already inherited human material of capitalism, in what is a chillingly functionalistic interpretation of personal transformation.[152]

The physical was an essential component in the creation of selfhood at Belomor. Jerrold Seigel's model of the self posits three layers: the biological, the social, and the reflexive.[153] While the latter two are often addressed in scholarship regarding Stalinist culture, the first, biological, self must be more fully integrated into our understanding of the Soviet subject. The prison camp is an ideal frame to allow for this incorporation. Not only was the penal philosophy of *perekovka* inherently physical, the prisoners were also performing labor with their bodies, bodies that were subject to pain and discomfort. The turn toward industrialization (and the implication of smelting metal contained in the term *perekovka*) further accentuated construction and the physical movement in which bodies were engaged. The industrial connotations of refashioning are essential—the camp is described by prisoners as a "smithy" (*kuznitsa*)[154] for new potential. Finally, water, the very foundation of the project itself, represented a physical element that was simultaneously natural and dangerous, peaceful and turbid—it was both the life-giver (waterway of the future) and the life-destroyer (road of bones).

The word *perekovka*, in its very morphological structure, emphasizes the notion of remaking or redoing. At Stalin's White Sea-Baltic Canal, everything would be re-made: geography, industry, nature, economy, country, culture, and, of course, people. People were built parallel to the construction of the canal, and both projects were equally important.[155] At Belomor, the administration could make people into honest Soviet citizens just as easily as they could make them into cement mixers, claims the *History of the Construction*.[156] The frequent use of the prefix "pere-" in the monograph reflects this near obsession with reconstruction. The idea of *perekovka* is echoed literally thousands of times while being applied to numerous different words and situations in the *History of the Construction*: *perestroit'* (to rebuild), *pererozhdenie* (re-birth), *perezhit'* (to survive), *perereshat'* (to change one's mind), "*rabota ikh pereuchit*" (work will re-teach, train them), *perevypolnenie* (overfulfillment), *peredumat'* (to change one's mind), *perechuvstvovat'* (to experience), *pereshchegoliat'* (to outflaunt)—the list could go on and on.[157]

The emphasis on remaking—with the prefix *pere-* as its vehicle—is so strong that there is an overall sense of forward motion in the book as a whole. Everything is in the process of being re-done and re-made, and not simply in order to make the same object or perform the same action over again; rather, it is to improve upon it. In this new society, old ways must die in order to give birth to a new system. Birth and death are the bookends of life, and the majority of rituals cluster around these two foundational life events. *Perekovka* in some ways resembled an initiation rite, where the old was destroyed to allow for a re-birth, with the initiation process allowing one to grasp a positive aspect within death itself.[158] There is also an inherent aesthetic aspect to this re-birth, since art not only facilitates re-forging but also documents its occurrence afterwards. In his 1933 book about the Karelian region *In the Land of Unfrightened Birds* (*V kraiu nepugannykh ptits*), author Mikhail Prishvin asserts that this, his first book, is the "first lock of his literary canal," a canal that brought him to a new homeland.[159] The canal metaphor is not coincidental. Prishvin was writing this book during his visit to the Belomor construction project in 1933, where he admired the reconstruction of people at the labor camp. He expresses a similar sentiment in his personal diary, where he writes:

> I place value on this cause of remaking geography for what it does to many homeless, desperate, joyless people, who become reborn in this creative process, and, having recreated the geography of this land, find a new motherland for themselves.[160]

Prishvin commends the Belomor construction project as well as Maxim Gorky in his volume, and he echoes the administration's perspective that through concentrated labor—labor that is a creative process—a prisoner can be re-forged.

The exposition of various personalities in the *History of the Construction* demonstrates how people can be created and constructed, either like a piece of art or like the building of the canal itself, since "the birth of the canal goes along with the birth of man."[161] This combined aesthetic-technological connotation in the re-forging of prisoners brings to mind the futurist concept of "life-building" (*zhiznestroenie*). At the canal, "the new man was created."[162] This birth of new people is accompanied by the birth of a new language[163] as well as the birth of the canal, since it is "as if Karelia itself was born along with the canal."[164] When there is a need for certain trades or specialties, these people will be created at the camp site alongside the project of re-forging: "You say that there are no cement makers here? This is true. But there are also no honest Soviet citizens here, so we must create both cement makers and honest Soviet citizens."[165] The repeated emphasis on birth renders the canal's construction organic, making an assault on nature appear to be a natural phenomenon.

Perekovka, with its goal being the "production" of new people, injects an industrial emphasis into the process of re-forging prisoners—an entirely appropriate tone given the concentration on manufacturing during Stalin's first Five-Year Plan. One prisoner likens the canal to a "smithy" where everyday life transforms consciousness,[166] and another compares the camp to a "life factory," where people are remade like so many products on a conveyor belt—albeit in a highly unusual way: "Yes, strange, unusual transformations are made here. Miraculous transformations, nothing about which you could even find in fairy tales."[167] Despite the industrial overtone of *perekovka*, texts often portray the process as organic in order to make it appear more like a natural phenomenon.[168] While capitalist construction sites such as the Panama and Suez Canals supposedly represent a pathway to destruction, misery, and death, the White Sea-Baltic Canal is a place of birth and beginnings, where new sounds and a new way of life are born; the project is both literally and figuratively a birth canal. The emphasis on birth[169] naturalizes the construction of the canal, allowing for the highly unnatural ideological construct of *perekovka* to take on the appearance of an organic re-birth. Naturalizing initiation rites is important, since the new birth is anything but natural, and instead represents a societal, cultural construction.[170] In the Gulag complex—where nature was plundered for its bounty and people were transformed for their psyches—the Soviet Union proclaimed itself the victor in the "war against nature," and in the process a new version of nature was created, with its own laws, rules, and processes. In this totalizing yet contradictory quality, the Soviet approach differed from other modernization campaigns. Not only was industry to be re-made, so were people—people who were supposedly freed by the very labor that served as a condition of their imprisonment.

The process is so complete and totalizing that the "new" person might not recognize the "old." This symbolized the utter finality of the transformation: "The engineer Magnitov thought about the old engineer Magnitov—for him this man was already a stranger."[171] The raw, physical acts of death and birth, in turn, are both inherent components of re-forging. *Perekovka* reveals the essential role that autobiography plays in the cultural narratives about Belomor; in order to articulate one's new life and devotion, it was necessary to recall where one came from and who one used to be. Just as the map could assess change in landscape and geography, the material text of the autobiography could document the change in a human being, a change that is itself understood spatially, in terms of a specified *put'*. The phenomenon echoed the construction of the canal itself; like "working the rough stone,"[172] building the person is a process that happens over time: "in the creation of great new projects the new great man is created."[173]

The production of new people privileges autobiography as narrative form. Maxim Gorky penned the opening and closing chapters of the collectively written *History of the Construction* (the only chapters to be written individually), and he served as the editor and organizer of the volume as a whole. The surprising amount of miniature biographies in the volume, therefore, signifies an extension of the writer's literary ideals. In order to achieve *perekovka*, you must tell the story of who you "were" in order to distinguish it from the person you came to "be." Such stories abound: there are biographies of the engineers Voler'ianovich, Maslov, and Zhuk; there are the narratives of criminal men such as Volkov and Rottenberg and criminal women, including Iurtseva and Pavlova, and there are even histories of the *nachal'niki*, including Frenkel', Rapoport, Kogan, and Firin.[174] Such a preoccupation with life stories also appears in the book *Liudi Stalingradskogo Traktornogo*, the first volume in the series "History of Factories and Plants" (*Istoriia fabrik i zavodov*). Gorky notes the importance of such biographies in the introduction to the book, claiming that they give a sense of the diversity of people who worked at the tractor factory:

> All of them are not literary figures, yet they managed to write their autobiographies so that I, a man of letters and a reader, can see how the *natsmen* Terkel-khan learned to work in difficult conditions, how the Red partisan Galushkin cries from joy that the factory has started working, I can see how Khloptunova trains girls by teaching them economy and machinery.[175]

This type of literature of fact—where reality can easily be embellished—lends credibility to the enthusiasm for the project. It also indicates the importance of journalistic writing and the *ocherk*, or sketch, which was the dominant literary form during the first Five-Year Plan.[176] The literature of fact not only blurs the lines between fiction and reality but also underscores the labor inherent in writing. Rather than a vague or undefined muse allowing for inspiration, here a concrete interest in lived reality serves as the raw material for written works. The plethora of writers visiting the far-flung reaches of the USSR and reporting back on their findings demonstrates physical work and tangible employment, as opposed to the "bourgeois" notion of writing from an armchair. The aforementioned "History of Factories and Plants," a series of publications that Maxim Gorky helped to found, represents perhaps the zenith of the literature of fact. The series produced nearly 30 books on Soviet workplaces from 1931-38, with the *History of the Construction of the White Sea-Baltic Canal* as one of its more infamous publications.[177]

Given the supposedly limitless potential of *perekovka*, the canal project was intended to be more than a pedagogical experience and much more than merely a collection of locks, dams, and dikes—instead, it represented life itself, a metaphorical and utopian homeland in which Soviet selfhood was transformed. As the prisoner Vasilii Atiasov explained in his autobiography, "I myself have a wife and four children and I once thought about them [but now] I'm happy to give everything to my beloved BMS,[178] it is our pride, our beauty. And here in this rock, in this water, I found my happiness, my pathway to life."[179] In a quasi-religious move, Atiasov was able to surrender all previous allegiances in glorious adoration of the canal, an appreciation that he was able to come to by way of a distinct path, or *putevka*.[180]

Path to Perekovka *as Socialist Realist Master Plot*

The New Man (*novyi chelovek*) was one of the key ideological concepts under Stalin,[181] and this omnipotent Soviet being shared many qualities with the re-forged prisoner at the camp site: both abjured their past in order to adopt a brighter future, both came to this realization through "correct" ideological training and education, and both were used as metaphors for the grandiosity of the Soviet Union. The creation of the New Man exemplified key tenets of socialist realism's master plot, wherein an unreformed, uninitiated main character comes to profess a new way of life with the help of a tutor or trainer, fulfilling the mythical narrative of the mentor-disciple dyad.[182] This narrative structure echoes the process of *perekovka* at the White Sea-Baltic Canal. A newly arrived, often untrained, prisoner might refuse to work or participate, setting up the task.[183] The *vospitatel'* acts as the mentor, guiding the prisoner along the path of reformation. While there may be initial setbacks, eventually a symbolic initiation occurs. Remarkably, this kind of narrative forms the key structure of most Belomor autobiographies even though these texts were written mainly in the summer of 1933, a full year before the formal declaration of socialist realism as official literary method at the August 1934 First All-Union Congress of Soviet Writers. In addition, prisoners composed these works in the relative isolation of a labor camp; although many had access to libraries and newspapers, the prison environment as well as Karelia's remote location necessarily restricted cultural life.

The stress on the life story in prisoner works about the canal also has a direct parallel with the biographical pattern evident in socialist realism after 1932.[184] The prevalence of the biographical mode stems in part from the importance of the "positive hero" as one of the most recognizable features of socialist realism.[185] The positive hero, emblematic of Bolshevik ideals, is often so generic and featureless that he appears not as an individual but more as hagiography.[186] Such is also the case with the re-forged prisoner: newly devoted and dramatically transformed, he is no longer discernible from the other convicts around him. Continuing the religious motif, the re-forging narratives are ritualized and repetitive, and they become conversion narratives. These texts subsequently represent liturgy. Other criminals can read of the transformations and understand the model they are supposed to follow in their voyage from darkness to light, from uninitiated to initiated. Prisoners perform selfhood through the narrative act in an attempt to assure their survival, and through this performance Soviet propaganda is internalized while most evidence of individuality is dissolved. Paradoxically, however, in order to re-fashion themselves, prisoners must first narrate the specific details of their past lives in their autobiographies.[187]

The short story "Karas'," by the prisoner A. K. Ivanov, is a productive example of a conversion narrative; although it is not written as an autobiographical submission, it follows the same pattern of a re-forging tale and addresses important aspects of identity formation. The title itself, which means a "wide-hipped woman" in criminal slang,[188] is a *klichka* (nickname) for the main character and represents his position within the criminal world (i.e., feminized and subservient). Significantly, the prisoner who submitted the story first wrote it in the third person, saying "he" (*on*) did this or that, but subsequently changed the third-person to first-person (*ia*), crossing out the previous pronouns in what was perhaps an attempt to render the story more realistic and personal. Similarly, while the story is signed by A. K. Ivanov, the name "Karas'" is scribbled more hastily next to his own real name, most likely another last-minute effort to make the story appear to be an autobiography.

This story has many of the characteristic features of the re-forging narrative. Most important is the role played by the *vospitatel'* (educator), who is likened to a father figure: "I listened attentively to the educator's speech. It seemed to me as if the educator was speaking to me like my father who was killed in the war."[189] While the physical speech of the reformer-educator frequently represents the first stage in the transformation,[190] the second could come at night, during sleep or dreams, when the ideas spoken of earlier have the opportunity to coalesce and take hold.[191] Some prisoners also imagine the dreams of their loved ones at home; in his diary, one prisoner pictures his wife Olia dreaming about her drunken, wild husband with a knife in his hands, and he tries to assure her that this really is just a dream—he is no longer a murderous maniac but is reading books and sitting in a Lenin Corner.[192] Dreams here are a schematic re-interpretation of the past, a way of acknowledging memories before transcending them.[193] Dreams also have a very specific function in the Russian criminal world, where they are believed to have the ability to forecast the future. Thieves, therefore, have a special respect for dreams and their content.[194]

Karas' could not fall asleep the night after a conversation with the *vospitatel'*, and he reviews his life history, in particular his difficult familial situation: "My thoughts sped away far into the past, remembering my father who did not return from the war. They killed him. I was seven years old. Finding out about the death of my father, my mother cried loudly. She also died in 1917."[195] Like so many other prisoners at Belomor, Karas' is an orphan and finds a substitute family in his re-educator and in the ethos of the state. The fact that so many of the prisoners were orphans who came from broken homes could explain their willingness to conform to ideological principles in order to garner the safety and protection of the regime as a substitute for their non-existent home lives. Karas' wakes up the day after his prophetic dream and decides to begin working. In the symbolic finale of the story, the character loses his old nickname of "Karas'," and now everyone calls him by his full name, Aleksei Ivanovich (very similar to the prisoner's real name of A. K. Ivanov), in recognition of his newfound appreciation for a dignified, laboring lifestyle.[196] Just as gaining a criminal nickname is an essential aspect of entering the thieves' world,[197] so would dropping it be a highly symbolic gesture of complete disavowal of lawless ways.

The prisoner Mikhail Koldobenko ends his autobiographical submission with a statement in all capitals, claiming this is "how the steel was tempered"[198] before signing his name. Such a pronouncement immediately brings to mind the identically-titled socialist-realist classic by Nikolai Ostrovskii, *How the Steel Was Tempered* (*Kak zakalialas' stal'*, 1932-1934), which—significantly—was published as a model socialist realist work only after Koldobenko wrote his autobiography, confirming how texts produced at the White Sea-Baltic Canal can prefigure what emerged outside the *zona*. In another parallel with a socialist-realist classic, the prisoner Fillipp Kabanenko (who interestingly refers to himself as "comrade" rather than "canal-army soldier," the officially accepted term at the camp[199]) recalls how he injured both his legs at the work site and had to be carried by his brigade, and despite not healing well insisted on continuing to work with his bandaged legs.[200] This autobiographical detail echoes Boris Polevoi's socialist-realist novel *Story about a Real Man* (*Povest' o nastoiashchem cheloveke*, 1946), which concerns the plight of a Soviet pilot who, despite losing both his legs, still flies in service to his country. Such examples confirm the compatibility between penal reeducation and the socialist realist master narrative and have important implications for the Soviet ideological system. Given that the prison program echoes the state-approved form of literature, it becomes easier to align the realms inside and outside of the *zona*. In addition, such correspondences between prison writings and the socialist realist narrative indicate that the master plot is rooted in Bolshevik ideology—and perhaps in even earlier cultural norms—rather than being spontaneously invented.

The presence of master plot elements in these criminal narratives demonstrates two central thematic undercurrents: the state as substitute family, and the process of *perekovka* as a ritualistic, religious phenomenon. Interestingly, many of the nuances of these characteristics also hold true for the *put'* of *perekovka* in the reverse direction: the fall into the criminal world, where the figure of a thieving mentor appears more vivid and durable.

The Inverse Trajectory of Perekovka

The words *doroga* and *put'* can both be translated as road or pathway in Russian, but the difference between the two terms is significant. While *doroga* implies simple back-and-forth movement, the perfunctory practicality of the path, *put'* implies an end result, a final destination that will be better than the point of departure. As Emma Widdis notes within the context of Soviet film, *put'* "was reconfigured not as progression to an elusive but significant goal but as the dynamic process of transformation itself."[201] *Put'* becomes equivalent to *perekovka*. Yet what could be called the inverse of *perekovka*—the fall into the criminal world—is also often reached by what the criminals call a *put'*, which must necessarily complicate not only how we view the prisoners' supposed transformations, but also our understanding of how their narratives were read by the authorities.

The prisoner autobiography by Grigorii Koshelev, entitled "My Path" (*Moi put'*), demonstrates colorfully how the road to crime can mirror the road to socialist labor. As is very common, familial problems serve as the generator of a life of crime for Koshelev: his father went to war in 1914 and his mother subsequently died of hunger, leaving him to search the streets, dirty and cold, for nourishment.[202] He soon met and befriended Vas'ka-Svistun ("Vaska the Whistler," or, in slang, "Vaska the Liar"), a vodka-drinking criminal, and asked him how he was able to procure so much food and drink. Enamored of Vas'ka's criminal lifestyle and the luxuries it affords, he "decides to start upon this path" himself.[203] It is significant here that the author uses the same—and very loaded—term in Russian for the pathway that brings him to a life of crime as for the one that brings him to a life of honest labor: *put'*. It is possible, in turn, to see Vas'ka-Svistun as a sort of inverse *vospitatel'*, a teacher or reformer who educates him about a life of stealing rather than about a life of labor, and also changes his world and habits.

Koshelev traveled from city to city, picking up supplementary nicknames and additional jail time along the way. While he at first followed

Vas'ka-Svistun like a devoted protégé, Koshelev eventually lost track of him. In 1929, he was sent to Solovki, where he still refused to give up his old ways and still dreamed of his former friend and father figure: "The whole time traveling in the train I was playing cards and thinking about the past, drunken, merry days, about Vas'ka Svistun, dreaming about somehow running away and meeting with Vas'ka once again to start thieving."[204] Then, the unexpected happened—one day Koshelev met his pal Vas'ka on the camp site but barely recognized him; Vas'ka was now the head of a shock-worker brigade, literate and cultured. Although Vas'ka continually tried to convince his friend to change to a working lifestyle, Koshelev did not want to hear about it, and he eventually began avoiding his former partner-in-crime. Vas'ka may have served as his *vospitatel'* for the criminal world, but he did not play this role in Koshelev's reverse trajectory—it was not a reformer who eventually convinced Koshelev to adopt a life of labor, but rather the peer pressure of his fellow prisoners:

> And so there was a despicable attitude against me. In the kitchen they opened the windows and hung loafers, they started to write my name on the black board of shame and in the wall newspapers, spreading it throughout the entire camp, through the radio and paper that I am a loafer, an idler, wherever I went everyone began laughing and making fun of me. I was alone in the company and every day the educator (*vospitatel'*) Zarybaev led discussions, talking about the free, Soviet country and how it was impossible not to work living in the USSR.[205]

This recollection is particularly revealing, because it suggests how massive the panopticon of propaganda was at the White Sea-Baltic Canal. In anticipation of what was to occur in the country as a whole, nearly every surface of the camp site was used as a place to disseminate slogans and ideological propaganda. Exhibits at the canal's construction were decorated with flags and banners, included notices and orders, and even showcased different kinds of Karelian rock. Yet although the *vospitatel'* and visual propaganda were omnipresent, shame and perennial teasing seemed to be the method of choice—one that was truly successful—in convincing recalcitrant prisoners to begin working.

Figure 8. A smattering of visual propaganda at the canal's construction, including announcements of the best workers, collections of local types of rock, administrative orders, and slogans. Photograph reproduced with permission of Iurii Dmitriev.

In a sketch submitted to the *Perekovka* newspaper, the prisoner G. Mel'nikov included work complaints as well as a more detailed description of the prisoners' work ethic. He understood the importance of worker collectivity in the context of the infiltration of two loafers named Rus and Mailov. After the two were subjected to a week of taunting by the rest of the work collective, they finally decided to start working. This was precisely the kind of psychological atmosphere the authorities wanted to create; a den of peer pressure where fellow prisoners began acting more like administrators than convicts, because they knew the group's collective work output depended upon the work completed by each individual member. So the "patience" (*terpenie*) of Mel'nikov's brigade finally gives out, and they show Rus and Mailov how to work, an effort that was couched in pedagogical terms: they decide "to teach" (*pouchit'*) those who were not producing, and their "studies" (*ucheba*) began the moment they arrived in the work brigade. This pedagogical terminology echoes the efforts of the *vospitateli* at Belomor, who saw their task of re-forging as an educational process.[206]

While the prisoner Koshelev does eventually begin working and reading newspapers, becoming literate, he claims merely that he "got used to the educator" (*ia privyk k vospitateliu*) and not that he was truly swayed by him. When he sees Vas'ka again, the former criminal is being freed early as one of the best shock-workers; Vas'ka later writes his friend that he is now working on the Moscow-Kurskii railroad line as a conductor. Vas'ka, therefore, exchanged his metaphorical *put'* for a literal one, leaving behind the pathway of crime to follow the more entrenched, straight path of the railroad tracks.[207] Koshelev ends his autobiography by thanking his comrades for putting him on the proper *put'*, one that no longer follows crime but instead a life of work.

Like Koshelev, the prisoner Orest Vziaemskii falls under the influence of a criminal-world educator, Semen, and Vziaemskii highlights the allure inherent in a life of crime in his description of Semen:

> I have to say the people who are used to a more refined life of the mind are worse off in terms of their personal qualities than people who are closer to life, who address danger as a trade. Maybe to blame them is not possible, because for them, as Semen said, life seems vapid if they are not exposed to danger. I advised him to become a pilot, or that he should understand the construction's fervor. He finished a ton of courses, he was a tractor driver, he was in Pioneer camp, but he always returned to the dangerous life. He remains one of the brightest of all my memories.[208]

Semen, unlike Vas'ka, cannot be re-forged even though he might try to re-educate himself. Almost like a drug user, he is addicted to a life of crime, and Vziaemskii is entranced by his colorful life more than he could be by any *vospitatel'* preaching about socialist labor.

The autobiography of the prisoner Mikhail Koldobenko is another re-forging tale that concentrates more on the pathway to the criminal world than on the road to socialism, its narrative offering a telling glimpse into the psychology of crime. Born in 1901, Koldobenko has memories of growing up with his drunk father whose life advice (in addition to quitting school) consisted of: "You struggle really hard—like fish beating against the ice—but still you have nothing to eat. And they suck your blood like spiders."[209] Koldobenko began working at the age of sixteen in a factory, and when World War I broke out he started to feel like a real man; he got married, he was not afraid of death, and he loved to work. With the sudden death of his wife in childbirth, however, his life fell apart: "right away life snapped [...] and so stretched on the boring, gray days."[210] He saw death everywhere and was solely responsible for his young daughter. Eventually, he took to drink. When he married again, his second wife turned out to be a "meshchanka" (a member of the petty bourgeoisie, or someone of narrow tastes and interests) who did not like to work and had a fondness for sweets. When she suggested to him that they could wound the child with a needle in the top of the head, causing her to die without anyone noticing, he decided to leave her, but his life only became more difficult.

While examples have already made evident the psychological thrill provided by a life of crime, Koldobenko's road to prison was related directly to alcohol. At the camp site, he claimed to be captured by the idea of physical work, which was the best way for him to address his drunkenness, "Prison is a good school for drunkards. It turns them towards a new life [...] I regret only one thing: that I landed late in prison, thank you Soviet power for returning me to life. Thank you to the camps of the OGPU for its humanitarian approach to criminals."[211] In this surprising affirmation of allegiance, Koldobenko reinforces the notion of *perekovka* as a successful way to refashion prisoners and also frames his transformation in pedagogical terms. In these inverse trajectories of *perekovka*, the role of guide or mentor and the notion of pathway remain essential elements. Narratives in which a criminal mentor plays an essential role seem to downplay the role of the official *vospitatel'*, with peer pressure from other prisoners emerging as a more convincing call to labor. While such a move may not have been a conscious effort on the part of the criminals, the fact that a different kind of *perekovka* emerges in the face of the absence of the socialist version is significant. Already having had their lives once transformed, the prisoners could have related easily to the *perekovka* concept and so been able to easily pen the trajectory of transformation, no matter in what direction.

CHAPTER ONE

Violating the Norm:
Subversive Criminal Narratives

Although most of these criminal autobiographies follow the formula of an initial stage of laziness, a second stage of contemplation (whether through the *vospitatel'*, reflection on earlier life, prophetic dreams, or intimidation by fellow prisoners), and a final stage of abandoning the past and becoming a productive worker, there are also narratives that violate this pattern to varying degrees. There are prisoner autobiographies in which there is no admission of guilt and no particular praise of the Soviet system. Begin a new sentence: Although such examples are rare, the mere presence of such texts indicates a lack of strict censorship—not only were less-than-positive tales kept (and left unmarked) by the administration, the prisoners themselves clearly felt comfortable with penning submissions that paint the canal experience in an unfavorable light.

One such example is the autobiography of Mikhail Polokhin, a criminal who practiced the seasonal work of stealing motorcycles and bicycles for three years before switching to thieving on railroad cars. Polokhin seems to take pride in his criminal life; he describes his various extra-legal professions with flair, explaining precisely the details of his criminal maneuverings. He had the nickname "Tashkent," and he moved to various cities before finally being caught stealing a large sum of money and sent to Povenets, where part of the Belomor construction was located. Included in his narrative was no allegiance to the Soviet state, and no description of re-forging, but instead only his success in securing false documents. With these documents, he went into the city of Povenets every day instead of working at the camp site and continued his former vocation of stealing from suitcases. He asserts that he lacked nothing in prison and was well fed. In an unorthodox description of the administrative organization, he claims the authorities are often entirely unapprised of the activities at the work site:

> The monitor and company apparently did not know who and how many people they had, and where to find these people. They are either sleeping or working. In short, an extremely advantageous situation was created for loafers and pretenders. The loafers went wherever they

pleased, especially those who were the smartest. But it wasn't even necessary to be particularly smart. And so I hung around for more than a month, but in the end I got sick of the idle life.[212]

It was utter boredom—and not a shock-worker mentality or allegiance to the Soviet state—that ultimately pushed Polokhin to form a work collective called "The Pathway to Socialism" (*Put' k sotsializmu*), a name that seems incongruous with Polokhin's laziness and distaste for work. Despite Polokhin's indifferent attitude, the all-important component of pathway remains, demonstrating how essential this element was in cultural narratives regarding the canal. In both utopian texts and travel narratives (including those of religious pilgrimage), the trope of the road is a vital element; in order to describe a fantastical, alternate reality or a literal one, one must explain how to arrive there. Even biographies that seem to violate the norm, therefore, still contain important ideological motifs central to the canal's construction.

Rather than suffering from mere disinterest or boredom, other prisoners criticize the regime for its lack of fairness. Iosima Korneevich Zhitkov claims that he received fewer privileges than his friend, who had worked less than he did. He goes on to assert that the recent atmosphere on the canal was negative because the Party was not strong enough. Cryptically, he says, "But that is all I can write," giving the reader a sense that there is more criticism he would like to air, but he is simply not free to.[213] The unexplained ellipses that appear in his text also allude to this possibility. Yet despite these criticisms, the prisoner does not demonstrate any clear anti-Soviet tendencies, instead writing of his desire for better Party organization.

Although they are not as long or descriptive as Polokhin's text, there are other prisoner autobiographies that also refute the supposed transformational potential of *perekovka*. The prisoner Fedor Tupikov declares in his text that he is not guilty and has never committed any crime. Although he claims he learned many things in prison, including how to read, he swears no allegiance to the Belomor project. There is no mention of *udarnichestvo*, although he does write that he would like to become part of the workers' family.[214] While not necessarily declaring their innocence, other prisoners use their autobiographies to point out shortcomings on the canal: "dampness in the barracks, the wind blowing through cracks, even no place to dry your foot wrappings on occasion," and only since they were young and their "blood is boiling" could they withstand such conditions.[215] The initial paucity of the cultural environment also becomes apparent, even if the situation improved as the canal was constructed:

> All of this work went on in very difficult conditions, there was no cultural life and not even any promises of it. The club corner was just beginning to be built [....] So I started to go to the [reading] corner, where they had some books, magazines, newspapers. I was especially interested in questions concerning the international situation, because in our division and camp there were gossips, and an out-and-out counter-revolution spread around rumors that Japan had taken the Baikal and now there is supposedly some secret council or congress that is discussing something. I looked upon all this with suspicion, and I wanted to report it, but I didn't see any power to whom to report; despite the fact that I'm in the camps of the OGPU, at our work point the KVCh[216] worked weakly.[217]

This passage illuminates several different aspects of life at Belomor, including hardship, gossip, and the attempt to self-aggrandize, most likely in the interest of protecting oneself politically. The passage's author, Abram Bessonov,[218] seems unabashed in his criticism of cultural life at the canal; in his opinion, although it did exist, it was not as productive or as thorough as other prisoners may make it out to seem. In addition, Bessonov acknowledges the existence of gossip and whisperers at the labor camp,[219] as well as the ideological and moral pressure to report those who do not fall into line, even when no one is looking or paying attention. His narrative is quite contradictory—he is at once interested in international news and gossip and trying to refute it. The end to his story, nevertheless, is a "happy" one—he himself becomes a *vospitatel'* and publishes wall newspapers. Although Tupikov and Bessonov both offer criticism of the Soviet regime, they would like to become members of its utopian reality. Such criticisms were not overtly publicized, but the mere fact that the prisoners felt comfortable writing in such a manner attests to the relative softness of the regime in comparison to later Gulag camps.

Beyond the existence of such potentially subversive texts, the existence of RUR (*rota usilennogo rezhima*), a type of special punishment zone in which recalcitrant prisoners were housed, made it evident that not all prisoners were willing to work or to accept the message of re-forging. Most of these prisoners flatly refused to work in any capacity, and they were a significant number: one memoir estimates about 750 people in the "stable" (*koniushnia*) section of RUR, which represented only one barrack.[220] These intractable prisoners were frightening even to other hardened criminals, who noted their savage cruelty. Since the inhabitants of RUR were not working, their food ration was much smaller, and the prisoners would steal and fight for one another's portions, often killing or maiming one another.[221]

In her autobiography, the shock-worker Elena Il'inichna recalled fewer prisoners in RUR—286, to be exact—and claims that the *pakhan* (crime-boss) played an important role in discouraging the prisoners from working. Her role as an educator-reformer was to convince the prisoners to begin participating in the canal's construction. When they asked for bread, she gave them bread. Once they had bread, they asked her for tobacco.[222] Supposedly, Elena's reading of an official order out loud to the RUR inhabitants inspired them to finally begin working, despite their recalcitrance.[223] In addition to the presence of RUR, the need for periodic *chistki* (purges) of the work collectives demonstrates the presence and threat of unruly prisoners, even within the supposedly law-abiding organizations of labor brigades.[224]

Given the presence of subversive texts, institutions like RUR, and the necessity of cleaning the ranks of the brigades, it is easy to doubt the successes of re-forging. It would be impossible to calculate its actual effect on recidivism, just as it is not possible to ascertain what the prisoners truly thought about the rehabilitative program. In Nikolai Pogodin's Belomor play *Aristocrats* (*Aristokraty*), the character Sonia's re-forging is preceded by heavy amounts of doubt and skepticism: "It's all a lie [....] It's a lie! Re-forging, remaking, education, newspapers [....] Who are they fooling? A prison's a prison!"[225] Yet as the genre demands, Sonia is re-forged and her educator-reformer is re-cast in the role of metaphorical father. Knowing Sonia is an orphan, the *vospitatel'* asks about her family situation and then compares himself to a paternal figure in an attempt to serve as a substitute father. Such familial recasting likely had a distinct appeal for criminal prisoners, many of whom were orphaned or abandoned.

The Re-forging of Homeless Children

The notion of *perekovka*—in the form of the New Man—has other important parallels in Soviet culture. One of the most relevant is the phenomenon of *besprizorniki*, or homeless orphans, in Russia. Not surprisingly, children were at the forefront of the campaign to indoctrinate individuals with socialist ideology. In many strictly controlled regimes, it is common to begin with the youth—their consciousness is not yet fully formed and so represents a *tabula rasa* for ideology.[226] Gorky promoted this point of view at the First Congress of Soviet Writers in 1934, acknowledging children's literature as "the most important 'front' of socialist creative labor and a natural ground for creating the 'new Soviet man.'"[227] In terms of Soviet literature of the time period, one needs to think only of the slogan-chirping Nastia in Andrei Platonov's *The Foundation Pit (Kotlovan*, 1930)[228] or the strapping soccer player Volodia in Iurii Olesha's *Envy (Zavist'*, 1927) to see just how easily younger members of society can become thoughtless ideological containers. The topic of the New Man was essential to children's literature of the late 1920s and early 1930s, since "children's writers were expected to produce books that reflected the new Soviet values."[229] The school tale not only included key aspects of socialist realism but also served as a pedagogical version of the *perekovka* narrative.[230] Children's literature often contained industrial themes that linked visual and textual images in homage to the Russian avant-garde, just as it was also, in a paradoxical move, being streamlined and institutionalized along Party lines.[231] This transitional period in children's literature reflects the nature of the artwork produced at the White Sea-Baltic Canal adeptly, since texts produced by the project exhibit artistic hybridity.

With the evolving role of children's literature also came a new interpretation of childhood. Spearheaded by none other than Gorky himself, the interpretation turned childhood into an "anti-utopia," a space of suffering and sadness, as is the case with the author's own childhood memoir, which mostly documents his harsh treatment by neighbors and relatives. The idea of a happy childhood was seen as anti-socialist and bourgeois, an outdated notion linked to the gentry class. Instead, Soviet authors chose to portray one's upbringing as lonely and difficult, with separation and alienation from parental figures.[232] These unhappy children characters, who use their sorrow and displacement as sources of strength and vitality,[233] are not so different from the criminals and thieves at the White Sea-Baltic Canal; they come from broken homes, have certainly had unfortunate childhoods filled with hunger and want, and use their troubled pasts as springboards to begin new futures.[234] The criminals at the White Sea-Baltic Canal were very often parentless, or if they still had a parent alive they were estranged from them because of their unlawful lifestyles. Both groups, the young orphans and the abandoned criminals, were ideal targets for *perekovka*, because they had no family structure on which to rely. The Soviet Union could easily become their ancestral replacement. Mikhail Nikolaev, orphaned in 1932 at the age of three, recalled:

> After all, we were deprived of family events, of conversations around the kitchen table—that non-official, and, in my opinion, most important source of information that forms man's notions of life and his relationship with the world. Our "window on the world" was the teachers, the educators, the camp councilors, the radio in the red corner, and the newspaper *The Pioneers' Truth*.[235]

Not only were both groups a blank slate for Soviet ideology, but the two were strategically targeted for reformation, since both wayward orphans and professional criminals represented a threat to the well-being of Soviet society at large.[236]

Anton Makarenko's pedagogical classic, *The Road to Life* (*Pedagogicheskaia poema*, 1935), tells the story of the appropriately-named Gorky colony for young delinquents, where orphans were taken in and "reformed" through education and hard work. The Belomor official Semen Moiseev makes a connection between Belomor and the juvenile education program, writing that the prisoners were taught "according to Makarenko's methods" (*po metodam A. S. Makarenko*).[237] Once again, the theme of the New Man comes to the fore, since one of the key goals at the colony centered upon the fact that "we have to find new methods for the creation of the new man."[238] Here the parallels with the Gulag prison camp are even more striking, since the orphanage is likened to a den of thieves, where crime and hooliganism run rampant.[239] The old forms of instruction—such as the rod in Tsarist Russia—are compared to the progressive education of the present day, just as official works about the White Sea-Baltic Canal contrast Soviet incarceration with its capitalist counterpart.[240] The importance of strict, military-type training at the Gorky colony for juvenile delinquents[241] parallels the militaristic jargon used in many Belomor texts.

As was the case with the convicts on the canal, it is supposedly a new life of construction and physical work that allows the children to change their lives and habits.[242] By extension, while rebuilding outhouses or clearing paths in the forest, they understand these physical actions metaphorically and see them as analogies for their rebuilt lives. The orphan-thieves of the Gorky colony admired the namesake of the institution because they could identify with his life and see it as not so different from their own. They idealize his rough-and-tumble biography as well as the romantic portrayals of thieves and criminals in his early short stories and plays. Once again Gorky seems to have become a symbolic persona for the era and its various hopes and struggles. The boys are reported to have reacted positively to Makarenko's explication of Gorky's life:

> At first they didn't believe me when I told them the real story of Maxim Gorky's own life. They were stunned by the story, suddenly struck by the idea: "So Gorky was like us! I say, that's fine!" This idea moved them profoundly and joyfully. Maxim Gorky's life seemed to become part of our life. Various episodes in it provided us with examples for comparison, a fund of nicknames, a background for debate, and a scale for the measurement of human values.[243]

It is significant that specifically Gorky's life story inspired the boys, since autobiography played an essential, motivational role in the re-forging of prisoners at the White Sea-Baltic Canal. Not only did Gorky champion the notion of *perekovka*, but his lived experience can act as an example of the phenomenon. His story inspires others, just as at Belomor the tale of one criminal's re-forging is intended to instigate it in another.

The Gorky colony gave many of the juvenile delinquents a new lease on life, offering them opportunities and support networks. However, some students left without being "reformed," or were forced to depart because of mischievous behavior. Although the transformative process at the orphanage was similar to *perekovka*, there were also key differences. One important difference is that the charges living at the colony were not prisoners and could technically leave of their own free will, according to Makarenko's text. More importantly, there was a decided lack of emphatically ideological instruction in their re-education, a component that was absolutely imperative in the re-forging of White Sea-Baltic Canal prisoners. Even when the boys living at the colony expressed interest in becoming members of Komsomol, the youth communist club, this path was initially forbidden to them, as Party members saw them as delinquents and ineligible for consideration. Only after their departure from the colony and their certifiable reformation could the topic of their inclusion in the organisation be discussed.[244] This is precisely the opposite of the situation at the White Sea-Baltic Canal, where the prisoners were encouraged from the very beginning to be trained ideologically, to understand Soviet mannerisms, speech, and traditions. Officials believed that the more a previously debased convict could take pride in his newly upstanding socialist status, the more likely he or she was to be transformed completely and permanently.[245]

In certain cases, juvenile delinquency and incarceration as reformation followed parallel tracks. The OGPU, which was in charge of operating the Gulag, also headed children's colonies to garner favorable publicity. In 1929, the OGPU sent juvenile delinquents to the Solovki prison camp in an attempt to quell rumors about the abominable conditions in the Gulag; such problem children were also sent to the White Sea-Baltic Canal. In addition, just as the canal administration ultimately viewed Belomor prisoners as wares processed by the "factory of life," so did Makarenko interpret unruly children as products in his pedagogical writings: "Every person reformed by us is a product of our pedagogical production. Both we and society must examine our product very intently and carefully, to the last tiny detail."[246] Although the homeless children problem had diminished somewhat by the mid-1920s, juvenile criminality soared in 1929 during the brutal process of collectivization.[247] Since most of the prisoners at the White Sea-Baltic Canal were peasants incarcerated for being kulaks, it is the State itself that created the massive homeless population. In an ironic twist of fate, the two groups—the homeless, basically orphaned children and their convict parents—were subject to the same propaganda of re-education and re-forging in the name of Soviet power. These families, broken apart by the very institutions attempting to indoctrinate them, were now supposed to look to the state itself as a replacement for their family, which may at some point have been intact. Yet many prisoners did not make this connection, instead blaming the "vile" elements of capitalism in the Russian Civil War for the deaths of their parents, which had left them homeless and set them upon the path of criminal behavior.[248] Similar to the paradox of prisoners being forged as free beings by the very labor that imprisons them, the predicament of homeless children demonstrates an additional contradiction. Both re-educational programs are totalizing and complete: there can be no alternative to the Soviet path.

Conclusion: Navigating Soviet Reality

While the relationship between *put'* and *perekovka* demonstrates the ironic parallels between a fall into a life of crime and a lift into a socialist reality, certain incompatibilities remain. The role of the criminal mentor is often more pronounced and durable than that of the *vospitatel'* counterpart, who is not necessarily always responsible for a criminal's re-forging. Often the peer pressure of other prisoners working in the brigade, or the allure of specific incentives (like a shortened prison term), is more successful than the typical educator's speech. There are also inconsistencies on schematic, symbolic planes. In what is a ritualistic, repetitive act, elements of the personal and individual become magnified; in what is an atheist country, quasi-religious conversion narratives are promoted; in what is a forced-labor Gulag camp, lax policies and disobedience abound and often remain unnoticed.

In the face of these divergent characteristics, one unifying thread remains: the *put'*, or path, of transformation. The names alone of various work brigades at the canal make this evident: "The Path to Correction" (*Put' k ispravleniiu*), "The Path to Studies" (*Put' k uchebe*), "The Path to Socialism" (*Put' k sotsializmu*), and so on. *Perekovka*, like its inverse voyage towards the criminal world, was figured spatially and linked with a sense of physical motion toward a defined goal, rendering the phenomenon a type of pilgrimage. While there may be a defined set of features accompanying a pilgrimage, each pilgrim participates in the voyage in an individualized way,[249] similar to how criminals performed *perekovka* at Belomor. Similarly, the writers' brigade completed a pilgrimage to the baptismal waters of the White Sea-Baltic Canal in order to pen their collectively written tome about the project. In the factory of life, the physicality of creation becomes apparent, and art and labor are inextricably bound in performing the cycle of alternating production and destruction.

II
THE ART OF CRIME

> In theory one would think that power belongs to brute force. In fact, this is not the case at all: power is wielded by the magician, by the man with the subtle sleight of hand. It belongs to the light-fingered cutpurse. Power belongs to art. Almost as in the case of poets, what counts most in the thieves' code of behaviour is style, the ability to project one's personality in terms of show, spectacle.[250]
> –Andrei Siniavskii, *A Voice from the Chorus* (1973)

Criminals often consider their profession an art, an elaborate performance requiring wits, timing, and costumes. Russian thieves respect the trade of pickpocketing above all other criminal jobs precisely for its performative flair and finesse; murder, on the other hand, was the least esteemed, despite its brutality.[251] Thieves' slang eloquently captures the artful connotations of crime: *risovat'*, or to draw, means to kill; *pero*, or quill pen, is a knife.[252] The craft of pickpocketing, which a criminal in RUR described as the most "clever" of all types of theft,[253] at times required some unusual techniques. The prisoner Praskov'ia Skachko writes in her autobiography about the skill of stealing in church, an art form her husband taught her:

> He began to convince me, assure me, that there shouldn't be any fear, since there isn't any god. [...] I must say, that there is not a better or less dangerous job—it's in the church. When god's sheep let loose their drool and all the strings of their soul, sweetly raising their eyes to the church heavens, asking for happiness and riches—at this time without any difficulty, you can freely clean out all of his pockets, and he will peacefully and reverently stare at some unseen point, and just as you've cleaned out his pockets, he begins to zealously cross his sheep's forehead.[254]

Skachko and her husband made an excellent living this way. They bought new furniture, had more children, attended luxurious parties, and sent presents home to their families. Even the Odessan police looked the other way for them, deliberately ignoring their infractions. Everyone is jealous of their lavish, charmed lifestyle. Yet Skachko eventually tires of her criminal life and the vigilance it takes to maintain. She never admits to wrongdoing, but simply claims that she was caught because she was "unlucky" and no longer had the proper clothes to ply her trade. In other words, she did not have the correct costume to act in the performance of crime. In a continuation of the previous chapter's metaphor, Skachko was produced into a new person at Belomor. The former thief ends her autobiography, "About camp I can say one thing: that it is not a camp, but a factory—a factory of people, where from the dregs of society and refuse of humankind the new man is forged."[255] The productive potential of manufacture and the creative results of art echo each other—both new works and new people would be designed and fabricated at Belomor, while simultaneously human lives and the natural landscape were being destroyed.

The criminal world has long had a distinct aesthetic quality. Even Aleksandr Pushkin makes the connection between art and crime: for the seminal Russian poet, "art clings to life through death, sin, lawlessness."[256] Not only was crime an art among Russian thieves, but art was often criminal. Bandit characters figured frequently in the traditional Russian *lubok* (early graphic prints with narrative stories), and they were the "the most important protagonists of the installment novels that gained popularity in the early twentieth century."[257] Bandit stories addressed issues of freedom and rebellion against the backdrop of the individual's relationship to society. Although such stories were not based on the real deeds of criminals—nor did they idealize bandits as figures—they nevertheless exposed Russian readers to the vocabulary of crime. Criminals, in turn, were historically objects of pity rather than contempt or derision. In a marked difference from their Western counterparts, Russian bandits were not Robin Hood figures. They did not commit good deeds on behalf of the common people, and they were not incorporated into society because of their community actions. Instead, the main occupation of the fictional Russian outlaws was grappling with the concurrent needs for freedom and a place in society, both individuality and collectivity. The bandits were redeemed through acts of patriotism or state service, much like the re-forging undergone by the Belomor criminals.[258] Thieves also figure prominently in traditional Russian folktales, where they commit seemingly impossible and practically magical robberies, making them seem more like skilled sorcerers than evil wrongdoers.[259]

The Belomor prisoners were real people, not fictional characters immune to violent realities. Art, however, could imitate life. A 1934 issue of the popular magazine *Thirty Days* (*30 dnei*) features a Belomor criminal in the short story "Bandit." With his waist girded by a sparkly belt, the fictional bandit Umarov commits crimes with finesse, dances energetically, and fights Soviet power with "rifle, saber, and dagger" before being sent to the Belomor construction. The story devotes more time to detailing Umarov's difficulties and frustrations at the site than to his re-forging—the bandit falls sick with angina, yawns in the face of diagrams and work-completion statistics, and curses his fellow work brigade members.[260]

The real-life events at Belomor inspired fictional tales, blurring the boundary between the true and the imagined. Prisoner N. A. Blium's play *Mister Stupid and the Shock-workers of Belbaltlag* (*Mister Stiupid i udarniki Belbaltlaga*) is another example in which the creative literally plays out in reality, with the work demonstrating Belomor's multilayered aesthetic environment. Blium's play won a 50-ruble prize in a literary competition organized by the camp newspaper *Perekovka*. It was subsequently performed on the banks of Belomor, a performance that was later recalled in the memoirs of a prisoner audience member.

Art—coupled with labor—played an integral role in the re-forging of prisoners at the White Sea-Baltic Canal, since creative expression "inspired" by physical work was intended to spur the transformative process of *perekovka*.[261] Officials, therefore, encouraged prisoners to participate in a variety of cultural activities. Figures and calculations for cultural production were included alongside, and were just as important as, technical figures regarding the canal's construction.[262] These activities took place across a wide range of media and disciplines, including everything from agitational theater performances to philosophical lectures.

Despite the frequent presence of highly charged ideological content, the prisoner narratives discussed here cannot be considered propaganda in the traditional sense. Some works openly criticize the regime in their texts, despite the fact that the prisoners were knowingly submitting their pieces to a panel of editors that included fellow convicts as well as camp officials. While such denunciations are more rare than expressions of unbridled enthusiasm for the canal project, their audacity is significant. In the more positive assessments of the canal project, which are themselves often tempered by complaints or padded by personal stories of thievery, declarations of praise were likely motivated by multiple factors, potentially including: a desire to curry favor with camp administrators, an attempt to receive special privileges (including early release), or real real enthusiasm for the project. Even texts that were not intended to pass through official hands (such as personal letters and private memoirs), and so would not necessarily have been meant to secure privileges, often echo the ideological messages of re-forging and transformation through labor.[263] The propaganda apparatus of the White Sea-Baltic Canal was so invasive that it could be interpreted as a metaphorical version of Jeremy Bentham's omniscient and all-pervasive Panopticon (see Figures 1, 8). One Belomor historian claims that this was one of the greatest public relations campaigns ever undertaken, worthy of study in business school for its many machinations and techniques.[264] Yet despite this administrative hegemony, prisoners had multiple approaches to and interpretations of incarceration, something that their participation in creative affairs facilitated. While it is impossible for us to access the prisoners' original motivations—motivations that for the convicts themselves were likely nuanced and shifting—it is possible to mine the textual evidence they left behind to look for patterns and make informed suppositions, as this chapter does. The results are complex and startling.

Perekovka: *The Camp Newspaper as Artistic Vehicle*

Many of the texts presented here come from literary competitions organized by the camp newspaper *Perekovka*, which was perhaps the most important organ for understanding Belomor's aesthetic dynamics. The newspaper was an essential, ubiquitous component of the convicts' lives. It served as an official barometer of daily life at the camp, acknowledging achievements as well as deficiencies in the construction and even printing prisoner complaints.[265] The newspaper was both an artistic and an ideological outlet, echoing the popularity of the reportage style in the

Soviet 1930s. Futurists, some of whom were incarcerated at Belomor and are discussed later in this chapter, appreciated the aesthetic and social appeal of the newspaper as a voice of the street. In the four-sentence manifesto of Igor' Terent'ev's futurist group 41°, which will be discussed in greater detail below, one quarter of the text is dedicated to the group's publication: "This newspaper will be a haven for happenings in the life of the company as well as a cause of constant trouble."[266] It was essential for art movements—and later, for Gulag camps—to have a journalistic mouthpiece to spread their ideological and artistic messages.

In what Elizabeth Papazian has termed "the documentary moment," a realist aesthetic dominated from the avant-garde period to the foundation of socialist realism in 1934.[267] The primacy of factuality informed many aspects of Soviet cultural life, and newspapers, in turn, garnered a privileged role as truth-bearers. The newspaper was so important in early Soviet culture that the constructivist writer Sergei Tret'iakov defined it as the epic of its time, likening the journalist to a present-day version of Tolstoy.[268] The predominance of the newspaper in the early 1930s stemmed not only from this new focus on documentary materials, but also from an inheritance of the avant-garde aesthetic, which relied heavily on newspaper fragments as a quotidien representation of authenticity. Collage, which required the insertion of everyday life into art forms, frequently employed the newspaper as a material object. The popularity of *Perekovka* at the campsite, therefore, echoed the larger trend of blended documentary-aesthetic products. While the analysis here is limited to *Perekovka*, there were other journalistic publications at the White Sea-Baltic Canal (mainly wall newspapers, or *stengazety*), and the communal reading of newspapers became a type of social activity at Belomor.

The documentary approach in Soviet culture was paradoxical, as it offered "apparent transparency of transmission of information," or supposed objectivity, when in reality there was a continuously growing contradiction between fact and artifact.[269] This slippage was particularly prominent in the dissemination of propaganda. Factual-fictional hybridity allowed for the infusion of artistic motifs into the documentary aesthetic; just as artistic products of the time exhibited a predilection for the factual—as exemplified by the production novel, which centered its activity at a real-life factory or construction site—so did newspapers have a penchant for poetry and artistic prose.

Figure 9. Prisoners reading wall newspapers at the White Sea-Baltic Canal. Photograph reproduced with permission of Iurii Dmitriev.

Figure 10. A newspaper kiosk at the White Sea-Baltic Canal. Photograph reproduced with permission of Iurii Dmitriev.

The newspaper encouraged literacy by training convicts to read and write and employing prisoners as the correspondents (*lagkory*) for the paper. Only the best workers were allowed to occupy the position of camp correspondent; as one inscription on a smattering of wall newspapers reads, "every shock-worker is a camp correspondent, every camp correspondent is a shock-worker" (*kazhdyi udarnik lagkor, kazhdyi lagkor udarnik*) (see Figure 11). Given their privileged role in editing and disseminating camp affairs and artworks, it is understandable that only the most dedicated workers were in theory allowed to hold such posts. Yet it is unclear if such guidelines were actually followed, and the matter of how difficult it was to receive the auspicious title of shock-worker is even murkier. *Tufta* (padding) was so pervasive that it figured into jokes about Belomor, and written narratives point to massive numbers of shock-workers. Both of these factors seem to call into question the veracity of shock-workers as elite, highly productive laborers. And despite the supposedly high status of being a camp correspondent, the paper had to actively recruit new candidates for such positions; an advertisement for *lagkory* in *Perekovka* requested that those interested in the job send along their full name, article of crime, length of sentence, and any previous newspaper experience.[270]

Figure 11. A collection of Belomor wall newspapers with the slogan above reading, "Every shock-worker is a camp journalist, every camp journalist is a shock-worker." Photograph reproduced with permission of Iurii Dmitriev.

In nearly every issue of the newspaper, there are examples of poetry, short stories, and other pieces of creative writing. Alongside such pieces are more traditional newspaper articles, containing facts and figures of plan-fulfillment and work collective output. The very different realms of poetry and production appear side-by-side on the newspaper's pages. Since most other Gulag newspapers do not exhibit this degree of factual-cultural hybridity, *Perekovka* is a particularly acute example of an aestheticized documentary style and a different refraction of the art of crime. In her monograph on the Gulag press, Alla Gorcheva cites *Perekovka* as the birth of the camp newspaper genre. She notes three primary goals for the publication: improving socialist labor and competition, increasing prisoner enthusiasm, and strengthening of party organizations.[271] I would expand this list by including what is perhaps the newspaper's most important feature, as it undergirds all three of the previous categories: artistic expression. If competition, enthusiasm, and party strength were the ends, artistic expression was the means. Here again the physical body and aesthetic inspiration are inextricably bound in the performance of transformative labor, a formulation that is emblematic of the Soviet approach to productive selfhood.

Sergei Alymov: Editor of Perekovka

The poet and prisoner Sergei Alymov performed many roles at Belomor. He edited the camp newspaper *Perekovka*, he contributed to the collectively-written volume *History of the White Sea-Baltic Canal*, he served as literary figurehead for the canal in his role as the "Belomorkanal poet,"[272] and he kept detailed records of all the artistic undertakings at Belomor. Other prisoners acknowledged his notoriety; in one essay sent to the newspaper, a camp inmate described fighting over a poetry collection in order to read Alymov's work aloud.[273] Alymov was also a meticulous record keeper. He carefully documented criminal slang,[274] collected games and charades from the camp, wrote a detailed diary, and fielded complaints and requests from other prisoners. His notebooks, in turn, are a type of collage, with drawings, facts and figures, vocabulary lists, conversation fragments, miniature biographies, and diary entries all pieced together in one text.[275]

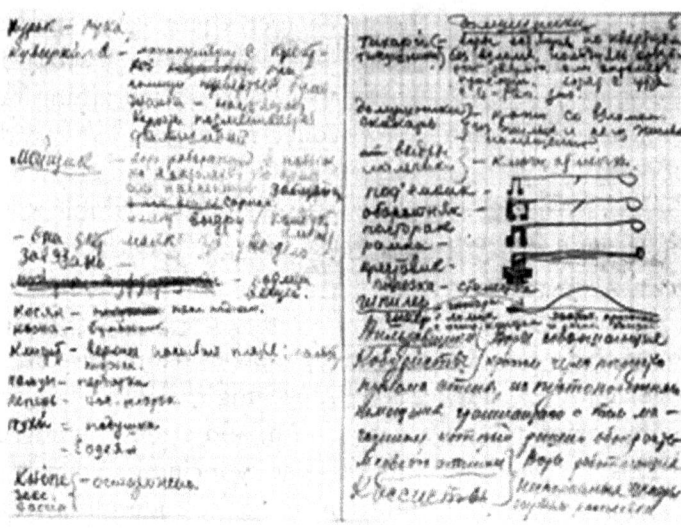

Figure 12. A page from Sergei Alymov's Belomor journal documenting criminal slang. RGALI, f. 1885, op. 3, d. 30, l. 5.

With his prominent status and proximity to the administration, Alymov served as a mediator between officials and prisoners. This unusual position demonstrates how indistinct the boundary between prisoner and non-prisoner could be at Belomor, a phenomenon that was replicated in later camps of the Gulag. In his January 1948 autobiography located in the RGALI archive, Alymov recounts his several arrests and imprisonments across Russia, but he excludes entirely any mention of his incarceration at the White Sea-Baltic Canal. He instead highlights his many travels (including to Australia and the Far East) as a sort of formative education à la Gorky, during which he had a multiplicity of humble trades (he notes a total of sixteen unskilled professions), including stevedore, lumberjack, digger, fisherman, and boot cleaner.[276] Alymov became a well-known songwriter after his release from prison, and for the rest of his life remained in favor with Stalin, who gave Alymov's mother and children a handsome pension after the poet's death.[277]

In his poetry—all of which seems to glorify the grandeur of the Belomor construction—one of the most effective metaphors is picturing the canal's construction as a "wedding of seas" (*svad'ba morei*), which serves as the inspiration for several poems, including "The Wedding of Seas" and "B. M. S." (an abbreviation for the Belomor construction), which are included in his notes and observations about the canal.[278] Other prisoners also explored this idea of romance between two bodies of water, perhaps demonstrating Alymov's artistic influence on the camp populace; one of the most sentimental prisoner submissions is a series of imaginary love letters between the White Sea and the Baltic Sea, entitled "The Love of Two Seas" (*Liubov' dvukh morei*). In this "correspondence," the Baltic Sea writes to the White Sea that they have loved each other for thousands of years, and that the hundreds of kilometers separating them has been a great source of despair. Now, however, thanks to Bolshevik intervention, their union would calm their "stormy hearts" (*burnye serdtsa*).[279] While such a submission would likely please the administration, it is important to acknowledge its creative reimagining of the canal's construction, a refashioning that is, importantly, depicted in romantic tones.

"The Wedding of Seas" was also offered, but apparently not used, as a title for a collection of prisoner poetry. This suggestion most likely became the inspiration for the title of extant volume of prisoner poetry published in 1932, *We Will Unite the Seas!* (*Moria soedinim!*). This "wedding" was not the only way in which the project was figured romantically; in their autobiographies, many prisoners expressed a fervent type of love for the canal, one that replaced the familial and spousal relationships they had left behind. One prisoner wrote in his diary, "BBVP (acronym for *Belomor-Baltiiskii Vodnyi Put'*, or the White-Baltic Waterway) ... these four letters are pronounced with love by the prisoners. Exactly like the name of a beloved girl."[280] It is significant that love—arguably the most common theme of and inspiration for artistic expression—is here recast, and the human lover is replaced by an aquatic, cold substitute. The administration wanted to harness not only the creative potential of the prisoners but also, in some ways, their emotional capacity to love. The State became a surrogate family for the orphaned prisoners just as the canal became a lover, a child, and a friend.

The "transformative" potential of *Perekovka* was highlighted in numerous ways. In a documentary film about Belomor, its printing press is shown with an intertitle claiming it as "one of the most important machines in the transformation of people."[281] The glossy journal *USSR* in Construction (*SSSR na stroike*) showcases the newspaper, claiming it serves as an essential organ in their transformation.[282] Numerous poems in *We Will Unite the Seas!* are dedicated to the newspaper, highlighting its general importance, the correspondents that work for it, and the actual artistic content of the paper itself.[283]

Perekovka also functioned as material—both literal and citational—for aesthetic projects. While many literary works from Belomor simply cite the newspaper, others have pieces of the publication physically glued into their texts. The copy of the *History of the Construction* held in the GARF archive has cut pieces of *Perekovka* adhered to the manuscript's margins.[284] The newspaper also functioned as a mouthpiece for everyday camp matters, since prisoners could send their letters of complaint, concern, or praise to the editors. The publication of one such letter regarding the prisoner work ethic served as an inspiration for a new slogan at the camp, "a shock-worker is not a chicken and does not fear the rain" (*udarnik ne kuritsa–dozhdia ne boitsia*).[285] An October 1932 issue was dedicated to the founding of the publication, and proclaimed that the two-year construction of the canal accompanied the two-year-long struggle for the new, re-forged human being; in a drawing, a stack of newspapers is pictured next to the Eiffel Tower (and is just as tall), and a quotation of some shock-workers notes that "their" newspaper "made them into people" (Perekovka *sdelala nas liudmi!*).[286] One early-released prisoner, A. P. Kupriianova, sent a canal-praising letter to Alymov, asking for its publication in *Perekovka* so that everyone could understand that the feats possible in the Soviet Union would be unthinkable in any bourgeois country. Kupriianova recognized that publishing her letter in the paper would be a way to reach "all camp prisoners" (*vsem lagernikam*), and this indicates the wide reach of the paper.[287] An entire collection of prisoner-written letters (some written on the back of the camp's library order forms) ascribed to the newspaper their supposed transformations: one prisoner thanked the newspaper for allowing him to become literate and so change into a new person (a sentence highlighted in red on the hand-written letter, most likely pleasing to the editorial board); another prisoner included a list of the best *udarniki*; a third convict divulged his life story, citing orphanhood after the Russian Civil War as the central reason for his life of crime. Much of this correspondence, replete with laboriously scrawled letters, was clearly written by newly literate prisoners.[288]

The rationale behind the newspaper-run literary competitions demonstrates the attitude toward artistic participation developed at Belomor. Just as hard labor was to inspire prisoners to poetic heights, so the creation of artistic materials in honor of the canal's construction was meant to make convicts work harder. The physical and artistic were collapsed in a self-sustaining circle. Yet the June 11, 1932, issue of *Perekovka* announcing a literary competition in honor of great feats accomplished at the construction site was actually filled with reports about the inadequate efforts of the laborers, with article headlines such as: "What explains this unallowable inactivity? The third month in which one of the most important shock-worker accomplishments is not fulfilled" and "The work tempo in all divisions is completely unsatisfactory."[289] The coupling of such negative news with a call for works aggrandizing the Belomor project demonstrates two important phenomena. First, the newspaper clearly saw no conflict in soliciting works that actively contradicted the real situation as reported in the newspaper's own pages. Second, artistic expression was meant to improve prisoners' work ethic—this idea resolves the preceding paradox. For this reason, a time of poor labor output would be precisely the correct moment to call for laudatory works regarding the construction, as such narrative contributions would ideally be mirrored by physical displays. The act of putting pen to paper is made equivalent to the act of lifting pick to rock. There is an element of performance in these physical acts; despite whatever the actual work situation was at the camp site, the prisoners could act out and internalize a different reality through the truth-producing act of writing.

Perhaps because of this disjuncture between expectation and truth, the first call for submissions was a complete flop. The competition was originally advertised on June 11, 1932, with three monetary prizes offered for each of three different categories of works: short story or *feuilleton* (250, 150, and 100 rubles), play (300, 200, and 100 rubles), and short forms such as sketch or "living newspaper"[290] (75, 50, and 30 rubles). Yet the deadline had to be extended from 1 July 1932 to 1 August 1932, presumably because the newspaper had not received enough submissions. Even with the new August deadline, the paper received only eighteen poems, seventeen plays, and twenty-five sketches: the prisoners most likely had a difficult time composing artistic works at the end of a ten-hour day unearthing rock, even with the appeal of a monetary prize. To further constrain them, the prisoners submitting works could not write on any topic of their choosing. Specific themes were suggested for the materials, all related to the canal's construction and described in militaristic terms: the "heroics of struggle" (*geroika bor'by*) for the on-time completion of the project; the "struggle" (*bor'ba*) for shock-worker labor; and the "struggle" (*bor'ba*) for quality in construction. The panel of judges was printed in the newspaper, and since the group included camp officials in addition to prisoner representatives of *Perekovka*, it may have further discouraged convicts from participating. The works eventually submitted by the 1 August deadline were not, in the editors' opinion, of high enough quality to merit prizes. Instead, the workers were encouraged to continue reading and writing, and to re-submit later.[291] Despite the announcement of some prizes in the 21 August issue, none of the pieces won the full award money because of the texts' inferior quality. This judgment indicates the editors' preference for aesthetic quality over ideological content.

The editors' impressions about the submitted works make their artistic standards clear; for example, the hand-written notes regarding poetry and theater submissions indicate aesthetic discrimination: "helpless" (*bespomoshchnaia*), "not poetry" (*ne stikhi*), "word choice in places ara illiterate and ungifted" (*nabor slov mestami bezgramotno, bezdarno*), "nonsense!!!" (*erunda*), and "boring piece" (*nudnaia veshch'*). Any complimentary notations are very moderate in tone, such as "pretty good piece" (*veshch' sdelana neplokho*).[292] By contrast, virtually no narrative notations are made in terms of the ideological correctness of the content, and if there are passages that would clearly be offensive to the administration, they are simply underlined. Ultimately, literary inferiority was more important—and frustrating—to the editors than ideologically suspect passages within the works.

It is time to return to the prisoner N. A. Blium's play *Mister Stupid and the Shock-Workers of Belbaltlag*. Paradoxically, it was both a prize-winner in the competition and mildly subversive in its content. Perhaps the play's most striking feature is its character names, all of which are English words transliterated into Cyrillic characters. In a manner reminiscent of eighteenth-century satire à la Denis Fonvizin, the names reflect something about the personality of the character or the subject matter of the play, albeit with English—and not Russian—words, thereby disguising their negative connotations. The main characters include: Sir Austin Waterproof (*Ser Ostin Voterpruf*) and his wife Lady Waterproof (*Ledi Voterpruf*) along with the Copper (*Kopper*) couple, and the two journalists Mister Hardbrain (*Mister Khardbrein*) and Stupid (*Stiupid*). Half of these names are related to water and an attempt to control it (Waterproof, Copper) and the other half insinuates that those who work in the newspaper industry are, to put it mildly, not the most intelligent of creatures (Hardbrain, Stupid). If the potentially insulting names for the journalist main characters (ironically sent into a *newspaper* literary competition) were meant to be a joke directed at the panel of judges, the humor was lost along the way, or at least was not seen as offensive: the piece won a 50-ruble prize in the contest.

Set in England, the play begins with a discussion on the future of the Soviet Union and communism, with Mister Copper arguing on the side of the Russians, praising the phenomenon of shock-worker labor, and Hardbrain claiming that prisoners work in "awful conditions"(*v uzhasnykh usloviiakh*) in concentration camps in northern Russia. In order to resolve the matter once and for all, Stupid goes to the Soviet Union as a newspaper correspondent to investigate. Stupid sends telegrams back to England describing the marvelous conditions at the camp site, which at first he could not believe was a prison; he realizes that the cramped buildings he assumed were prisoners' quarters are actually greenhouses, he talks to convicts walking around with no guards, and he observes orchestral accompaniment on the work site. While the latter two elements certainly were true of Belomor, the overall description of the camp is clearly exaggerated optimism. Stupid loves the prison so much, in fact, that he decides to stay and never returns to England, claiming that he has found a real utopia. Hardbrain cannot believe it and wants to send someone to look for him in the Soviet Union. Once again, while the connotations of the story are clearly positive, a moderate amount of reading between the lines reveals a different significance. Surely, it is not entirely coincidental that the character that visits and falls in love with the White Sea-Baltic Canal is named "Stupid," just as the one who refuses to believe in the potential of the place is called "Hardbrain." Similarly, the fact that Stupid never returns from the canal—despite the explanation that he loved it so much he did not want to leave—has a chilling resonance with real-life disappearances in the Soviet Union. Despite its generally positive representation, the fact that such a play would not only be accepted by the editors but would actually be selected for a prize shows the potential for a certain malleability and even humor among the judges, since at least some of them most certainly understood the English words.²⁹³

Subversion in Criminal Art: "The Moan of Stones"

While it is important, and at times even surprising, to acknowledge which works won the camp newspaper literary competitions, it is also necessary to contrast these texts with works that did not win prizes. Although most of the non-prize-winners still portray Belomor and its machinations in a positive light, there are a few exceptions wherein daring convicts openly criticize the regime. Iosif Kitchner, a prisoner of the first *lagpunkt* (or *lagernyi punkt*, meaning camp section), wrote a subversive short story called "The Moan of Stones" (*Ston kamnei*). Despite the controversial content in "The Moan of Stones" and other pieces, the editors seem to have had a rather relaxed attitude towards such deviational texts. The judges made no commentary on Kitchner's overtly critical text, only underlining particularly inflammatory passages. Similarly, the short story "Breaking Point" (*Perelom*), about two criminals who possess a great disdain for working on the canal and claim that the camp site will be their grave, has only a rather tepid editorial comment written across it: "primitive" (*primitivno*).²⁹⁴ The notation need not refer only to the aesthetic quality of the piece; it could also suggest the editor's opinion of the criminal figure as unformed, not yet fully realized, still primitive in writing and mentality. Just like labor itself, art could process the "crude" criminal on the Soviet path toward transformation.

"The Moan of Stones" provides a nuanced view of camp dynamics, as its author is critical not only of the regime itself but also of fellow prisoners. The seemingly autobiographical short story is about a kulak named Aleksandr Donskoi, sentenced under article 58 for counter-revolutionary crimes. This would already set him apart from the typical criminal prisoner eligible for re-forging, as his crime was an ideological one. He arrives at the White Sea-Baltic Canal after serving time in other prisons, most likely for what the narrator calls his "bold tongue" (*smelyi iazyk*). Immediately upon his arrival, he has the premonition that the landscape will be a place of death—a feeling that troubles him all the more when he realizes that the others around him are silent, and "not merely silent but actually take part in the administration and help the production."²⁹⁵ Even though this piece was submitted as a fictional story, it is impossible not to understand such a statement as describing the factual reality of the camp. Given the written, material evidence of many prisoners praising the canal, it is highly plausible that such allegiances occurred and exacerbated tensions among prisoners. While it might be tempting to speculate as to whether these dedicated affirmations were "genuine" or not (i.e., did prisoners praise the camp administration because they truly believed in the project, or only because they were looking for material rewards?), such an investigation is, in some ways, beside the point. Given that we will never know what the prisoners truly thought, as we can never climb inside their minds, any suppositions here are scurrilous. The prisoner-authors likely had a very complex relationship with their own motivations, on the one hand desiring rewards and recognition while on the other hand being potentially reworked by their own artistic production. This likely caused antagonism between prisoners who wanted to collude with the administration and those who did not; from Kitchner's writing, it seems as if there were plenty who fell into the first category, and this fact should be recognized as an important aspect of camp life.

Kitchner's character Donskoi also undergoes a transformation in "The Moan of Stones," although it is not the typical story of re-forging in which a lazy prisoner suddenly finds dignity in work. Instead, the main character becomes sluggish and indifferent to everything around him, a wordless and obedient piece of machinery. Although he attempts to fight against this phenomenon, he finds himself "sinking under the universal pressure of slavery."²⁹⁶ Eventually, he becomes like those around him, with an almost primitive (recalling the editor's aforementioned comment of *primitivno*) mentality towards work and obligation. Unlike some of the other prisoners, Donskoi's ability to function silently as a cog in the machine does not imply that he harbors any true enthusiasm for the project. He does not read or occupy himself with cultural matters, and he finds comfort only in his dreams.

Dreams and sleep are a frequent motif in Belomor prisoner narratives, since they offer one of the few escapes from tedious prison life and also have particular significance in criminal culture.²⁹⁷ In a short story entitled "Bura" written by Mikhail Koldobenko, for example, a criminal suffers through sleepless nights, thinking about his past life and how most of his friends have likely forgotten about him.²⁹⁸ The profound pleasure of sleep is matched by the extreme stress associated with its absence. In another unpublished short story entitled "The Factory of Life" (*Fabrika zhizni*) and signed by the prisoner "Endi"[299] Dmitriev, the narrator discusses sleepless nights in order to demonstrate devotion to the project: "The windows of the little town *Belomorstroi* do not know dreams. In the rooms calculators chirp like starlings. Inclined on drafting tables are old and young faces. Why are these sleepless people doing a work project? What motivates them? Words? Money?"[300] In Andrei Platonov's novel *The Foundation Pit*, completed just before construction began at Belomor, dreams individuate the builders of the All-Proleterian Home:

> Every worker dreams his own dreams at night—some represent the fulfillment of a wish, while others are premonitions of lying in a coffin in a clay grave—but each of them gets through the day in one and the same stooped manner, all doggedly digging in the earth, so as to plant in a fresh abyss the eternal stone root of a building designed to last forever.[301]

The difficulty of physical labor shackles Donskoi's brain and, along with general camp life, paralyzes him; he likens the workers and himself to laboring livestock. Nevertheless, Donskoi is not entirely broken and still has "the spark of human love for freedom" in spite of the harassment—and heavy hand—of his fellow brigade worker, who is a particularly ferocious criminal prisoner (*urka*). The interaction between the political prisoner Donskoi and the criminal prisoner brigade worker makes apparent the friction between these two distinctive groups, who were afforded different privileges by the regime. On the one hand, political and criminal prisoners at Belomor were perhaps closer than they were at other Gulag camps—working, writing, and performing alongside one another. On the other hand, the fact that only criminal prisoners (in theory) had the potential to be re-forged—and so were clearly favored by the administration—likely caused a lot of animosity between the two groups.

A similarly fiendish portrayal of the criminal realm appears in another non-published fictional submission, Dmitriev's aforementioned "The Factory of Life" (*Fabrika zhizni*), where the abysmally long train ride into the dark Karelian landscape is punctuated by the crude language of the criminals: "In their stories, sprinkled with vile language, there was quite a bit of open cynicism, bragging and fabrication. The sinewy *pakhan* recounted his thefts and escapes from prisons [...] the thieves laughed enthusiastically after all of his stories."[302] Even though Dmitriev's story ultimately portrays a positive atmosphere at the camp site, acknowledging it as a factory of life, where absolutely "unusual, miraculous conversions" (*strannye, neobychainye prevrashcheniia*) occur, the narrator makes a point of underscoring the rough and raw character of the criminal prisoners.[303] The narrator in "The Moan of Stones" also indicates the power and cruelty of the criminal population. Since criminals were the primary targets for *perekovka*, they were more likely to become shock-workers and to be assigned the duties of cultural-educational workers. In fact, official documents completely deny membership in work collectives to any prisoner convicted of counter-revolutionary acts under article 58. The only exceptions to be made to this rule are for workers, the poor, and the middle class, and even in these cases a prisoner must first be included only on a trial basis.[304] Yet this standard was clearly not always maintained, as the presence of numerous autobiographies by 58-ers in various work brigades attests.

While the petty criminals were certainly the most privileged of all groups, this population was ironically the most ill-equipped to have the responsibility of *vospitatel'*, or ideological educator. This topsy-turvy situation led to mass disorganization, abuse of power, and a re-configuration of the social environment along the lines of criminal mores. The rearrangement is reflected by the criminals in the short story "The Moan of Stones," as they transform the barracks into a veritable den of filth and vice, where convicts are endlessly playing cards, swilling vodka, and engaging in drunken orgies. The unbelievable racket in the living quarters robs Donskoi of the only peace he has—his dreams—and his situation becomes more and more unbearable.[305] Donskoi likens the criminal population to stupid animals, and is unable to see anything worthwhile in their characters: "With disgust [Donskoi] thought about how little in them was human, and the very worst was that these unfortunates were doomed to a slow death since in reality no one was interested in their fate."[306] This phrase, underlined in wax pencil, clearly caught the attention of the editorial board. Kitchner's deep cynicism, as expressed through Donskoi, sheds light on the motivations and attitudes of both the colluding criminal prisoners and the administration trying to harness them.

Yet perhaps the most damning aspect of "The Moan of Stones" is neither the portrayal of mass disorganization at the camp nor the deflation of the entire system of shock-workers and cultural educators; rather, it is Donskoi's blaming of the prisoners themselves for their predicament. Those who refuse to disobey orders and who silently work as requested are the true source of shame for Kitchner and his character:

> Donskoi raised his voice. "We ourselves, ourselves are guilty." Donskoi ardently began speaking. "We are many, almost everyone is unhappy, and everyone is quiet [...] they talk to us like cattle, and we work [...] you really think someone will free us? No! It is only our own hands that can bring us to freedom."[307]

Once again, physicality reigns supreme. It is physical labor that enslaves the prisoners, and it is physical action that can free them. When Donskoi's interlocutor claims that overtired workers do not have the strength to stage a rebellion, the main character merely insists that the time is not far off when the entire country will stand up for itself and issue a verdict on the injustices done to them. The prisoner's call to arms makes it apparent that he is condemning the oppressive atmosphere in not only the prison camp but also in the entire country, linking Belomor to the Soviet experience as a whole. When Donskoi is confronted about his anti-Soviet agitation and ordered to collect his things, he aggressively provokes the administration, in a response that garnered wax pencil underlining by the editors: "You are the executioner and I am the victim, but remember well that roles often change."[308]

Even though Kitchner emphasizes the misery of day-to-day life at the camp, his fictional narrative based on real events demonstrates how easily prisoners could become engulfed in the power apparatus at work on the project. During a noisy card game in the barracks, one prisoner brags about his belief in the Soviet system, as if making this proclamation will assure him some sort of status, "One of 'their own' was already loudly, drunkenly crying out, 'I am for socialist competition, I am an *udarnik*, and do not dare touch me.'"[309] It is highly significant that the prisoners would use the very administration's term of valuation—shock-worker—in attempting to demand respect from fellow prisoners.

This quasi caste-based system of shock-workers is re-addressed when Donskoi discusses the potential for early release with an old peasant acquaintance of his. While his friend Pankratov maintains that there will be an early release for all those who work hard, Donskoi contends that only the thieves—and not those sentenced under article 58—will receive such privileges. In the face of such injustice, Donskoi insists that the only way to spur any amelioration of their situation is to stop working. Yet, of course, this is precisely what the administration cannot accept, even if they can be permissive in other areas. In fact, Kitchner's story demonstrates how the authorities were willing to accommodate a certain amount of deviance in exchange for work, with one official promising Donskoi he can stay up late and play cards and drink if only he will help work on the construction.[310]

The overt criticism of both Belomor and the Soviet Union in Kitchner's story is brazen, daring, and brave. The text raises many significant and controversial issues: the privileging of criminal prisoners over their political counterparts, the general mayhem and disorder in the barracks, and, most importantly, the guilt of the general populace for what was occurring both at the campsite and in the country. It is difficult to imagine a prisoner having the panache to contest the regime so directly while being incarcerated. Furthermore, the contribution was not anonymous, and there is no evidence to suggest the use of an assumed name. Yet surprisingly, the editors did not seem to react very strongly to the short story, at least not on paper. Although they underlined the seemingly more offensive excerpts in pencil, there is no written commentary, as there is with the pieces the editors judged as artistically inferior. There is no evidence indicating that Kitchner (and other writers of his ilk) did or did not experience any particular punishment for their more critical writings. Although it would be impossible to deduce the precise power dynamics at work just from this evidence, it certainly suggests that the administration's control over the prisoners as well as the ideological atmosphere was less than ideal. Notations in Alymov's notebooks make evident a high degree of disorganization: "Where is the plan? We know nothing. We know that it is necessary to build a canal. But how, what—no one knows anything—and the plan is not clear to anyone."[311]

A closer look at *Perekovka*'s literary competitions defies our expectations for a Gulag newspaper. The editors often seem more concerned with the literary merit of submissions than with their ideological correctness; the pieces chosen to win prizes do not necessarily portray the project entirely positively; the reactions to overtly critical pieces submitted to the literary competitions seem lukewarm. These inconsistencies demonstrate an odd state of affairs: what might seem like a straightforward propagandistic organ of state ideals actually contains much more complicated messages. While art and physicality continue to reign supreme in the prisoners' narratives in an affirmation of the aesthetic-physical whirligig at Belomor, the discourse is otherwise hybrid, varied, and complex.

Criminals as Performers: Igor' Terent'ev's Agitational Brigades

At Belomor, the criminal population had the opportunity to transform the theatrics of thieving into literal performance by participating in agitational brigades (*agitbrigady*). These productions were a type of assemblage—a three-dimensional collage of humans, music, backdrops, and props. Igor' Terent'ev, a famous avant-garde poet and Belomor prisoner, was the most notable agitational brigade leader. The troupes' instruments included mandolins, accordions, and guitars, and Terent'ev wrote the musical numbers for his troupe, or used verses from Soviet poets. The songs were short and rhymed like *chastushki*, making them easy to memorize and repeat and so fulfill their propagandistic function all the more readily. Like a mobile art brigade, the troupes would perform everywhere: at the barracks, in the cafeteria, and on the work site. Actors who participated in these performances were not freed from their work duties, and yet they somehow found the energy to perform after a long day of hard physical labor.[312]

Before his incarceration Terent'ev was a member of the futurist group 41° and active in the creation of youth theater ensembles in Ukraine. The group 41°, whose members included Aleksei Kruchenykh and Ilya and Kirill Zdanevich, held eccentric performances at the Tiflis nightclub The Fantastic Tavern (*Fantasticheskii Kabachok*) and proclaimed *zaum'* ("transrational language" or "beyonsense") as the cornerstone of aesthetic inspiration. One of the goals of the group 41° was to "to put the world on a new axis," a task that sounds remarkably similar to the one undertaken at the White Sea-Baltic Canal,[313] and that alludes to Boris Groys' argument regarding avant-garde complicity in the Soviet project.[314]

Figure 13. An *agitbrigada*, or agitational brigade, performance troupe at the White Sea-Baltic Canal. Photograph reproduced with permission of Iurii Dmitriev.

Figure 14. A self-portrait of the futurist and Belomor prisoner Igor' Terent'ev from Vladimir Markov's *Russian Futurism: A History*. Reproduced with permission from the Vladimir Markov Trust.

As one of the most avant-garde of all the futurist groups, 41° members sought radically to transform the world and the language used to express it. Their laconic manifesto—it contained only four sentences—made evident the need for a re-orientation of the world by affirming "transreason as the mandatory form for the embodiment of art," and proclaiming, "let's roll up our sleeves."[315] The group even looked upon such "classic" futurists as Vladimir Mayakovsky and Velimir Khlebnikov as obsolete figures.[316] Terent'ev claimed that the absurd was "the only lever of beauty and a poker of creativeness," and the futurist was acknowledged an "apostle" of nonsense and "an apologist for aggressive mediocrity."[317] Yet *zaum'*, the aesthetic and philosophical backbone of Terent'ev's version of Russian futurism, was not intended as a mere synonym for gibberish or nonsense. Instead, *zaum'* proposed a new understanding of language, appreciative of the sounds of speech and words in and of themselves. This approach rendered Russian futurism distinct from its Italian counterpart, while testing the boundaries of language itself.[318] *Zaum'*'s stress on the auditory component of language recalls the poetry and short stories of Belomor prisoners, which often focus on the sounds of the work site and the "symphony of labor" that it produced (or, in more somber notes, "the moan of stones," as the prisoner Kitchner described it).

In the "Declaration of Transrational Language" (*Deklaratsiia zaumnogo iazyka*, 1921),[319] the importance of sound is underscored and eventually linked to image, since *zaum'* often begins with a rhythmic, musical agitation, a "protosound" that may eventually "give birth to a transrational protoimage."[320] While sound remains the most important element of this aesthetic philosophy, it is deeply connected to the visual. Paralleling this approach, Terent'ev's theater performances at the Shuvalov palace in St. Petersburg used surrealistic paintings complete with visible organs, veins, and arteries in the theater's foyer as a "kind of visual prelude to Terentiev's [sic] productions."[321] Such art pieces brought the physicality of the human body directly into the spectacle. Exhibiting merry, crude, and brutally naturalistic qualities, Terent'ev's performances were veritable romps with sound effects, multiple languages, and scandalous behavior. All of these factors contributed to his notoriety as a particularly daring and obscene director.[322]

Sergei Alymov, editor of *Perekovka*, also had connections to the futurist movement. As an ego-futurist, Alymov wrote the collection of poetry

Kiosk of Tenderness (*Kiosk nezhnosti*, 1920) and helped to organize the journal *Creation* (*Tvorchestvo*) with fellow futurists in Vladivostok.[323] It is telling that two of the most important cultural personas at the White Sea-Baltic Canal hailed from a futurist background, and it may not be entirely coincidental that some of the prisoner poetry has a choppy, avant-garde style. Aleksei Kruchenykh, a fellow 41° member, identified the following characteristics dominant in their variety of futurism: "richness of sonic orchestration, gaudy metaphorism, variety of rhythmic patterns, and structure based on shift."[324] In this respect, the core dilemmas at the foundation of futurism and the construction of the canal were quite similar: the re-making of a new world and a new language to accompany it, the privileging of the culture of the streets as well as everyday life, and a spotlight on the criminal realm.[325]

From April 1931 until the completion of the canal, Terent'ev headed an agitational brigade named after camp official Semen Firin (*agitbrigada im. Firina*), a name the prisoners themselves suggested, since Firin took a particular interest in learning about individual criminals' lives at Belomor.[326] Terent'ev also coordinated the exceedingly popular Povenets agitational brigade (*Povenetskaia agitbrigada*), named for a town near the camp. A journalist visiting the White Sea-Baltic Canal in 1933 describes the excitement of watching a Terent'ev performance:

> The numbers follow one after another and the artists come out one after another. Such richness and different genres! From the lyrical scene of *Shalman* to lively ditties and mad dance. [...] People who are re-forged through labor look upon their past with pain. And here is Lelia Furaeva, in the past a thief and recidivist, and now she is freed early, one of the best shock-workers, singing songs, the thieves' song of Shalman, a hopeless and despairing song, and there was a coldness in the air from the stage. And it is Lelia Furaeva with her comrades who led the scene in the club to such an ascent [...] that the room roared with applause, and invisible threads of sympathy, love, and admiration tied together the stage and the spectators.[327]

The troupe's numbers were equally popular among the prisoners, who had their favorite performers among the criminal participants: the former thieves Iurii Sobolev, Vladimir Kuznetsov and Mikhail Savel'ev as well as the former prostitutes Lelia Furaeva (described in the passage above) and Marina Bannikova.[328]

Terent'ev's daughter Tat'iana Terent'eva recalls her father's performances as "funny and sharp vaudeville on the theme of prison life," and claims that it was only thanks to their production that prisoners began to over-fulfill their work quotas.[329] Not only is labor meant to inspire art, but art inspires labor. Despite the repression and eventual execution of her father at the hands of the regime, Terent'eva chooses to acknowledge his achievements in terms of Soviet standards. She is proud not only of her father's personal efforts and records, but also of his ability to inspire others to work. The regional journal *Karelo-Murmanskii krai* makes clear the necessity of such performances, noting that "art is in the service of man's reforging at the canal's construction."[330]

Terent'ev, therefore, was achieving precisely the art-labor synchronicity that Gulag officials so encouraged. Not only was he a highly successful agitational brigade leader, but he also regularly fulfilled 400% of the work norm, wrote for the camp newspaper, and organized concerts. The administration immediately noticed his dedication and value to the cultural arena, and they rewarded him with separate living quarters.[331] Given his success, Terent'ev and his actors were freed early from prison, and the futurist eventually moved to Moscow, where he voluntarily participated in the creation of agitational brigades at the Moscow-Volga Canal.

In yet another example of the absurdity that permeates Belomor narratives, Terent'ev was arrested in Moscow because of supposed anti-Soviet themes in his theater productions, even though all along he had been staging enthusiastically pro-Soviet pieces in the camps. Terent'ev had continued his efforts in agitational theater in Dmitlag (the camp of the Moscow-Volga Canal) as a free citizen, choosing to live at the Gulag camp to facilitate his work. Ironically, the namesake of one of his most popular brigades, the seemingly untouchable Gulag official Semen Firin, eventually suffered the same fate as his protégé; after the downfall of Genrikh Iagoda, Firin was arrested and killed in 1938. Despite this tragic end for Terent'ev and the official who had served as his protector, the futurist's daughter was able to remark upon the unusual atmosphere at the White Sea-Baltic Canal where she visited her father. "The camp at

BBK remains in one's memory, I would say, as some sort of democracy," where the Kulaks lived better than they did in exile.[332] This comparison, although at first glance controversial, merits elaboration. Although many people assume the Gulag to be the nexus of Stalinist evil, where all of communism's horrific machinations were concentrated, the reality is that exile, collectivization, and forced famines were often much more brutal and certainly more deadly.[333] Such recollections also point to the rather unique aesthetic environment at Belomor.

Yet Terent'ev's dedication and talent were ultimately not appreciated by the regime. In May 1937, the innovative performer was arrested without the right to correspondence—a declaration that ultimately meant execution. Although his official death certificate states that he died of a heart attack in March 1946, Terent'ev was actually shot on 17 June 1937 in the infamous Butyrka prison in Moscow.[334] It is through this personal story that just one of the many Belomor tragedies comes to light: the unapologetic assassination of a brilliant mind who in fact greatly—and enthusiastically—contributed to Soviet ideals and cultural life at the White Sea-Baltic Canal. By applying his artistic skills to novel, experimental projects, Terent'ev was able to ease the pain of prison. As his daughter Terent'eva recalled, living was always interesting to him, "even in prison, even in camp," and "he survived [in prison] thanks to his talent, intelligence, character. Later he told us about how he started drawing portraits of prisoners so as to not fall into grief."[335] For both political and criminal prisoners, art served simultaneously as escape mechanism and ideological expression. The regime favored the latter function, attempting to co-op aesthetic inspiration and bind it to labor production.

Criminals and the Theatrics of Deviance

Performance occurred at Belomor in a literal way, with theater productions, agitational brigades, and musical numbers as regular occurrences, but it is also possible to interpret performance at the White Sea-Baltic Canal metaphorically. This is especially true with regard to the criminal realm. The criminal prisoners at the White Sea-Baltic Canal often took great pride in their former professions in the underworld, and prisoner autobiographies stress the amount of finesse and care necessary to carry out a successful crime. The criminal resembled a performer, with an elaborate set of requirements to get into character: frequent and specific gestures, speech characterized by intense emotion and slang words, a particular type of gait, certain clothing (with the type of hat being of utmost importance), and the ubiquitous presence of tattoos.[336] The criminal act, in turn, became like a performance, an art form that one must master and for which some had more natural talent than others, as Andrei Siniavskii notes in the epigraph that opens this chapter. Art could also function as a survival tool within the criminal world; since the thieves loved amusing yarns, being able to tell entertaining stories could afford one special privileges or even save one from death.[337] In Nikolai Pogodin's play *Aristocrats* (*Aristokraty*, 1934), based on Belomor, a character called simply "tattooed woman" (*Tatuirovannaia*) teaches other prisoners about the "art" of killing. In pre-war Odessa, one of the bastions of the criminal underworld, thieves would perform their acts with stunning flair, acquiring notoriety and fame for their elegant maneuvers. A reporter at the time likened such criminals to "artistes" and "ballet dancers."[338] Many of the prisoners at the White Sea-Baltic Canal likely came from Odessa, and this magnetic city served as the inspiration for some of the cultural works to be discussed here. Perhaps no other place in Eastern Europe is as synonymous with crime as Odessa, the "city of thieves."[339]

Odessa played a major part in a criminal-written song about the White Sea-Baltic Canal from the early 1930s, "Music Is Playing in the Moldavanka" (*Na Moldavanke muzyka igraet*). The neighborhood Moldavanka was a type of city-within-a-city, infamous for its "dark alleys, filthy streets, crumbling buildings, and violence."[340] It was also a distinctly Jewish neighborhood, in which middle-class business affairs took place alongside more seedy activities.[341] Although there are several versions of the song,[342] the same basic story remains the same: the pickpocket Kol'ka is sent to Belomor as a prisoner from his native Odessa, and the local *pakhan* (crime boss) decides to send the beautiful Masha after him to facilitate his escape from the labor camp. What she finds, however, is unexpected; Kol'ka has been "re-forged" into a hard-working citizen, and does not want to return to Odessa nor to his former criminal life:

> Ah, hello Masha, my dear darling,
> Say hello to Odessa and its rose gardens.

> Tell the thieves that Kol'ka is developing
> Into a hero of the canal in the flames of work!
> Also tell them, that he doesn't steal anymore,
> He has ended his criminal life forever,
> He has understood a new and different life here,
> Which the Belomorkanal gave him.
> Goodbye, Masha, my dear darling,
> Say hello to Mother Odessa.[343]

It is significant that Kol'ka refers to himself in the third person; like the engineer Magnitov in the *History of the Construction*; he has become a new person and so can speak about himself from a distance, objectively. His transformation matches the idealized rehabilitation of *perekovka*: through the physical strain of hard labor, he has found a new code of morals and given up his old life. Yet the criminal code of behavior is just as strict as the Soviet penal system, and since Kol'ka has broken the trust of his gang, the *pakhan* orders for him to be murdered immediately. It is crucial to highlight that even a representative text from the thieves' world includes a re-forging narrative, thereby echoing the official ideology of Belomor and demonstrating the tenacity of its philosophy even in informal criminal realms. Given that thieves' songs typically highlight a successful robbery,[344] it is all the more significant that here the achievement is reversed as a successful re-forging.

The song highlights important elements of the criminal world: thieves' jargon, like the words *pakhan* and *fraer* (the slang terms for a crime boss and a non-criminal, respectively); the criminal profession of pickpocket; the unforgivable sin—punishable by immediate execution, according to the laws of the criminal world—of colluding with the State; and the sinister realm of Odessa, its dark and mysterious dens coupled with the tender nickname of "mother." Given the all-important status of the mother figure in criminal culture, the maternal nickname for Odessa demonstrates how much the thieves adored their unique and colorful city.[345] Like the Moldavanka neighborhood, Odessa was a conspicuously Jewish city, and many of its gangsters and crime lords were Jews.[346] Interestingly, the Belomor construction had a similarly Jewish flavor, with scholars noting that Jews occupied top administration posts[347] and acknowledging the significant Jewish elements of the project in the *History of the Construction*.[348]

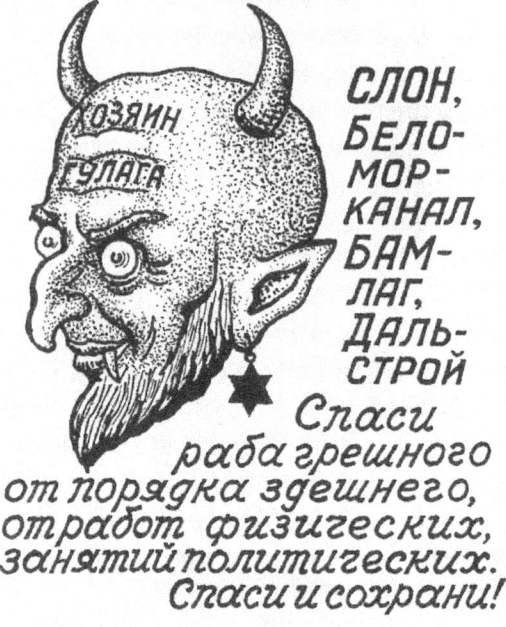

Figure 15. © FUEL / Danzig Baldaev. An anti-Semitic criminal tattoo. Across the forehead reads "Boss of the Gulag" and next to the image is "SLON [Solovetskii camp], Belomorkanal, Bamlag, Dal'stroi. Save thy sinful servant from the regime here, from physical labor and political lessons!"
Reproduced with permission from *Russian Criminal Tattoo Encyclopaedia* Volume I, FUEL Publishing, London 2004.

Figure 16. © FUEL / Danzig Baldaev.. A tattoo of three skeletons digging the White Sea-Baltic Canal. The caption reads, "Dig Deeper, throw further, farting steam. 1931-33. The White Sea-Baltic Canal." Reproduced with permission from *Russian Criminal Tattoo Encyclopaedia* Volume II, FUEL Publishing, London 2006.

Figure 17. © FUEL / Danzig Baldaev.. A tattoo of a Belomorkanal ration cup. The caption reads, "The extra rations of a convict-hero of socialist labor." The letters on the ration cup are an acronym for the White Sea-Baltic Canal. Reproduced with permission from *Russian Criminal Tattoo Encyclopaedia* Volume II, FUEL Publishing, London 2006.

One criminal's tattoo from the Gulag represents graphically—with antisemitic connotations—the association between Jewish power and the prison camps. It shows a devilish-looking character across whose forehead is written "Ruler of the Gulag" (*Khoziain Gulaga*). Next to him are written the names of various labor camps, including Belomor. There can be no doubt about the anti-Jewish allusions: the beastly character has a hooked nose and horns, a pointed beard and bulging eyes, and wears the Star of David as an earring in his left lobe.[349] Tattoos—a complex and ubiquitous art form in the criminal underworld—often referenced Gulag camps, with Belomor a particularly frequent allusion.[350] Another Belomor-themed prisoner tattoo depicts three skeleton-prisoners, digging furiously as they smoke and fart steam in what is a highly sarcastic—and physical—rendering of camp life. A third tattoo indicates the malnutrition prisoners faced at the canal. In the star-shaped (clearly a reference to Soviet power) ration cup labeled "the extra rations of a convict-hero of socialist labor," the only contents are a hammer and sickle and shackles. The prisoners are fed with ideology and forced labor, as the image makes apparent. The cup is bordered with barbed wire laced with carnations, yet another way of equating Soviet ideology—carnations are the flower of the Revolution—with the prison camp.

Chapter Two

The practice of tattooing, ubiquitous in the criminal realm, had the paradoxical nature of being both the *cause* and the *effect* of exclusion—existing outside the limits of society, a thief obtained a tattoo to signify their allegiance to the underworld, but this very tattoo also ended up demarcating the subject as a member of a lower order.[351] The criminal tattoo language in the Soviet Union was highly codified and complex, allowing a prisoner's biography to be written on the skin: nickname, birthdate, criminal specialty, number of sentences, locations of incarceration, ranking in the criminal hierarchy, sexual preferences, and more could be gleaned from markings on the body. Using dictionaries of criminal tattoo images, police could literally read the life of an unknown corpse through the images on their skin to ascertain its identity.[352] The practice of criminal tattooing encapsulates many of the central tenets of this research; it is creative and destructive, aesthetic and violent. Some prisoners could not have their tattoos completed due to the extreme pain of the makeshift procedure.[353] The process is also performative: one prisoner must tattoo another, and the images in turn play a vital role in a criminal's "costume," or operational identity.

The massive influx of thieves at Belomor allowed criminal motifs to emerge in many of the cultural products from the project. The only woman truly respected according to criminal mores, the mother, was the subject of much prisoner poetry, some of it quite sentimental, with titles like "Romance" (*Romans*).[354] There was also the ubiquitous presence of card games, that all-important activity in the world of thieves. Such games were a type of performance, since other prisoners would typically crowd around and watch the contests in action.[355] Just like in the criminal world as a whole, these card games had strict rules, and criminals could play only specifically criminal—not *fraer*—games with fellow convicts. The outcomes of such games could have drastic consequences, with losses incurring anything from the removal of a gold tooth by hammer to the ripping off of an ear to the end of life itself. Much like dreams, card playing could also have a predictive function; good luck in a game forecasted good luck in a crime, according to the criminal tradition.[356] The obsession with card playing serves as a metaphor for the criminal realm as a whole, since the element of risk in gambling parallels the excitement of committing crimes.[357] The adrenaline rush experienced when stealing, in turn, was described in the memoirs of many prisoners as a feeling that made a life of crime addictive. Some skills inherited by a thieving life were reconstituted as special talents that could actually help the canal's administration; in his story "Filter" (*Fil'tr*) the prisoner Mikhail Koldobenko claimed that his years in the criminal world had allowed him to develop a keen eye for recognizing mistakes, including technical ones: "Believe me. After ten years of criminal life, I can punish things exactly. My eye is a microscope. Reliable. For one ruble I can offer a hundred. And I know what mistakes smell like."[358] The criminal eye, which must be observant and astute at all times, can here apply its skills to a drastically different context.[359]

Through the process of re-forging, the prisoners at Belomor were also meant to become "cultured" in the larger, more Russian sense of the word.[360] The authorities hoped that, thanks to the learning of manners like cleanliness and respect, and skills like reading, writing, and professional training, the prisoners' reeducation would extend beyond the physical work of building the canal. This kind of training was occurring in the Soviet Union more generally as an important aspect of the Cultural Revolution of 1928-31.[361] An article in *Perekovka* addressed the significance of living properly, claiming that the prisoners had to be careful about cleanliness and garbage and needed to take care of their living spaces in order "to live pleasantly, civilly, and healthily."[362] The prisoner G. Mel'nikov, in his essay "From the Baltic [Sea] to the White [Sea]" (*Ot belogo do baltiiskogo*), claims that at the canal "a new manner of life was born," with the usage of the Russian word *byt* implying everyday customs, household matters, and cultural life.[363] In his essays, Sergei Alymov also pointed to cleanliness as a vital aspect of maintaining the proper atmosphere at the canal, noting particularly the importance of keeping kitchen areas clean, since prisoners were going to the infirmary with dysentery.[364] Maintaining cleanliness, therefore, was nearly as important as working on the canal itself. Even the *History of the Construction* contains a lengthy section on washing laundry at the camp site, a mundane and everyday task that was elevated to a matter of supreme importance in the larger battle of the Cultural Revolution.[365] During Stalin's rule, uncleanliness could signify the violation of sociopolitical norms as well as physical dirtiness, as evident by the term *chistka* (cleansing, or more familiarly, purging) being used for the systematic rooting out of political enemies.[366] Given its removed position and strictly regulated atmosphere, the prison is an ideal site for undertaking such methodical cleansing.

During the Cultural Revolution in Russia, aberrations had to be minimized in what was a total societal makeover. Such a process necessarily brought out the more unsavory elements of society, such as hooligans, a demographic of concern in the 1920s. In her groundbreaking work on hooliganism, Joan Neuberger examines the relationship between class conflict and cultural identity against the backdrop of crime. Neuberger claims that the rise of hooliganism in the 1920s created a clash between barbarism and civilization, thereby prompting a discussion of culture and definition of identity.[367] Crime is an ideal backdrop for such a discussion, "because it provides one of the few instances in which classes actually interact, right on the street"[368]—or, as in the present research, at the site of the labor camp, with its diverse working population. Neuberger links hooliganism to revolution in the socially tumultuous arena of 1905 St. Petersburg. I would also connect hooliganism with revolution, but in this case with the dynamics of the Cultural Revolution of 1928-1931. The large proportion of criminal prisoners at Belomor, often externally described as "hooligans" (khuligany),[369] alongside more educated (as well as international) convicts necessarily introduced class and cultural conflict and prompted discussions of identity. While hooliganism may still have been controversial in the early twentieth century, by the early 1930s it was already a popularized phenomenon. Its rise was helped in part by Maxim Gorky's romantic tales from the criminal world, the futurist and avant-garde embrace of hooliganism, and the massive influx of newly literate citizens into public discourse.[370]

The privileging of criminal prisoners at Belomor in and of itself foregrounds their experiences, with even the propagandistic *History of the Construction* seeming to glamorize the *blatnoi* lifestyle by including thieves' slang and customs in its pages, rather than condemning it.[371] The criminals at Belomor are ensnared in the destructive/creative cycle both physically and metaphorically; as Vera Inber, the writer, notes in her diary after visiting the prisoners on the canal: "The bandits love the rock labor most of all—in other words, to explode rock. The thirst for destruction, turned towards creation."[372] With every explosion of rock, the criminals were also intended to feel that they were destroying their old habits, their old predilections, in order to clear space for the construction of a new Soviet identity. This work was accomplished collectively and with a sense of larger purpose—the stitching together of waterways for the ultimate goal of Moscow as the port of five seas.

The 1930s also witnessed the emergence of a new type of criminology, in which the focus shifted from the supposedly inherent characteristics of the criminal to the society that produces the prisoner.[373] Similarly, the foundational work of the re-educative Soviet penal system, *From Crime to Labor*, focuses on how capitalist societies produce criminals rather than attributing crime to some type of innate quality of the prisoner—with the latter tendency identified as part of Nazi deterministic philosophy. The adoption of this stance is necessary for the possibility of *perekovka*; in order for prisoners to be re-forged, their personalities must be malleable and not intrinsic. Just as the rise of hooliganism allows for a discussion of culture and identity at the beginning of the twentieth century, so does the privileging of criminal prisoners at Belomor create a particular environment in which issues of class, tradition, and custom are not only discussed but also significantly altered.

Conclusion: The Art of Criminality

The criminal categories examined here—the camp newspaper, agitational brigades, tattoos, subversive texts, the performance of song—demonstrate the polyphony of artistic voices and experiences at Belomor. In all of these examples, the body is linked to art, with the performance of labor often facilitating this connection. Physicality plays a literal and metaphorical role in the articulation of criminality; creation and destruction are coupled. The criminal profession requires a certain amout of artistry, and at Belomor criminals became artists by participating in literary competitions, performing *perekovka*, and acting in agitational brigades.

The art of crime, therefore, not only includes the aesthetic aspects of the criminal profession but also how prisoners more generally contributed to the Belomor project as artists. All of their contributions include a level of spectacle. Blium writes a play that is performed at the work site; Kitchner writes a story in which the main character is performing a false reality; Terent'ev organizes performative brigades that employ artists and are meant to inspire others. These two aspects of performance—the criminal profession itself and the performative works of prisoners—embrace both the creative potential and the violent reality of the prison camp.

III
THE SYMPHONY OF LABOR

> In order that the center can not only advise, convince, and debate with the orchestra—as has been the case up to now—but really to direct it, we need detailed information: who is playing which violin and where? What instrument is being mastered and has been mastered and where? Who is playing a false note (when the music starts to grate on the ear)—and where and why? Whom to relocate to where and how in order to correct the dissonance.
>
> –Vladimir Lenin, *What is to Be Done?* (1902)

In Grigorii Aleksandrov's 1936 musical *Circus* (*Tsirk*), the acrobatic performer Marion Dixon is chased out of the American town "Sunnyville" by an angry lynch mob because of a black baby who is the evidence of her interracial affair. Welcomed in the USSR as a talented entertainer and a potential future citizen, she is eventually incorporated into the socialist family, one that does not draw distinctions along ethnic or racial lines, as the universal acceptance of her baby demonstrates. Her child is passed from the arms of one Soviet "family" member to another—Russian, Georgian, Jewish—and just as in Mel'nikov's aforementioned sketch "From the White (Sea) to the Baltic (Sea)" (*Ot belogo do baltiiskogo*), the many groups working in the army of labor are highlighted (Uzbeks, Tatars, Armenians, Ukrainians, Russians, Georgians, Belorussians, Poles, and Germans). Instrumental in Marion's transformation—her re-forging, if you will—is the importance of music. As Marion begins to learn Russian, she is also able to learn the words to "Song of the Motherland," the Issak Dunaevskii hymn that peppers the entire film. She stumbles through the words with her Soviet admirer and fellow circus performer Ivan Martynov—her *vospitatel'* (educator), if you will. In the final scene of the film, Marion exclaims, "Now, I understand!" in Russian as a collective of white-clad Soviet citizens march through Red Square. Her comprehension is both literal and metaphorical. She has learned not only the Russian language but also what it means to be a member of the collective in the Soviet Union, and song and performance are what helped her to achieve this transformation.

Mass song, like Isaak Dunaevskii's "Song of the Motherland," had a particularly strong effect on the Soviet populace and was an ideal vehicle for state-sponsored ideals. The songs were catchy and memorable. They incorporated the individual voice into the chorus of the collective and allowed for ideological messages to become part of one's internal contents, one's inner consciousness. Song is of the body and from the body, yet must leave the realm of flesh in order to be heard. Music's rhythm likens it to the human organism. The first beat is the heartbeat. The cadence of song can then accompany the cadence of labor, another one of the human body's productions. It is no surprise, then, that Trotsky would encourage socialist efforts to be accompanied by music, and Lenin would liken the socialist collective to an orchestra. Yet perhaps the most ideal Soviet re-conceptualization of music was the phenomenon of the "conductorless orchestra." Begun in 1922 as an experiment in radical egalitarianism, Moscow spectators were greeted by musicians with their backs facing the audience at the first Persimfans (*Pervyi simfonisheskii ansambl bez dirigera*) concert. By 1928, there were eleven such ensembles playing across the Soviet Union, embodying the revolutionary capabilities of music.[374] While the experimental atmosphere of the art world allowed for such novel approaches to music, it is perhaps song's relationship to labor and the physical body that is most relevant to the Gulag context. Given these connections, musical performance was ubiquitous at Belomor and in Belomor narratives. This chapter will focus on the role musical motifs played in criminal Belomor narratives, on both the levels of content (hymns, oratories, songs) and form (various aural literary devices). As a metaphorical and artistic technique, collage—and its close relatives, montage and photomontage—best exemplify the chorus or orchestra, as all of these art forms must assemble their final creations from numerous parts. The collage technique also combines the physical (such as the tearing apart of materials) with the aesthetic (such as a popular avant-garde art form), making it an ideal vehicle of expression for both the corporeal-artistic and destructive-creative tensions in Soviet culture. Collage, in turn, informs the development of both film montage and photomontage in the Soviet Union.[375] A thorough explanation of music in the Belomor context, therefore, will be accompanied here by a sustained analysis of collage and its related terms.

Chapter Three

Music and the Gulag

Song comes from the body or is pieced together by numerous bodies, incorporating physical activity. Long before the Bolsheviks, the Russian folkloric tradition recognized the connection between the corporeal and the musical instrument. Created by the human body, the musical instrument served as a link between this world and the next. Furthermore, the body itself can be used as an instrument, just as instruments often take the shape of a human body. In a circle of artistic-physical connections, the body makes music that makes the body dance. Even during the most difficult work in peasant communities in pre-revolutionary Russia, music and dance took place.[376]

In the Gulag, music played a somewhat different but equally important role. As is evident by the chain gang blues or the simple motto "whistle while you work," music often accompanies labor. It serves as a distraction and rhythmically imitates repetitive work tasks. Vera Inber, the famous Soviet writer mentioned above who visited Belomor and participated in the collectively-written *History of the Construction*, wrote in her diary about Gorky's interpretation of the music-labor connection:

> The continuousness of human efforts during work processes and their rhythms he compares with music. Gorky perceives the human collective, united by a common, goal-oriented task, as its own type of orchestra, where everything is subordinated to the whole. The grand symphony of labor captures Gorky.[377]

Inber respects Gorky precisely because of his strong work ethic, and she recognizes him as an author who has been able to combine aesthetic production with the concept of *trud* (labor).

While the labor-music connection played a theoretical role in the musings of Soviet writers, it played a tangible role in the prison camps. Given the link between labor and song and the naturally creative environment of incarceration, the prison setting accentuates the connection between the corporeal and the aesthetic. Music had the potential to save prisoners. Both the administration and the criminal prisoner population appreciated a good performer, and the possession of such skills often promised easier workloads or special privileges.[378] Musical performance, in addition, offered great comfort to Gulag prisoners as a method of mental escape.[379]

In the Gulag, music was ubiquitous. Seemingly paradoxically, full orchestras accompanied prisoner laborers at Belomor and were present in many other Gulag camps as well. Music and physical labor often fuse, echoing each other's melodies and attesting to the role musical bands played in many prisons in the Soviet Union. Kazimierz Zarod, a Polish prisoner in the Soviet Gulag, remembers distinctly his experience with music in the camps:

> Our departure each morning was bizarre. Among so many prisoners there were represented all the professions, and very soon after our arrival the commandant had organized a "band" of musicians. Some were professionals, others amateur, but together they made quite good music. Each morning the "band" stood near the gate playing military-style music, and we were exhorted to march out "strongly and happily" to our day's work.[380]

The American Alexander Dolgun recalls a similarly uncanny musical scene when he was in a Kazakhstan prison camp:

> I began to feel as though I was hallucinating again because I could hear music, a band, playing some kind of bravura march. It sounded weak and the instruments were not well tuned, but the rhythm was fast and I was sure it was coming from inside the gate. I had a sense of deep cosmic horror that made me dizzy. In the distance I could see the silhouette of the corpses on the wagon. The band seemed to be playing some kind of grotesque farewell. Then it got worse. Out of the gate came, in lines of five abreast, a column of *walking* corpses in black cotton jackets with white number patches. [...] The band kept playing.[381]

To the outside observer, such musical scenes in a prison camp setting seem peculiar. Yet perhaps Russian prisoners had become accustomed to such a paradox. The documentary film *Stalin Is with Us (Stalin s nami,* 1989) includes a small trumpet group performing as prisoners nonchalantly walk by in a Krasnodar jail, allowing the contemporary viewer to understand more tangibly the incongruity of such a tableau.[382] In the film, the prisoners do not seem at all surprised by the presence of a brass band in the prison's courtyard; instead, they are much more interested in the camera that is filming them. While there is something uncanny about the combination of musical performance and the duress of hard physical labor, the symphony of labor is yet another way in which the paradox of creation in the face of destruction can be articulated through performance. Such a paradox is emblematic of Stalinism and the Soviet experience, as everyday citizens experienced such idiosyncrasies on a regular basis.

Musicality and Collage in Belomor Narratives

Belomor was full of the noise of machinery and the sounds of industry that prisoner and editor of camp newspaper *Perekovka* Sergei Alymov described—as a good futurist would—in what he calls the "Belomor Symphony": "The electrical stations hum. The perforator drills chirp. The loads rumble. The locomotives groan."[383] In a separate essay entitled "Explosions and Music," Alymov describes the ubiquity of music:

> The Canal Army Soldiers arrive with an orchestra in the "land of unfrightened birds."[384] Music begins the day. Music accompanies the work. Rest is full of music. Music and explosions. The explosions groan, like the voice of the construction itself. Explosions accompany and complete the music.[385]

The futurist symphony of noise and machines and the rehearsed performance of music were not at odds with one another. In the socialist symphonic landscape, both were necessary. Alymov likens the noises on the canal to the construction's heartbeat—a rhythm that never stops. In his extended metaphor, he claims that the arteries of the various divisions—project, production, financial, cultural-educational, supplies, transport, and many others—lead to the construction's heart, likening the canal to the human body.[386]

With Sergei Alymov at its head, the camp newspaper *Perekovka* collected many literary works with significant musical or aural features, often including detailed descriptions of the Belomor sound landscape.[387] The three prisoner works—Mel'nikov's sketch, Kremkov's hymn, and Iansen's "literary-theatrical montage"—discussed in this section are varied in form and content, despite their musical commonalities. As an echo of depictions of the rapid industrial construction during Stalin's first Five-Year Plan and Alymov's own statements, the prisoner G. Mel'nikov claims that "new sounds" were born at Belomor in his sketch "From the White (Sea) to the Baltic (Sea)" (*Ot belogo do baltiiskogo*). Audible motifs pepper his entire essay and serve as its aesthetic backbone, from the *tuk-tuk* of the train wheels that forms the opening onomatopoeia to the final observation, poetically rendered, of all the various sounds at Belomor: the cry of beasts and the occasional firing of a hunter's gun, the resounding whistle of train engines hurriedly speeding along with their deliveries, the nighttime cries of forest and lake, the knock of shovels, the ring of picks, and the bump of pile-drivers; all of these sounds compose the "new symphony of the new life" (*novaia simfoniia novoi zhizni*).[388] Once again, this submission reads quite similarly to Alymov's own sketch, cited at the beginning of this section, and prompts the question of the futurist poet's influence on newly literate prisoners.

Mel'nikov's sketch emphatically exemplifies the canal project's ethos, with its inclusion of work stimulation's importance, the feeling of collectivity among the workers, the physicality of hard labor, the psychology of the red and black boards, the potential for re-birth, and the use of militant diction. Mel'nikov's essay, therefore, demonstrates different motifs on the level of content and form. Mel'nikov is proud of the canal project and compares favorably to with other "failed"— and more importantly, capitalist—construction projects. He claims that the Panama and Suez Canals will be "sad poetry from that land" (*mrachnoi poezii etogo kraia*), since the Panama Canal is merely a "route to gold" (*put' k zolotu*) and the Suez is a sandy grave for the bones of Africans and Arabs (ironically, the motif of building on bones became a trademark of Belomor itself).[389] Yet while the content of the piece is highly ideological and in line with the regime, the form, with its onomatopoeic devices and layering of sounds, has more commonalities with an avant-garde aesthetic. This slippage between form and content occurs frequently with prisoners' artworks, and exemplifies the idea of what I would call "avant-realism," the period of time between the end of the avant-garde movement (1930) and the official beginning of socialist realism (1934), during which elements of the two aesthetic approaches combined.[390]

Mel'nikov's essay embodies the notion of collage. The prisoner compares the workers to a giant colony of ant, all of whom are working together as a unified mass, inspired by labor. Despite this suggestion of cohesiveness, Mel'nikov unwittingly acknowledges the diversity of the camp population by enumerating the various nationalities and ethnicities, "On the path of the grand route there are not Uzbeks, Tatars, Armenians, Ukrainians, Russians, Georgians, Belorussians, Poles, and Germans—here there are only soldiers in the Canal army and their commanders."[391] With its battle terminology, this example illustrates the notion of unity through diversity that reappears in many Belomor texts. Individuals from diverse backgrounds fight in the name of a singular cause, just as their artistic works of varying styles exhibit a similar, unified message, like the many voices in a chorus or instruments in an orchestra.[392]

The prisoner Kremkov is also the author of a short piece entitled "Tournament of Labor" (*Turnir truda*) that won a prize in *Perekovka*'s literary competition. Remaining consistent with the auditory motifs under discussion here, Kremkov subtitled his work "Hymn to Labor Competition" (*Gimn trudovomu sorevnovaniiu*). This more schematic, condensed piece repeats the word "competition" (*sorevnovanie*) with different definitions and clarifications: it is the key to victory, the path to the better world of socialism; with it the entire world can be rebuilt. The piece clearly pleased the editors, who wrote "conscious" (*soznatel'nyi*) across the submission in blue wax pencil, in one of the rare instances of ideological commentary on a work. The repetition, or anaphora, of the word "competition" on nearly every line amplifies the sense of combative production and renders the text a slogan or ditty. Both the form and the content, therefore, would likely appeal to the panel of judges. Not only does the piece stress work competition—the backbone of production at Belomor—but it also uses a highly stylized format, replete with repetition and dashes,[393] mirroring the futurist Igor' Terent'ev's poetry. This invocation of the avant-garde is also present in works that the judges found unappealing. The short piece "How to Build a Waterway at the Belomor Construction" (*Kak stroiat vodnyi put' na Belomorstroe*) with its unusual format—a series of chants and replies—exhibits avant-garde characteristics and has "boring" (*skuchno*) written across it by the editors. Surprisingly, however, the piece won a prize, and its aural format of a parade of voices likens the piece stylistically to other winners in the literary competition.

The camp newspaper *Perekovka* recognized the new, innovative genre of "lito-montazh," or literary montage, by awarding a piece in this category with a 75-ruble prize, and the futurist poet and prisoner Igor' Terent'ev espoused lito-montazh as a theatrical aesthetic for his Belomor agitational brigades. The term referred to the organic combination of heterogeneous texts, through which an entirely new work is created: in essence, another version of collage.[394] Although Terent'ev used the word for theatrical performances, it also had a more general, literary application. The prisoner and author D. Iansen described his prize-winning piece "How to Build a Waterway," as a "literary-theatrical montage" (*literaturno-stsenicheskii montazh*), and described himself as attempting to "write a theatrical work on contemporary-production themes with a range of the most important moments of the construction, cultural work, and everyday life of the canal army workers."[395] The piece seems more like a musical composition than a theatrical submission, with a chorus of eight different parts and a separate "oratory" (*oratoriia*).[396] Iansen addresses the question of construction throughout his work, with the physical building of the canal as the most significant theme. Just as the prisoners are building the canal, step by step and lock by lock, so does Iansen's work build itself out of a multitude of voices, employing an auditory format.

Terent'ev notes his interest in lito-montazh as early as 1925 in the theater journal *The Worker and the Theater* (*Rabochii i teatr*). According to Terent'ev, the term montage[397] is not only important in "lito-montazh," but rather will help to change the world entirely:

> We don't need—composition!
> Not music—but sound montage!
> Not decoration—but assembly!
> Not painting—but light montage!
> Not plays—but literary montage![398]

The construction of a new world demanded new literary forms in order to express it, with both environment and technique embracing industrial motifs in the construction of a new socialist reality. Labor was not only the subject of and necessary ingredient for photomontage, but the images also demand significant labor in their interpretation.[399] The fact that the photomontage was often attributed not to an individual artist but rather to a work brigade proves that the toiling masses were both the subject and the *means* by which graphic images were created.

Terent'ev's concept of lito-montazh and the collage of workers at Belomor emerge from the avant-garde legacy in Russia. As early as 1914, Russian artists were experimenting with the collage method. Kasimir Malevich's cubo-futurist collages are some of the first examples of the technique. Russian futurists, in turn, formed important collaborations with poets, painters, and costume designers. The Russian futurists were fascinated with texture (*faktura*), which led to artistic experiments including such varied materials as wood, metal, tar, and glass.[400] These materials not only allowed avant-garde artists to transform reality but also gave them the opportunity to commune with a mass audience. With the outbreak of the Russian Revolution, futurists embarked upon the ideological education of the people by creating agitational propaganda not unlike Terent'ev's performative brigades. Within the context of mass education, collage expanded to include photomontage, a medium that would be even more accessible to the public. The photographer Aleksandr Rodchenko explored photomontage extensively for the 1933 Belomor-themed issue of the Soviet magazine *USSR in Construction* (see Figures 21, 25, 26). It has now become perhaps the best-known issue of the glossy periodical. In the 1920s, Gustav Klutsis split photomontage into two categories: photomontage in form, and photomontage with political aims. German Dadaists and Russian Constructivists argued regarding who first invented the form of photomontage, and the two groups used it to different ends—the Dadaists to criticize the German regime, the Constructivists to support the Soviet one.[401]

Perhaps due to his backing of the socialist vision, Terent'ev believed that it was through the separate bits and pieces composing a montage that the whole of proletarian culture could best be expressed. The art forms of this newly created proletarian world were framed in organic terms: "The living book instead of the play! The living book is: literary montage plus sound plus bio-montage (the actor)."[402] Many Soviet artists, in turn, wanted art to reflect the active realities of life itself. This was especially true at Belomor, where the regime encouraged prisoners to base their compositions solely on the *quotidien*. Reality and fiction, just as in the larger Soviet context, were blurred. This focus inevitably imbued artistic texts with the physicality of hard labor, demonstrating how creativity and work were inseparable at the camp. The Povenets agitational brigade had as their motto an inspirational speech that underscores the corporeal:

> Guys, tell us,
> Where, in what brigade
> Are you trudging along from behind?
> We will go there and we will help!
> Not only in word but in deed,
> Not only in soul,
> But in body,
> Not only with Russian folk songs,
> But with muscles,
> Not only with a singing round dance,
> But with actual sweat,
> Not only with art and culture,
> But with cubic capacity....[403]

Terent'ev attributed the Povenets brigade's success to this slogan, and he claimed these words spring naturally from, and bring them back to, their labor efforts.[404] The motto makes it clear that the members of the brigade are prepared not only to perform for their fellow prisoners, but also to put down their instruments and work alongside them; once again, art and labor are inextricably connected, and participation in performance brigades did not excuse prisoners from general work. This emphasis on physicality resonates with the larger Soviet project; a character in Fedor Gladkov's socialist realist classic *Cement* (*Tsement*, 1925) explains, "'The future is in our brains, but we must realize it with our muscles."[405]

Musicality in Nikolai Pogodin's Aristocrats

Nikolai Pogodin's play *Aristocrats* (*Aristokraty*, 1934) is based on the construction of the White Sea-Baltic Canal and includes a cast of Belomor characters. The play incorporates significant musical elements into its plot, and has an accordion-playing main character who explores his criminal identity before eventually being re-forged. Pogodin, a former journalist, enjoyed a lengthy career penning works that trumpeted the achievements of the Five-Year Plan. Criminals are the main characters in the ironically-titled *Aristocrats*. This type of tongue-in-cheek titling was actually a common phenomenon among Gulag prisoners. Criminals even had sarcastic nicknames for the most sinister of prisons: Sukhanovka was "the monastery" and Lubianka was "the hotel."[406] The play's realism and provocative subject matter is perhaps part of the reason for its great success among audiences—it was declared the best play of the 1934/1935 theater season.[407] It was also adapted into a feature film directed by Evgenii Cherviakov, *The Prisoners* (*Zakliuchennye*, 1936), for which Pogodin wrote the screenplay and Sergei Alymov composed the songs.[408]

Figure 19. A scene from the 1935 production of Nikolai Pogodin's play *The Aristocrats* (*Aristokraty*) at the Moscow Realist Theater.

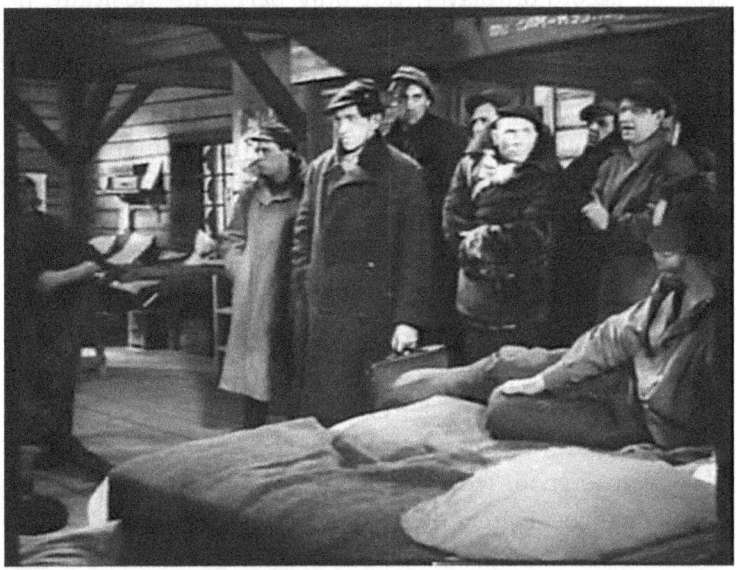

Figure 20. A scene inside the prisoners' barracks from Evgenii Cherviakov's 1936 film *The Prisoners* (*Zakliuchennye*) based on Nikolai Pogodin's play.

Selfhood emerges as a central subject in the play, and Pogodin most often chooses music as the medium that expresses the utopian ideal of collective selfhood. At the end of Act Three, the main character, Kostia claims he wants to sing a Hungarian Rhapsody about the marvelous night that passed, the work they accomplished, and the potential for human love. The "former" Father Bartholomew (former because he "realized" his errors in subscribing to Orthodoxy instead of the socialist brand of religion) follows Kostia's serenade with his musical ensemble's performance of a foxtrot. Kostia asks for a dance called Peter the Great (an appropriate choice, since this famous Russian leader was another empire-builder, reformer, and landscape modifier of northern Russia), and the camp dissolves into the merriment of music and dance. When water rushes through the newly-constructed canal at the end of the play, it is "singing through the locks,"[409] making it appear as if nature—like the prisoners—is musically joyful in appreciation of being transformed by socialist labor. This is a chilling re-writing of events, since the route of Belomor has been more often accompanied by cries of anguish than harmonious melodies.

CHAPTER THREE

Kostia, an accordion player, not only performs musically, but also uses music in his final, grand metaphor about the magic of re-forging. Before relating song to the camp itself, he recalls a vivid childhood memory—reinforcing the crucial role of individual autobiography and past experience—of seeing a Jewish boy play the violin in a concert hall. Kostia makes an analogy between this performance and the one that he is about to give regarding the canal's glory:

> The rhapsody isn't finished yet: there are still a few notes to be struck, still a few bars out of tune. The Bolsheviks know this very well. To go through the conservatory of life is no easy job, especially for folks like us. Sonya, you're not pleased with my speech, I can see. Sonya, I can't sing a Soviet serenade with a cheap tune now. This serenade of mine has cost a great deal.[410]

In what sounds like an unintended double entendre, the Soviet serenade did indeed cost prisoners a great deal—in many instances, their lives. The musical metaphor here is so apt because it sufficiently describes the unification of many voices into one whole, a collective composed of many individual pieces, similar to a collage. The camp chief Gromov notes after Kostia's speech, "Yes, comrades, it's true, our destinies have become intermingled and in this intermingling of thousands of lives there is much that is touching."[411] The composition of the camp population is diverse: "Sluices, dykes, rocks, dynamite, boulders, marshes, crooks, bandits, wreckers, kulaks, ministers of the Provisional Government, colonels, pickpockets ... thousands of them with spades and shovels and wheelbarrows and saws—like a battle tonight."[412] War serves as an aggregating force to bind everyone together in a type of human assemblage.

The Kostia character is practically a stock figure in Belomor cultural narratives, and with his rakish expression, cigarette-stub dangling from his mouth, and simple clothing, he is immediately recognizable. Yet perhaps the most important component of the Kostia-thief guise is his instrument—an accordion. The accordion plays an essential role in Pogodin's play (Kostia gets into trouble when he is looking for glue to fix it), and the classic picture of a thief in the Belomor issue of the magazine *USSR in Construction* shows a prisoner playing an accordion. In the criminal song "Music Is Playing in the Moldavanka," Kostia is the *pakhan* (crime boss) in Odessa, and the name Kostia figures frequently in such *blatnye pesni*. Sergei Alymov remarks in his sketches that in every brigade, in every work collective, one will necessarily find some sort of instrument—be it string, wind, accordion, or a portable phonograph.[413]

Not only was music important in the symphony of labor, it was an absolutely vital component of the criminal world, where thieves entertained themselves by singing songs and playing musical instruments. This perhaps made it easier for the regime to exploit this natural proclivity for song.

Figure 21. A Kostia-like figure playing an accordion in the Belomor-themed issue of *USSR in Construction* (*SSSR na stroike*). Reproduced with permission of Productive Arts.

The Symphony of Physicality: Collage and Related Terms

As an artistic technique, collage (as well as film and photomontage) mirrors the physical presence of a chorus, orchestra, or agitational brigade performance. Piecing together various performers from numerous backgrounds in a musical number is the corporeal articulation of collage. In order to understand why musicality was so important at Belomor, it is necessary to examine thoroughly the process of collage and its connection to the canal project. Collage—from the French word *coller*, to glue—combines different media in order to draw attention to the relationship between art and everyday life. The word collage itself indicates the cobbling together of disparate elements, with their rough edges still showing, an apt metaphor for the prisoner narratives from and the prisoner population at Belomor.[414]

The cubists Pablo Picasso and Georges Braque are largely credited with developing the style of collage and making it into a legitimate art form in pre-war Europe. Following the cubists, the futurists expanded the technique for their art experiments. Photomontage—pioneered by Soviet artists such as Gustav Klutsis and Aleksandr Rodchenko—continued the exploration of fragmentary and open structures in the articulation of technological modernity. Since the often jarring juxtapositions in collage collapse the boundaries between the low-culture *quotidien* and the high-culture art world, the style is apt for the futurist movement, which had as its goals the abolition of museums and the delivery of art to the people in the street. As the futurist manifesto "Slap in the Face of Public Taste" (*Poshchechina obshchestvennomu vkusu*, 1912) proclaims, "The past is restricting. The Academy and Pushkin are less intelligible than hieroglyphics. Throw Pushkin, Dostoevsky, Tolstoy, etc., etc., overboard from the Ship of Modernity."[415] This formulation echoes the philosophy of the avant-garde itself, which asserts that both art and literature must become components of everyday life.[416] Collage represents the "falling together" of modernism, with its qualities of disintegration and fragmentation leading to subsequent integration.[417] As a style, collage refutes norms and tradition, just like the avant-garde worldview.[418] The collage elements evident in so many Belomor artworks attest to an avant-garde inheritance, an influence that substantially informs creativity at the White Sea-Baltic Canal.

Collage also embodies the precarious tension between important pairs of opposites: high and low culture, the individual and the collective, truth and falsity.[419] Everyday objects could be combined with more formal images such as depictions of classical instruments, and an art piece could represent a collection of fragments, yet typically be an individual's work; the collage is simultaneously a fabricated reality and an attempt at uncovering a deeper truth. Such oppositions were ubiquitous at Belomor, and collage served as an appropriate way to channel this tension between opposites like freedom and incarceration, life and death, individual and collective, prisoner and non-prisoner. The inherent reproducibility of newspapers, as well as their capacity to transform language into a commodity, made them a suitable and frequent insertion in collage works; Picasso and Braque often included newspaper fragments in their paintings.[420] Similarly, prisoners and officials at Belomor often cut out poems and slogans from the camp newspaper *Perekovka* and glued them onto other texts.[421]

Collage emphasizes the active process behind art rather than the finished product, and the focus shifts from the result to the ongoing artistic process. The labor involved in creating a collage, therefore, is part and parcel of the art object itself. The primacy of labor in this context makes it an even more appropriate style for Belomor narratives, "Time is not necessary for the collage artist to achieve mastery, itself an ideological token. Rather, he or she plugs directly into the instantaneous present of cultural artifacts. Craft becomes equivalent to labor, which is time itself in a material sense."[422] Collage, therefore, reconfigures the relationship between space and time. With its unique potential to address and assess society, collage has the possibility of not just commenting upon the contemporary world but also "interact[ing] with it so as to change it."[423] This capability points to collage's potential revolutionary quality—a world-changing capacity, not surprising given collage's challenge to the art world's privileging of painting as preferred medium.[424] In art history's important transitional moment to modernism, creativity is no longer mimetic, and works no longer need to produce a mere copy of the outside world. Instead, art faces and challenges the multiplicity of contemporary realties, with an infusion of the everyday creating, but not dictating, an art piece.[425] In this newly constructed reality, art may have the guise of *realia*—defined here as "things in themselves and their immediate reality"[426]—but such realistic-looking artistic works actually challenge the very possibility of a "knowable" world.[427]

The notion of *realia* comes into play in a controversial way in Belomor narratives. Texts often have the illusion of veracity while nevertheless remaining creative, imaginary works, which complicates their status as historical documents. The *History of the Construction* is a prime example of this phenomenon, evident in its very title. While the phrase "History of the Construction" leads the reader to believe this will be a documentary, encyclopedic source, the text is far from representing an objective historical reality. Even other contemporaneous, more sociologically-based sources emphasize that the book is a mere "fictional sketch" (*iavliaetsia khudozhestvennym ocherkom*) and should not be taken seriously as a theoretical model.[428] The text itself is a collage of various materials: *chastushki* (ditties), *prikazy* (orders), menus, life stories, photographs, agitational slogans, newspaper articles, and poetry. The collage style of the work appears not only in its content, but also in its form, since the *History of the Construction* is an "experiment" of collective writing wherein various segments comprised of various contributors' words are literally pieced together.[429]

The integration of radically different elements serves as a metaphor for the canal population, with its profound diversity representing a type of human assemblage—the medium that is collage's three-dimensional twin—including a pastiche of criminal and political prisoners, murderers and intellectuals, Russians and *natsmeny* (national minorities). The end product of the convicts' labor, the canal, is itself a type of assemblage, since the project was built according to the *metro-metod* (subway method) whereby various *punkty* (points) were brought together by separate groups prisoners working toward one another, rather than in a straight line.[430] The great armies of labor who erect a wall in Franz Kafka's short story "The Great Wall of China" employ this same work method, an approach that proves problematic both literally and metaphorically in Kafka's story.[431] This work technique was almost disastrous for the White Sea-Baltic Canal as well. Most of the canal structures were completed by the beginning of 1933, but gaps between watersheds remained and threatened to cause the breakage of dams with the coming of spring floods. Work was accelerated to close these gaps, and the canal opened on May 28, 1933, even though it was not entirely complete.[432]

The workers of varied languages, customs, backgrounds, and religions at Belomor became a single working organism, however oddly shaped, toiling in the name of building socialism and completing the first Five-Year Plan. This very direct and intense encounter with various nationalities and ethnicities often made a strong impression on the prisoners. The priest, historian, and convict P. A. Florenskii wrote in a letter to his wife about how the large barracks in which he was living was filled with national minorities,[433] and he would sit back listening to their various languages with awe and wonder.[434] Diversity could have positive effects, since the camp experience introduced prisoners to situations that would have been impossible in their everyday lives. For example, the linguist Teodor Shumovskii was able to further his research on the connections between the Arabic and Russian languages thanks to the time he spent as a tree-feller among the highly diverse, often Eastern, population at the White Sea-Baltic Canal.[435]

Yet the diversity of the prisoner population could also be a source of tension and conflict, as multiplicity existed in so many aspects: culture, class, gender, ethnicity, and religion. The canal administration devoted particular attention to the religious differences among the prisoners. Apparently, the mullahs (religiously educated Muslim men) in particular proved to be a challenge to authorities, and frequently disrupted the camp's discipline.[436] Such episodes demonstrate not only the difficulties created by a diverse prisoner population but also the officials' lack of control in unruly situations.[437] It also shows another battle faced by prison authorities—the fight to quash religious devotion. The presence of national minorities agitating for the observation of Muslim holidays and the formation of anti-religious discussion circles to counter such activity underscore the fact that faith was an important concern at Belomor.[438] Russia's deeply entrenched spiritual history would have made it impossible to eradicate all religious devotion within the first generation after the Russian Revolution. Devout Orthodox peasants most certainly worked alongside highly religious Muslims.

The division of the prisoner population at the camp mirrors the segmentation that occurred in the construction of the canal itself. At Belomor, *punkty* (points) and *uchastki* (sections) divided areas of the work site just as *trudkollektivy* (work collectives) and *brigady* (brigades) delineated various groups of prisoners. Despite the fact that convicts constantly identified their *lagpunkt*, *otdelenie* or divisions, and *brigada* or *trudkollektiv* in their texts in what is the Belomor version of an identity card, they often considered themselves not so much individuals members of the larger working "family" of the White Sea-Baltic Canal or the Soviet Union itself, reiterating official ideology.[439] One's individual identity had to be destroyed in order to facilitate the creation of the workers' collective. Just as Mel'nikov pieced a metaphorical ant colony together out of individual groups of prisoners, the White Sea-Baltic Canal—with the subsequent completion of its "sister project," the Moscow-Volga Canal—demonstrated the "uniting of five seas." This was an important slogan inspiring the completion of both waterways, as the *nachal'nik* of the eighth division of the White Sea-Baltic Canal construction, Semen Moiseev, remembers it.[440] Similar to what happened to the identities of individual prisoners, destruction (here of the natural environment) was necessary in order to piecing together the seas with the desired, newfangled creation.

The term montage in Russian (*montazh*) beautifully captures the art-labor divide so important in Belomor ideology, since the word refers both to the assembling of machinery and to the artistic technique of montage, which is most often used in film editing. Montage, a cousin to collage, is present in other construction narratives touting the moralizing force of *perekovka*; the prisoner Vasilii Azhaev at the Baikal-Amur camp titles a report about his life and transformation "The Montage of Life" (*Montazh zhizni*).[441] Aleksandr Rodchenko uses constructivist montage in much of his Belomor photography, in particular in the 1933 issue of *USSR in Construction* (*SSSR na stroike*) which was dedicated to the canal. Agitational propaganda in the Soviet Union itself often used montage, with agit-prop trains representing a giant, moving montage. Experimental artists like the film director Dziga Vertov combined the use of sound with the technique of montage to create an elaborate noise symphony in his homage to socialist labor, *Enthusiasm, the Symphony of the Donbas* (*Entuziazm: Sinfoniia Donbassa*, 1931).[442] Montage and collage embody aesthetic physicality and combine the creative with the destructive in narrating the Soviet story. Yet the unbridled modernity endemic to these experimental artistic styles could also be dangerous. Photomontage was challenged as a style in 1931, when Gustav Klutsis was scolded for what was deemed too "impersonal" a portrayal of Soviet workers.[443] This turn of events demonstrates why the concept of avant-realism is so appropriate for the Belomor aesthetic—while the innovative photomontages of Aleksandr Rodchenko depict the canal, the much "safer" texts of prisoners' reformations narrate the achievements of the construction according to the dictates of socialist realism, replete with uninitiated laborer and consciousness-raising moral reformer. It was as if at Belomor one foot was in the experimental and revolutionary past, and the other was on the threshold of the organized and radiant future.

Photomontage and Belomor Tourist Guides:
Maps for a Newly Realized Utopia

The technique of photomontage is ubiqutious in Belomor travel guides. Similar to the criminals' musical performances, these guides take unrefined fragments and transform them into a holistic narrative. The final version ends up being something that does not quite exist in reality: the cheery sound of a trumpeting orchestra did not reflect the actuality of Belomor, just as these tourist guides depict a non-extant utopia (as is discussed in Chapter Five of this monograph). At first thought, the existence of Belomor tourist guides seems absurd. Why would anyone want a map to a deadly prison camp? Yet in keeping with the dictates of socialist pride in technological achievements, it is only fitting that such texts would be created to advertise Soviet progress.

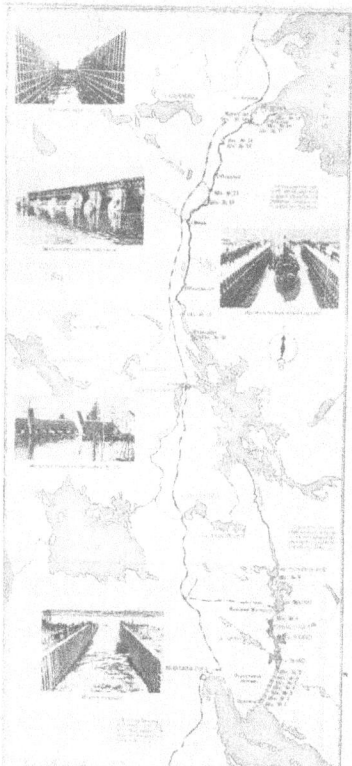

Figure 22. A map-guide to White Sea-Baltic Canal, published in 1934. Russian State Library, Moscow, Russia.

"Map-guide" (*Karta-putevoditel'*), was published in 1934, immediately after the canal's completion. The small volume consists of generously-sized foldout maps on thin, tissue-like paper, accompanied by an introductory text. Not surprisingly, the text addresses the alteration of the country in terms of the map and the first Five-Year Plan by quoting Stalin: "Look at the map of the USSR; the Five-Year Plan has re-carved the country's face."[444] The introductory texts defines the White Sea-Baltic Canal as one of the most important socialist achievements and a major part of the first Five-Year Plan. Many factors contribute to Belomor's significance, according to the guide: it creates a long-awaited connection between the Baltic and White seas; it is longer than the Suez and Panama canals; it has "exceptionally great" (*iskliuchitel'no veliko*) transportational significance; it is important to the production strength of Karelia; and the on-time construction of the project in such harsh territory represents an unbelievable technical feat.[445]

While the text regurgitates the standard, official proclamations about the canal, the images are somewhat more complicated. The diagrams of the canal shift from general to more specific, moving from an overview map of the area, including the Ladozhskoe, Onezhskoe, and Beloe lakes, to a localized image of just the very beginning of the canal and its surrounding landscape, to a close-up of the canal itself. This zoning-in serves both a geographical and pedagogical function: as readers, we are slowly exposed to the landscape and guided to the final locale of the canal itself. While the text has a straightforward, totalizing message, the images employ photomontage techniques in order to create a fantastic reality, sometimes including the juxtaposition of jarring pictures. The second map in the guide contains two inserted photographs: one of the Karelian forest and another of a leisurely bather. In the depths of wild nature, the bather seems like a parody.

Figure 23. Images from Photo-Tourist (*Foto-turist*), a small collection of photographs documenting the canal. The bottom right image includes Stalin, Voroshilov, and Kirov. Russian State Library, Moscow, Russia.

The miniature, postcard-like book "Photo-Tourist" ("Foto-turist") of the White Sea-Baltic Canal uses photographs—all of which have photomontage elements—as a version of a travel guide. The titles of the photographs are typed and inserted, lending a homemade, collage-like feel. Other photographs are also inserted into the photomontages. In the inset of one of the collection's images, Lazar' Kogan's head looms above the administrators Semen Firin and Matvei Berman, as if he were guiding them from a physically and intellectually higher vantage point. Yet perhaps the most interesting photo in the whole collection is that of Stalin, Voroshilov, and Kirov sailing through the canal. Although Genrikh Iagoda, with his easily recognizable pencil-thin moustache, is also present in the photograph, he is not included in the text of the caption underneath the image. The photograph eerily echoes a painting by socialist-realist artist Dmitri Nalbandian, in which Stalin and company are sailing through the canal.

Chapter Three

Figure 24. Dmitri Nalbandian painting of Stalin sailing through the White Sea-Baltic Canal. Note the overcoat hanging over the railing, which replaced the then-purged Genrikh Iagoda. Russian Pictorial Collection, Box 29, Hoover Institution Archives.

The painting looks as though it could easily have been created using those very documentary photos. Nalbandian finished his painting in 1937, the same year that Iagoda was declared an Enemy of the State. Nalbandian, a devout Stalinist, was required to touch up the painting, removing Iagoda altogether and replacing him with a much less substantial—and ideologically neutral—overcoat. The fate of Iagoda, who went from Belomor administrator to purge victim, was typical of Stalinism and of Belomor. Like Terent'ev or Firin, he was at one point a much-lauded figure at the camp site, but no sort of accolade—even the Order of Lenin Iagoda received for his work at Belomor—could save him from his eventual execution.

Although the 1933 Belomor issue of the oversized, illustrated monthly magazine *USSR in Construction* is not a travel guide *per se*, it can be likened to one. The magazine exposes the landscape in a series of photomontages created by the famous photographer Aleksandr Rodchenko, and under-

The Symphony of Labor

Figure 25.
The front cover of *USSR in Construction*, featuring an inset map. Reproduced with permission of Productive Arts.

Figure 26.
The back cover of *USSR in Construction*, featuring a map overlay. Reproduced with permission of Productive Arts.

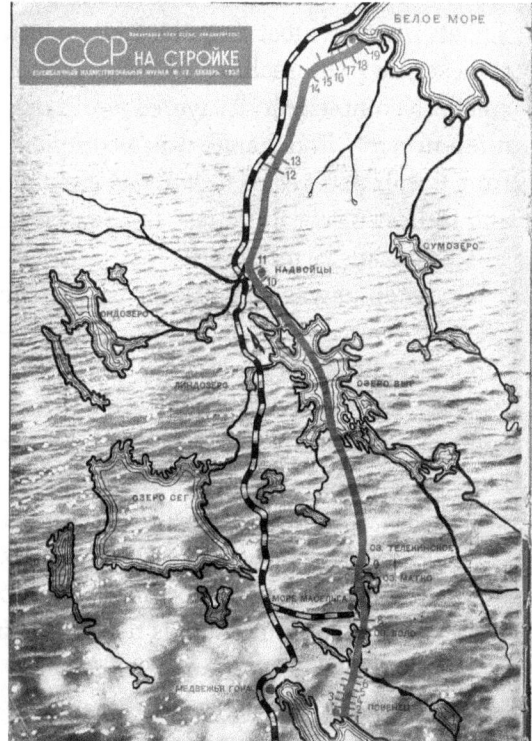

scores the importance of the map by including artistic diagrams of the waterway as both the front and back covers of the issue. Not only this particular issue but the magazine itself serves as a guide to the Soviet Union; it was published in German, French, and English editions to showcase Soviet achievements to an international audience. Other issues systematically document the country like a travel narrative—the magazine's stories in 1933 include a tour along the Volga River, a showcase of the "new culture" of industry, the opening of a tractor factory, and a voyage through Mongolia. The editorial board, headed by none other than the omnipresent Maxim Gorky, clearly wanted to showcase both the technological feats of the Soviet Union and its great geographical diversity. The ideological messages of the magazine were clear and heavy-handed—a Russian-language issue of the journal was included in a painting of Stalin as his reading material, making the leader both subject and consumer of the monthly—and yet its aesthetic was avant-garde.[446]

The map images that open and close the Belomor issue of *USSR under Construction* are not mere diagrams; they are innovative photomontages that creatively reconfigure the landscape. Photomontage is an adept style for utopian, world-recreating visions—a cruder equivalent to today's airbrushing. Artists could create a landscape that physically did not exist. Aleksandr Rodchenko, Belomor photographer and the Soviet Union's most famous photomontagist, was not interested in representing the reality of Soviet political life. Instead, he wanted to create "a complex, multilayered world of poetic imagination and private references."[447] Rodchenko was a complex figure, both removing himself from public debates concerning the social purposes of photomontage,[448] and indicating a willingness to collaborate with the state in the goal of society's transformation.[449]

Rodchenko was enthusiastic about the canal project, even if his excitement was limited to the creative potential he could explore at the camp site; he spent more time on the canal than any other outside artist, with estimations running from three months (in English-language sources)[450] to nearly two years (in Soviet sources).[451] He completed three trips to the canal and took a large number of photographs there, coming away with more than two thousand negatives. These images are often considered some of his best photography.[452] While some are critical of Rodchenko's role in the documentation of a harsh labor camp, his artistic corpus from the canal is not an aberration in his career but rather an exemplification of it, since transforming a Gulag camp into an aesthetic project would perfectly embody constructivist artists' desire to remake the world through photography.[453] Leah Dickerman asserts that Rodchenko participated in the documentation of Belomor only to salvage his own career; through the laborious craft of his photomontages, he was constructing an ideologically safe path for himself as an artist.[454] Nevertheless, it is clear that Rodchenko took a particular interest in the project: the number of photographs vastly outnumbers those he took of earlier projects; he made several trips to Belomor; he created some of his finest narrative pieces there. Even if Rodchenko had no interest in the project other than to secure his future, it is nevertheless telling that he would have embraced a kind of *perekovka* in order to re-make himself and accept the transformative potential of creative labor—just as Mikhail Prishvin later does when working on his Belomor-inspired book, *In the Land of Unfrightened Birds*, where he acknowledges the inspiring and admirable potential of criminals to transform themselves.

In a 1935 article titled "Reconstructions of the Artist" (*Perestroika khudozhnika*), Rodchenko celebrates the remaking of criminals at Belomor:

> Man arrives downcast, punished, and embittered, and leaves with a proudly held head, with a decoration on his breast and a start in life. And it reveals to him all the beauty of real, heroic, creative labor. I was staggered by the sensitivity and the wisdom with which the reeducation of the people was fulfilled.[455]

Like other prominent Soviet authors who wrote about Belomor, Rodchenko does not appear to be feigning his enthusiasm. Nevertheless, there remains a stubborn tendency to interpret all artists' support of the project as self-serving and careerist, as if such an explanation is necessary to explain the conundrum of how thoughtful artists could end up finding inspiration at a labor camp. While political designs certainly could have been a motivational factor, it is erroneous to exclude the possibility of genuine interest in the canal project because of the prison site landscape; such a move immediately imports our present-day moralism onto the past. The concentration of—and potential for—avant-garde experimentation extended well into the mid-1930s. Propaganda, in turn, could have an agitational effect on the artists themselves: "It seems there is no better way to convince people than to ask them to agitate. [...] The Soviet propagandists were not cynical; they spoke the same language among themselves as they did in their work."[456]

In another example of a Belomor tourist guide, the Central Council of the Society of Proletariat Tourism and Excursion (*Tsentral'nyi sovet Obshchestva Proletarskogo Turizma i Ekskursii*), in existence from 1927-1936, published "The White Sea-Baltic Canal and the Polar Region" (*Belomorsko-Baltiiskii kanal i zapoliar'e*) in 1936. Despite being published only two years after the other guides discussed here, the work has an entirely different physical appearance.

Figure 27. An image from the publication *BBK and the Polar Region (BBK i zapoliar'e)*, published in 1936. Russian State Library, Moscow, Russia.

Gone are the photomontages, the inserted titles, the recreated landscapes; instead, there is a much more straightforward, documentary guide that privileges text over image and includes simple, un-embellished photographs as mere factual accompaniments to the surrounding words. A comparison of these tourist guides demonstrates, along with the larger Soviet interest in cartography, that the map is of primary importance in creating an alternate landscape. This is a theme that will be discussed more thoroughly in the final chapter of this monograph. The map, in the end, is the result of the socialist "war against nature." Maps are not "inert records of morphological landscapes or passive reflections of the world of objects," but rather "refracted images contributing to dialogue in a socially constructed world."[457] Ironically, these power-laden texts were adept at realistically depicting a fantastical world, a non-existent utopia. The destruction of the physical environment would accompany the creation of documentary texts, with collage as handmaiden.

Aleksandr Lemberg: Film Montage as Ideological Weapon

In addition to collage and photomontage, film montage offers another way to piece together an alternate reality. Despite arguments for the non-reliability of the visual image,[458] documentary film offers the most tangible "proof" of the canal's heroic completion. There is something altogether different—and more powerful—about seeing the Belomor story unfold on the big screen. Other than the feature film *The Prisoners*, based on Nikolai Pogodin's play, the filmic texts regarding Belomor are all documentaries by one director: Aleksandr Lemberg. Lemberg was affiliated with official Party affairs long before he began documenting the White Sea-Baltic Canal. He worked as a cameraman on the front lines during World War I; in 1918-1922 he filmed Lenin, eventually becoming responsible for recording the leader's funeral; and in 1919-1920 he worked as a filmmaker on agitational ships and trains (*agitparokhody* and *agitpoezdy*).[459] It is not surprising, therefore, that Lemberg would take up the ideologically-charged task of recording one of the great achievements of the first Five-Year Plan. With its ability to prompt particular associations, the burgeoning medium of film represented a powerful new tool for expressing propagandistic themes.

As the famous Russian filmmaker Sergei Eisenstein argued, audience manipulation was possible mainly through montage. Rather than understanding film purely as a visual medium, Eisenstein combined shots—which he defined as hieroglyphs that became intelligible only within a particular context—in order to stimulate the brain physiologically and make the viewer "feel" cinema rather than simply see it.[460] This stimulation was achieved through the combination of drastically contrasting shots, with the "collision between two tendencies" ultimately intensifying the viewer's experience.[461] For Eisenstein, therefore, cinema could not be reduced to individual shots. Instead, it was their assembly and context that made the medium. Film did not just *use* montage as a technique; film *was* montage.

Montage, according to Eisenstein, had the ability to not only create new realities but also to act physically upon the viewer, since it "enhances perception from a *melodically emotional colouring to a direct physiological sensation*," shifting one into what he would call the "fourth dimension" of cinema.[462] This fourth dimension is a type of alternate reality, a non-existent realm, and this radical re-conception of space mirrors the avant-garde experimentation with photomontage as an exercise in creative geography. The discussions of both photomontage and film montage—which were heatedly debated in the 1920s and early 1930s—allowed artists to explore the possibility of creating realistic-looking fantasies. Early experimentation with montage is likened by one scholar to a type of total vision or "panoptic," in which a universal eye akin to Dziga Vertov's "cine-eye" is capable of capturing the entirety of space simultaneously. Like the all-seeing Panopticon, here the "cine-eye sees everything inaccessible to the ordinary eye and is not bound by the old model of perception. It allows the new society to free itself from the old canon of representation and to shape a new one along with new body language and new living spaces."[463] The eye of cinema, therefore, is adept at capturing the pre-determined reality of panoptic life in prison.

Lemberg's films offer stunning examples of the montage technique at its most ideological. He reiterates the trope of the war against nature with an examination of the pathway to *perekovka*. The ability of montage to articulate contradictions allows the director to transform a motif into its opposite—for example, the development of sleepy Karelia into an industrial powerhouse, or wayward criminals into honorable socialist citizens. Lemberg's 1934 film *The White Sea-Baltic Waterway* (*Belomorsko-Baltiiskii Vodnyi Put'*) opens with dramatic, anxious music that eventually flows into a softer, more relaxed melody. Music, just like montage itself, is essential in communicating the film's ideological content. The music's tempo is echoed by the particular succession of shots: first the viewer sees pictures of the Karelian landscape, with intertitles acknowledging its imposing rock and deep forest, its lakes and rivers and crashing waterfalls. Yet in a socialist country, the film informs us, such waters must be made "navigable" (*sudokhodnymi*). In order to accomplish this goal, prisoners arrive at the work site beginning in 1931. There is no attempt made by the film to mask the fact that the canal was built with prison labor or to make the criminals appear—at least initially—to be anything other than lawbreakers. The convicts, the film informs us, have no education or training, but instead only multiple prison sentences. Montage, with its facility for combining opposites, helps to document the miraculous transformations of the prisoners; first we see the original tools of their respective professions—skeleton keys to break into homes, tools to break into safes, brass knuckles to ward off enemies—and then we glimpse their substitutes: saws, shovels, and wheelbarrows. After seeing the instruments of their transformation, we travel to the actual worksite, where prisoners swiftly use their new tools to cut down forests. The literal tools become metaphorical ones, and the change in nature and the change in man occur side-by-side. One would not be possible without the other. Film, more than any other medium, can eloquently depict this transformation.

Shots of logs collected on the water (being readied for use in locks or makeshift roads) and images of rocks piled into dikes and dams allow the viewer to visualize vividly how "nature's riches" are being reoriented to serve the purposes of humankind. While the first half of the film concentrates on Karelia's wild landscape and its subsequent transformation, the second half focuses more on the cultural apparatuses at the camp site—making the change in nature equivalent to the change in humans. Alongside the picks and axes showcased in the beginning of the film, one of the "most important machines" at Belomor is the printing press, which we see churning out issues of *Perekovka*. The portrayal of an agitational brigade shows its members merry and animated, grinning broadly and playing guitars. They sport identical uniforms with kerchiefs akin to those that young Pioneers would wear.

In addition to the cultural endeavors at the White Sea-Baltic Canal, like the agitational brigades and the newspaper reading, *byt*, or everyday life, is also portrayed. We see a prisoner joyfully taking a bath in conditions that were surely ameliorated temporarily for the purposes of what is a propaganda film. We even see a prisoner being examined by a doctor, and the juxtaposition between the pair is jarring. The criminal prisoner, revealing a large tattoo of an eagle on his chest as he lifts his shirt, offers an odd contrast to the bespectacled physician, in his crisp white lab coat. As if the disparity were not already evident, the next shot shows an even closer view of the prisoner's tattoo, which spreads across his entire chest. The image of an eagle, in the language of criminal tattoos, symbolizes authority within the thieves' world, as well as freedom—sometimes denoting a past attempt at an escape.[464]

The film ends on a musical note, with an orchestra playing as the laborers put the finishing touches on the final lock. The lock chambers—all composed of precisely aligned wooden beams that look almost like graph paper on the screen—appear majestic and grand, especially when seen in contrast to the now-Lilliputian people who walk on the floors of the rooms. As the lock doors slowly close, the conscious use of montage throughout the film can be understood to have elicited the desired emotional response: it seems unbelievable that the piles of rocks and logs, the furious work with primitive tools, and the difficult landscape could actually have been transformed into such a neatly articulated finished product.

In Lemberg's 1933 documentary film *Belomorstroi Reports* (*Belomorstroi raportuet*) offers an even more dramatic example of the use of montage to facilitate specific viewer reactions. Eight images of workers in the opening of the film are interspersed with scenic images of Karelia, bringing the transformation of nature and the transformation of humanity even closer together. By juxtaposing a pair of opposites—the active walking of men with the stillness of untouched nature, for example—the film inextricably links the two and prompts viewer association. Under the "firm direction" of the OGPU, this sleepy landscape is transformed and the White and Baltic Seas are connected; even if nature is described as "stubborn," man "is even more stubborn." The initial, peaceful shots of the Karelian *paysage* are drastically contrasted with a subsequent series of images of men "working" on nature: hammering away at rocks, sawing down trees with great speed, and deftly wielding jackhammers. Yet this film does not highlight individual prisoners in photographs as the first film did; instead, it shows a group of criminals dancing merrily around a toothless accordion player, another example of the stock figure of Kostia showing the importance of musical accompaniment.

A third Belomor-themed Lemberg film, *Port of Five Seas* (*Port piati morei*, 1932-33), highlights the war against nature and brings it to an international stage. The intertitles are entirely in French, suggesting that the film was produced for a foreign audience, as was the glossy magazine *USSR in Construction*. Although the use of montage in articulating the transformation of nature remains, there is a major difference in this film, namely a predilection for documenting facts and figures regarding the construction project. *Port of Five Seas* is a veritable statistics report: 83,000 kilometers of railroad are built; 8,000 illiterate prisoners learn to read; 6,000 nearly illiterate prisoners receive an education; 15,000 prisoners finish advanced courses; 4,000 prisoners receive a technical education; 75 kilometers of rock is destroyed; 1,000,000 cubic meters of wood are claimed; 118 "works of art" (*ouvrages d'art*) are created (including 19 locks, 15 dams, 40 dikes, and 32 channels). The film's penchant for detailing specific numbers perhaps speaks to the necessity of offering concrete and precise documentary proof of the achievements made in the Soviet Union to a foreign audience.

Alongside this fixation on facts, there is also an emphasis on the concrete image of the map. The film opens with a spinning globe with USSR written across it—reminiscent of the opening of Grigorii Aleksandrov's wildly popular musical *Circus* (*Tsirk*, 1936)—followed by a map in which the cities of Stalingrad, DnieproGES, Magnitogorsk, Gor'kii, Khilingorsk, Cheliabinsk, Kuznetsk, Moscow, and Volkhov appear. Their names are followed by a railroad track's appearance, with animated trains moving to connect all the cities. After the first map documents the achievements of the first Five-Year Plan, a subsequent map notes the projections for the second: the Belomor Plant, The Palace of the Soviets, Bobriki, Lugansk, Solikansk, and Sverdlovsk. A third map denotes important cities in Russia: Rostov-on-Don, Odessa, Moscow, Leningrad, and Arkhangel'sk. Finally, yet another map indicates bodies of water: the Black, Caspian, Baltic, White, and Azov seas, with animated lines that link them all to Moscow. This is followed by a close-up on a map of the Karelia region. This film, unlike the previous two, strides into the future: it does not end with the construction of the White Sea-Baltic Canal, but rather asserts that in 1935 Moscow will be the port of five seas.[465] This accomplishment seems even greater than the feat of building just one canal—this is a radical re-drawing of the map in light of the projects completed during the first and second Five-Year Plans, and the ultimate collage of canal pieces. This even larger message—one that must be buttressed with statistical numbers and visual diagrams—is perhaps what would be most appropriate for export, so as to maximize the sense of achievement and pride that the Soviet Union attempts to portray. In all of Lemberg's films, montage and music help to facilitate the creation of fantastical realities both at home and abroad.

Conclusion: Performing Collectivity in Music and Collage

"Begin and complete your work to the sound of socialist songs and anthems": this was the message Leon Trotsky gave his countrymen in the spirited days following the Russian revolution.[466] Music became for the Bolsheviks an inspirational and motivational art form, one that aptly gave voice to the members of the collective. In the artistic world, futurists seized the revolutionary moment as fertile ground for their artistic experiments, organizing such performances as noise orchestras, concerts in factories, and conductorless orchestras. The New World demanded new sounds in different contexts, whether they were the hum of machines or the lilt of orchestras at prison camps.

Although composed of individual voices or separate instruments, music embodies a whole that emerges from discrete elements. In a tangible way, therefore, music could come to represent both the composition and the solidarity of the masses. Mass song played a significant role in Stalinist culture, and the songs of Issak Dunaevskii and others provided both entertainment and patriotic outlet. It is not surprising, then, that the regime would do its best to support the production of inspirational musical numbers. In his *Foundation Pit* (*Kotlovan*, 1930), Andrei Platonov depicts the jubilant yet disturbing march of the Komsomol band:

> The Pioneer band moved some way off and then began to play a youthful march. Precisely in step, conscious of the importance of their future, the barefoot girls marched past the forge. [...] Each of the girls was smiling with a sense of her own significance, an awareness of the seriousness of life that was essential both to the unity of the column and the impetus of the march.[467]

The girls might recognize their individual significance, but they are ultimately absorbed in the collective, with their integration facilitated by the homogenizing power of music.

Perhaps the best-recognized image from the construction of the White Sea-Baltic Canal is Aleksandr Rodchenko's photograph of an orchestra playing within one of the lock's chambers, as it so adeptly captured the paradoxical nature of the project's propaganda. This photograph, unlike other Rodchenko photomontages, was not posed or manipulated—in their reminiscences, many prisoners mentioned orchestral accompaniment at the work site as a particularly vivid memory. Sergei Alymov discusses the strange acoustics of the music within a frozen chamber[468] and the Belomor "symphony" (*simfoniia*) that combined stringed instruments and loud explosions to create the unique "voice" (*golos*) of the construction.[469] Vlasa Kirichenko, a mother of three and prisoner sentenced under article 58, recalls in her autobiography the orchestra playing and claims that it made work "still more joyful" (*rabotat' stalo eshche veselee*),[470] an echo of Stalin's famous statement that "life has become better, life has become more joyful" (*zhit' stalo luchshe, zhit' stalo veselei*).[471] Pogodin's play *The Aristocrats* ends with a soaring melody, and the Belomor-themed issue of *USSR in Construction* showcases the orchestral presence at the construction site.

The presence of an orchestra created a strange, almost cultured, atmosphere in a landscape of death. Mikhail Prishvin notes the ubiquity of music in his *In the Land of Unfrightened Birds* when he arrives at the Belomor work site: "We were met with music. The fine art of music is everywhere here: during the shock-worker labor the orchestra plays without fail in the help of work; during rest, actors perform and sing good songs."[472] The regime intended for rhythm to improve work performance; music, ideally, would accompany the over-fulfillment of norms. The sounds emerged from physical effort just as labor did, and the performance of labor was parallel to musical performance. In both, socialist ideals were achieved; in both, the creative and the corporeal were combined.

The labor that transformed the environment was eventually depicted in maps, tourist guides, and films about Belomor. In all of these products, montage was necessary as a technique to craft this new, not entirely extant, world. The pastiche of workers created segments of the canal through their labor, forming a collage that was in turn stitched together and re-imagined by creative outside artists. The mapping of utopia—an important aspect of the proof needed to win the ideological war against nature—is a central Belomor theme that will be examined again in a contemporary context in Chapter Five. The creation of a new environment accompanied the destruction of the old one, and montage helped to aid in the performance of this idealized reality, one that was central in maintaining the artifice of Stalinism.

IV
The Performance of Identity

> The performer can be fully taken in by his own act; he can be sincerely convinced that the impression of reality which he stages is the real reality.[473]
> –Erving Goffman, 1959

At an October 1932 meeting of Soviet writers at Maxim Gorky's house, Stalin spoke about the importance of theater in creating a new proletarian culture: "What is there to write? Poetry is good. Novels are even better. But right now we need plays more than anything else. Plays that are easy to understand; our working man is busy."[474] Theatrical performance—especially of the highly ideological agitational variety—was deeply influential in the Soviet Union during the 1920s and 1930s.[475] The Russian avant-garde movements, particularly futurism, in which the Belomor prisoners Alymov and Terent'ev took part, highlighted a performative aesthetic. The futurists—with their garish yellow blouses, wooden spoons in buttonholes, and ironic gestures—were natural actors and actresses. In a poem written fifteen years before his suicide, the great futurist poet Vladimir Mayakovsky wrote, "More and more often I think: / it might be far better for me / to punctuate my end with a bullet. / This very day, / just in case, / I'm staging my final performance."[476] The famous Russian critic and Belomor participant Viktor Shklovskii claimed that Mayakovsky was more of an event or an action than an author, and the futurist's final performance—his suicide—was exactly as he described: a bullet through the heart.

Performance played an integral role at Belomor. Not only was identity theatricalized at the camp, but performance was an essential aspect of cultural life: the regime intended for theater, like all art forms, to serve as a motivational tool for the prisoners. The regional Karelian newspaper *Karelo-Murmanskii krai* highlighted the integral role of performance at the White Sea-Baltic Canal, noting that of all the artistic endeavors at the construction site, the agitational brigades were the most popular and most important.[477] In his memoir, the Belomor prisoner Vatslav

Dvorzhetskii cites the theater as the administration's most noteworthy endeavor.[478] In a prison setting, theater could also serve as a coping mechanism, because the act of adopting a new name and pretending to be someone else allowed prisoners to escape their own realities for a brief respite.[479] The category of performance can ultimately be applied to the Belomor experience in numerous ways: prisoners performing *perekovka* and crime as performance, fulfillment of labor norms as work performance, literal performances on the banks of the waterway, and gender as performance. In this way, performance is not just another Belomor trope, but rather a concept that ties together all of the themes discussed in the present book.

Crime and Perekovka as Performance

The prisoner N. Argunov has a life story similar to that of many Belomor convicts. He was born in St. Petersburg—which was then called Leningrad—and grew up without knowing his mother or father. After serving in the Red Army, he fell into a life of crime and eventually lost his freedom in a game of cards. Although he had no desire to work when he entered prison, he writes in his autobiography that the White Sea-Baltic Canal construction "captured" his imagination, and he soon became a shock-worker, with his highly productive labor receiving recognition from the regime. While the story is familiar, the ending is a bit different from that of many of the other memoirs. He candidly notes in his autobiography that he is not quite sure why he "became another person," but speculates that it is from reading books in prison. Art, therefore, facilitated his supposed transformation. The reasons given for "conversion" from common criminal to socialist citizen through re-forging (*perekovka*) were numerous: psychological shame, peer pressure applied by other prisoners, desire for special privileges, dedication to labor and the Soviet project, and "persuasive" speeches by educators were all mentioned. There were also, of course, individuals who refused to reform altogether.

While it is often impossible to follow convicts' paths to see if their supposed "re-forging" was genuine or not, Argunov is to a certain degree an exception. We can trace at least a bit of what happened to him, in contrast to most criminal prisoners, who disappeared—literally or metaphorically—after the canal's completion. An editorial note across his file informs us that after his time was served, he continued to commit a series of crimes, including the sale of false documents. Argunov may have written that he was a new person, may have even believed it himself, but in the end his role as a shock-worker was just that: a performance. Criminals, as skilled practitioners of the arts of trickery and prevarication, were likely quite successful in creating these alternative identities. Since people tell stories to discover who they are, it is only in the act of narration that we "become" our selves. The declarations of conversion—whether "real" or not—are significant unto themselves, especially since they could appear quite believable to others. As the Goffman quote opening this chapter indicates, a performer can be taken in by his own performance and truly believe it to be real. The performance of identity within the criminal world dissolved the boundary between art and life, leaving spectators to wonder what was true and what was artifice.[480]

The need to constantly see oneself outside of oneself, as an object, is itself a remarkably creative phenomenon. W. E. B. Dubois wrote of the African-American population—another historically enslaved group—that they must develop a double consciousness, a "peculiar sensation [...] of always looking at one's self through the eyes of others."[481] This is precisely what the Belomor prisoners had to do: imagine their lives and work in the context of the regime while internalizing much of the ideological worldview forced upon them. The characters in Pogodin's Belomor play perform their re-forging literally and metaphorically while disparaging the idea of *perekovka*: "There's nothing reforged or reformed about me and all this play-acting isn't worth a god-damn," says the character known simply as the "tattooed woman" (*Tatuirovannaia*).[482]

While Argunov's story magnifies the potential for role play, Praskov'ia Skachko's story demonstrates the need for props as well as a role. Skachko's life changed dramatically after her husband's death in 1910. Tragedy encircled her: the passing of her husband was followed by that of one of her children, and shortly thereafter came the death of the man she re-married. These events made her afraid and more careful in her thieving. Without her former life of luxury and comfort—and the self-confidence that accompanied it—Skachko could no longer successfully ply her trade. In the art of stealing, exterior image is of the utmost importance. As Skachko explains, "My misfortune lay in my external appearance—in my clothes, and I had lousy clothes, which, of course, did not suit my work. And I must say, that a good pickpocket must be well-dressed, for only then is it possible to work."[483] Skachko lacked the costume that was

Chapter Four

necessary to perform the act of pickpocketing. The thief Argunov was engaged in a different type of performance: he acted out being a dedicated prisoner until he was caught making false documents.

The criminal aesthetic is inherently performative. Thieves' language is a "tool of production," a catalog of words that immediately implies action. The impulsive nature of criminals, according to Belomor prisoner and scholar Dmitri Likhachev, means that there is very little time between a thought and its expression; the thieves' language is emotional and causes action in a concrete way.[484] Requiring a particular costume, significant gestures, symbolically charged tattoos, and emotive language, a criminal makes his or her way onto the stage of delinquency. The specific abilities of criminals in regard to wordplay—what might be characterized as a sort of emotive "magic" in their verbal creativity—is ultimately rooted in pretense, in spectacle.[485] Criminals' cultivated talents for artifice is perhaps what allowed them to perform the show of *perekovka* in an ultimate ruse—swearing allegiance to the Soviet system in order to garner the benefits such a proclamation would provide. Artistic abilities, therefore, gave prisoners a modicum of power at the prison camp, while at times unfortunately obscuring the very real violence endemic to it. The criminal-actors' performances of *perekovka* took place on the carefully manicured stage of the Belomor camp, a stage that appeared artificial to some but quite believable to others. The actress Tamara Ivanova recalls her emotions while visiting the Belomor camp with her husband Vsevolod:

> We were shown what was apparent even to me to be "Potemkin Villages." I could not restrain myself and asked both Vsevolod and Mikhail Mikhalych Zoshchenko, "You really cannot see that the speeches of the 'reforged' criminals are theatrical performance and that the cottages in the little gardens with pathways sprinkled with clean sand, with flowers in the flower beds, are only theatrical decorations?" They answered me sincerely (both believed in the possiblity of the so-called "reforging"), that for a person to be re-educated, before anything they needed to be put in very nice surroundings that do not at all resemble those of the criminal world from which they came. And among the criminals there were, undoubtedly, talented actors. They delivered to us such fiery speeches,

shed such genuine tears, according to the Stanislavsky system! And though it might seem incredible, both Vsevolod and Mikhail Mikhalych believed them. And what's more important, they wanted to believe!⁴⁸⁶

This observation illuminates the power of performance as well as key tenets of the Belomor project as a whole. First, it is important to note that Ivanova's recollections are from a 1989 newspaper interview. Many years had passed since her visit to the canal, years in which her memory of her perceptions could have shifted. While she claims that she immediately disbelieved the performance of *perekovka*, it is significant that both Vsevolod Ivanov and Mikhail Zoshchenko, well-educated intellectuals, so clearly believed it. It is all the more significant that theirs was not an officially pronounced belief—and so one that might be informed by a need to curry favor with the State—but rather a private exclamation declared to a personal friend and relative. This demonstrates how believable these performances of *perekovka* could be. Yet most importantly, as Ivanova herself notes, was the fact that they *wanted* to believe—not just believe the performance of these individual actors, but believe in the project as a whole. Clearly, Belomor had a distinct appeal.

Yet in this belief there was necessarily a tone of falsity: after all, Belomor was still a prison camp where thousands perished. Art helped to obscure this reality, if only briefly, and paint a different portrait of the everyday at Belomor. Performance adeptly embodies paradoxes likes these, contrasts that are also inherent in Stalinist culture. On the one hand, the notion of performance brings forth the suggestion of a suspension of belief: one is merely play-acting. On the other, it is precisely through the physical act of such a performance that one is able to believe, or make others think that the performer/prisoners themselves believe. In creating a new science and a new world, straightforward rationality no longer held true: just as Fedor Dostoevsky's Underground Man would finally realize that two and two does not equal four, but five,⁴⁸⁷ the first Five-Year Plan would be completed in four, not five, years. Belomor would radically transform not only the natural environment but also the mechanisms of time that governed it, paralleling the larger Soviet project. At Belomor and in the Soviet Union, old worlds would be destroyed, and fanastical, artistic mirages would be propped up in their places through the performance of a new reality.

CHAPTER FOUR

Shock-Workers and the Performance of Labor

The competition in in the Soviet Union as a whole for better jobs, bigger apartments, and Party membership was mirrored inside the Gulag with the phenomenon of shock-worker labor (*udarnichestvo*) and the perennial demands to continuously outdo previous work norms. In 1931, the building with the largest seating capacity in the Soviet Union was the movie theater called Udarnik, which was created by Boris Iofan, the architect who later won the competition for the Palace of the Soviets design.[488] *Udarnichestvo* became all the more popular after Aleksei Stakhanov's celebrated mining feat in 1935, an achievement that inspired a burgeoning movement in his name and was dedicated to the over-fulfillment of work norms. The development of shock-worker labor at Belomor, we can see, foreshadowed future developments in the Soviet Union. Although the concept was not created at the White Sea-Baltic Canal,[489] the project's construction arguably witnessed its most rapid growth and systemization. The importance of the *udarnichestvo* phenomenon cannot be overstated; one's labor output was one's meal ticket, and the shock-workers received numerous special privileges. Countless poetic works and articles were devoted to the shock-workers and their abilities; slogans, chalkboards, and banners reminded everyone of their presence. Yet the vast number of shock-workers and the ubiquity of *tufta* (padded work reports) necessarily call into question the legitimacy of *udarnichestvo*. Did these feats of labor truly happen, or was this simply another example of performance at Belomor?

Given the rapidity of the canal's construction, it seems that at least some of these labor accomplishments were real. The emphasis on speed is central to one of the most common sayings about the canal in the *History of the Construction*: that the canal must be built "quickly and cheaply" (*korotko i deshevo*).[490] The use of local materials (such as Karelian pine for the wooden locks) and minimal technology was meant to keep down costs, just as work storms—particularly grueling and extended shifts—and shock-labor were meant to increase work production. References to "tempo" and "on-time completion" of the canal are everywhere in both prisoner and non-prisoner works about the canal, and according to the *History of the Construction* time is the most important aspect of the project: "For the realization of the project three things are needed: time, time, and once again time."[491] The Belomor construction was an important project within Stalin's first Five-Year Plan, an economic blueprint that was completed ahead of schedule, in four years, allowing for a new understanding of time. This re-definition of time was a source of great pride in the Soviet Union, and it represented the zenith of labor performance. The slogan "five in four" was ubiquitous, and the motif was included in the *History of the Construction*: "Only the Soviet Union surmounts all difficulties, fulfilling the grand plan of socialist construction—the five-year plan—even earlier than in four years."[492] Even though the canal had already been completed, work on it is often described in the future tense in the *History of the Construction*, locating the project in an imaginary temporal realm.[493]

On the pages of *Pravda*, one of the most ubiquitous Soviet newspapers, Stalin is pictured alongside shock-workers in connection with a 1931 campaign bearing the slogan "The Country Needs to Know Its Heroes." The article about the campaign included the photographs and life stories of more than a dozen such high-producing laborers.[494] Similar to how modern employees are judged during a performance report, shock-workers were examined and categorized by their labor output. However, while the present incarnation of such reports is most commonly an intra-company phenomenon, Soviet performances were made unapologetically public in the most brutal of ways. During the Stalinist period, major political holidays were transformed into opportunities to "review the year's achievements" in fulfilling and exceeding the first Five-Year Plan. The efficiency of an individual factory, in fact, determined its marching order in May Day parades.[495] At Belomor, red and black chalkboards indicated the best and worst workers respectively, and these boards provoked shame and resentment among many prisoners. Years after the White Sea-Baltic Canal was completed, work achievements in the Soviet Union continued to be tallied on chalkboards, providing a visual source of both pride and competition (see Figures 28 and 29). In a contemporary labor analogy, "performance reviews" are an integral aspect of the modern workplace and help in part to tabulate efficiency. Feedback is the most essential element for determining whether performance is "on target," in what sounds like a current day reiteration of "plan fulfillment." Management and technology, in turn, become contemporary performance acts.[496]

Figure 28. A chalkboard at the Belomor labor camp noting the output percentages of prisoner labor. Those who underperform are included in the column "our shame," while those who overperform are in a column titled "our pride." Photograph reproduced with permission of Iurii Dmitriev.

Figure 29. A factory chalkboard documenting workers' production levels that was included in a Moscow photo exhibit in 1945. Russian Pictorial Collection, Box 29, Hoover Institution Archives.

Parades celebrating the day of Physical Culture (*fizkul'tura*) combined physical performance with theatrics. The massive parades through Moscow's Red Square before the entire Party leadership were entirely orchestrated affairs. Rather than a sporting event or a spectator sport as one might imagine in an athletic context, the parades were thoroughly rehearsed and scripted as a performance, with a theater director in charge of the choreography. Such parades highlighted the beauty of the physical body and linked it to the aesthetic of efficient machines.[497] Athletes were glorified as imagined warriors in the class struggle against the bourgeoisie.[498] A physically fit athlete could run faster on the battlefield, jump higher over trenches, and shoot more precisely in combat. Youth, in turn, were often described in militaristic terms for upholding the ideals of the revolution (see Figure 3). During the period of War Communism, the "battlefield virtues" of "bravery and self-sacrifice" were encouraged among young adults. The regime imagined the young as future fighters for the socialist cause, full of energy and determination—the ideal advocates of Bolshevik policies.[499] Militaristic rhetoric, therefore, occurred in the battle for the New Man as well as in regard to labor performance in the war against nature. Yet the destruction of one element was combined with the creation of another—while nature may have been destroyed, new industry was developed in its wake. The creative-destructive tension inevitably introduces physicality and blurs reality with fiction.

Work performance and creative performance were closely linked at Belomor, and the connection exemplifies the Soviet art/labor duality. The camp newspaper *Perevovka*, in an article about the success of agiational brigades, records several instances in which workers who previously could not fulfill the work plan suddenly began over-fulfilling the norms after a troupe's performance. The entertainment potential of these shows, while present, was always supposed to come second to their motivational goals. The canal administration, realizing that the best way to teach people to work was to lead by example, encouraged the agitational brigades to engage in working on the canal while performing. The simultaneity of theatrical performance and physical labor, according to *Perekovka*, filled other Belomor prisoners with a newfound enthusiasm during the last days of the construction.[500]

Repetition is an integral part of performance as well as labor. In Russian, the word for rehearsal—*repetitsiia*—embodies this connection. Repetition more generally is how we come to know life, how we come to play the many roles it demands of us. In childhood, a youngster learns how to function in the world by repeating various acts until they become automatic.[501] Similarly, the repetition of the master narrative of re-forging as an echo of socialist realism's master plot allowed for the internalization of propaganda. In Pogodin's play *The Aristocrats*, the prisoner Sonia compares the educator-reformer to a "gramophone" (*grammofon*),[502] since he is constantly repeating that she needs to begin working. Although she insists that she never will, by the end of the play the message has sunk in: Sonia gives up vodka and becomes a diligent worker. Repetition, however, does not imply identicalness,[503] and every re-forging narrative has its unique aspects.

The shock-worker concept also provided a bridge between the individual and the collective: although an *udarnik* was honored specifically by name, his achievements were possible only within the context of the working masses and the brigade that helped him outperform other workers. As a Soviet publication assessing the legacy of the first Five-Year Plan explained, shock-worker labor is "a summons to pleasurable, cheerful work, in the name of a glorious goal, where the little 'I' becomes just as proud and significant as the big 'we.'"[504] The individually-listed names of shock-workers and Stakhanovites belonged to people who were ultimately imagined as laborers in the collective. Soviet selfhood, in turn, was simultaneously specific and general. A similar tension between the individual and the collective permeates the criminal persona. The criminal act is both a mass phenomenon and an attempt at individual expression; one hears of both crime tendencies and famous criminals. As Mikhail Bakhtin writes, "events acquire a public significance as such only when they become crimes. The *criminal act* is a moment of private life that becomes, as it were, *involuntarily* public."[505] The art of crime becomes material performance.

Political Prisoners as Performers:
Vatslav Dvorzhetskii and Lev Losev

The theater director Vatslav Dvorzhetskii, sentenced to ten years in prison as an enemy of the state under article 58, credited his survival to his art; his "actor's nature" (*akterskaia priroda*) helped him in the all-important task of remaining a person in a concentration camp. As he put it, "art helped one to survive."⁵⁰⁶ It is also possible to understand the "actor's nature" in relationship to the performance of Soviet selfhood; perhaps Dvorzhetskii is implying that his ability to act parts and play roles assured his survival. First sent to Solovki, Vaigach Island and Moscow, Dvorzhetskii finally arrived at the White Sea-Baltic Canal in 1933. His first impression of the city of Medvezh'egorsk is pervaded with excitement about the local theater and its professionalism:

> A real, big, comfortable theater! A wonderfully equipped stage, auditorium, lobby, backstage help—everything! And a real, large, professional company: a manager, head director, administrators, directors, actors, singers, ballet dancers, musicians, artists—and all are prisoners. And the audience is also all prisoners. It's true, though, that the first two rows are separated for free people and two side boxes are for the administrators.⁵⁰⁷

In addition to the spaces reserved for non-prisoners and the administration, there were frequent guests in the theater, including journalists, representatives of various commissions, and sometimes even foreigners.⁵⁰⁸

The theater in Medvezh'egorsk was indeed a lifesaver for Dvorzhetskii, especially since the productions were of high quality and the audience was hungry for art and incredibly diverse—the spectators were from all over the Soviet Union, of varying ages, and had committed assorted crimes.⁵⁰⁹ The actors in the main theater lived in their own barracks, with women and men divided. Although Dvorzhetskii recalled life in the barracks as strict—any infraction of the regime would land prisoners in a punishment cell or in the general workforce, and all communication with non-prisoners was strictly forbidden—it also seemed relatively relaxed. There were no fences or barbed wire, and the security paid little attention to the fulfillment of the administration's demands, he wrote. Most importantly, since Dvorzhetskii lived in the actors' barracks with other performers and *Perekovka* workers, he had the privilege of meeting many other interesting intellectuals, including literary critics, philosophers, and scholars.⁵¹⁰

Figure 30. A performance stage at the Belomor construction site. Photograph reproduced with permission of Iurii Dmitriev.

Figure 31. An agitational brigade's performance for spectators at the Belomor labor camp. Photograph reproduced with permission of Iurii Dmitriev.

Dvorzhetskii's memoirs about the Belomor theater provide an unusual glance into the daily life of prisoners and administrators, since he gives a summary of the overall power structure in play. The theater director was the prisoners' sole link to the administration, and he had the ability to alter the convicts' lives in dramatic ways. The actor-prisoners, all sentenced under article 58, did not talk about their punishment or crime, since the various *punkty* of the article did not much make difference. Only the criminal prisoners could be released early, and Dvorzhetskii recalls the camp official Rapoport announcing the freeing of *udarniki* and the strong impression it made on the other prisoners, regardless of whether they could verify that such discharges actually happened.[511] Even though the actors did not have the possibility of early release, they did have other advantages: with permission from the administration, they could stay in the hotel opposite the theater for a day, a week, or even a month; they could travel as far as Kem' to give performances at various worksites, and they could make voyages to perform without the accompaniment of guards. While many of the prisoners involved in theater at the White Sea-Baltic Canal note their relative ease of movement, the ubiquitous disorganization, and the lack of strict patrolling, this set of circumstances did not necessarily make it easier to escape. As Dvorzhetskii notes, the train tracks themselves were strictly guarded, and a prisoner—with his or her gray skin and skinny frame—would easily be recognized from afar. Besides these difficulties, there was really nowhere to run, given the remote location of the construction project. Finally, while criminals caught escaping were merely beaten and returned to their barracks, those imprisoned under article 58 who were caught escaping would be shot.[512]

Unlike Terent'ev, Dvorzhetskii worked exclusively with other political prisoners, rendering his prison experience different from that of the agitational brigade leader's. Also unlike Terent'ev, Dvorzhetskii managed to survive the Stalinist regime, dying of natural causes in Nizhnii Novgorod in 1993. Yet both artists relied on creative expression in order to endure the prison experience, Terent'ev with mobile performance groups and Dvorzhetskii with the comfort of a professional-style theater.

Like Dvorzhetskii, Lev Losev was a political prisoner and a cultural luminary at Belomor. A philosopher, Losev uses the foxtrot as a metaphor in his short story "From a Conversation at the Belomor Construction" (*Iz razgovora na Belomorstroe*, 1932-33), which he wrote during the canal's construction. Losev describes how prisoners' work on the canal has a direct connection to the performance of selfhood. The prisoners, Losev's short story claims, were energetically "dancing" on the outside, but empty and soulless on the inside:

> We and our work are a foxtrot. We are cheerful, joyful, alive; our tempo is jerky, garish, against any type of lethargy. But on the inside we are empty, we don't believe in anything, we mock and deride everything. We don't care about what we sign or what we vote for. We are sluggish, anarchist, profligate. We become numb, tremble, lisp; and everything there, in the depths, is rickety, corrupt, everything crawls, sticks, languishes sickly, aches, suffers dissolutely, laughs at its own weakness and solitude. The colossal energy of the Belomor construction is our intellectual and technical-expressive, industrial and social foxtrot. Our rhythm is buoyant, fresh, young; and our souls are empty, anarchistic, and profligate. For us at Belomorstroi it's tedious, cheerful, frightening, hysterical, joyful, empty, profligate!...[513]

Losev's description here aptly and disturbingly captures the paradox of Belomor by interweaving seemingly incongruous qualities, particularly in the last sentence. While the prisoners are cheerful on the outside, they are disintegrating on the inside. Productive work, again, becomes a type of performance, one whose cheap mendacity puts into ever greater relief the magnitude of human pain.

The foxtrot metaphor was complex and far-reaching; not only did it appear in many other Soviet literary works both related and unrelated to the canal, but it was also emblematic of modernism itself. The dance symbolized the "decadence" of the West, and the allure of its profanity increased its popularity in the Soviet Union. As Edwin Ware Hullinger, an American traveler in 1920s Moscow, noted in his appropriately-titled monograph *The Reforging of Russia*, "From ballet dancers to former princesses, former manufacturers' daughters to former janitors' daughters, every girl in Moscow has one great social ambition—to learn to fox-trot."[514] Hullinger asserted that the cabarets and cafes of the early 1920s were packed with foxtrotters, thanks to the introduction of the dance by American relief workers.[515] The dance was so popular that one concerned observer claimed it happened everywhere except on public transportation and in graveyards.[516] Some explained that their passion for the dance stemmed from a desire to escape the bleak realities of the revolution and civil war they had just lived through; as one girl explained to Hullinger, "I am now trying to live on the surface of life [...] I have been in the depths for five years. Now I am going to be superficial. It hurts less."[517] Just like Losev's description of the dance, the foxtrot was all surface, meaningless, vapid performance, making it an apt metaphor for the role-playing of selfhood at the White Sea-Baltic Canal, where many prisoners performed a certain part either to obtain privileges or because of ideological indoctrination.

Although the foxtrot was eventually outlawed in the Soviet Union because of its supposed "bourgeois" tendencies, not everyone agreed that the dance and the building of socialism were entirely incompatible.[518] As a reflection of its popularity, the foxtrot appeared in numerous literary works during the 1920s, including Mikhail Bulgakov's novel *Master and Margarita* (*Master i Margarita*, 1928-40), Il'ia Erenburg's novel *Trest D. E.* (1923), and Vladimir Mayakovsky's play *Bedbug* (*Klop*, 1928). In *Bedbug*, the main character Prisypkin—an avid foxtrotter—claims that he cannot possibly change society if he is forbidden to dance.[519] Prisypkin, like the dance itself in Soviet society, must be removed from the cultural arena, only to re-appear later as farce. In 1935, however, the regime's attitude towards the dance softened, and official protocol stated that the dance should be neither forbidden nor propagandized.[520]

The Role of Gender in the Performance of Identity

Judith Butler, in her seminal work on feminism *Gender Trouble*, theroizes that gender is a kind of performance. Gender is not an identity one has in accordance with their biological sex; instead, it is defined by what one does.[521] Women prisoners at Belomor faced specific problems, and many of these issues related particularly to the performance of gender. While Soviet criminologists often attributed female transgression to sexual deviance,[522] women were ideally supposed to represent the purity of the motherland (*rodina*). Perhaps this explains why women's crimes seemed all the more heinous and inexplicable to criminal researchers: their wrongdoing threatened the very moral fabric of society. Such a double bind is perhaps why female criminals generally exhibited more shame and emotional trauma in narrating the art of their crimes than men did. Women also posed specific problems for the administration: a regional journal at the time noted that women had more difficulty getting used to "social life" in prison, and that they needed a "taste" of incarceration to improve their cultural-political level.[523]

Male prisoners' autobiographies often cite the lack of money, the death of parents, and hunger as reasons for falling into the criminal world. They acknowledge the Russian Civil War as the most traumatic event in their lives, in which they often lost loved ones as well as all means of sustenance. Female criminal prisoners explain their "fall" into the criminal lifestyle somewhat differently, emphasizing psychological elements of shame and humiliation rather than the outside influence of physical, material circumstances. The female prisoner Lidiia Isaeva, after living on the streets or at friends' houses and occupying herself with pick-pocketing, drunkenness, and sex, finally rejected this lifestyle because of the shame it caused her.[524] In writing her autobiography, Isaeva chose to emphasize the difficult psychological elements comprising the criminal path—the disgrace of her drunkenness and the peer pressure of the friends who encouraged her to commit crimes[525]—rather than her newfound love of labor at Belomor. While she does include the latter in her life story, she does so only with common, generic-sounding phrases such as "through work comes correction" and "there will be no return to the old ways."[526]

The prisoner Praskov'ia Skachko describes the humiliation of her childhood family poetically, claiming that constant need, hunger, and cold "surrounded her entire family like a black cloud" (*kak chernaia tucha okruzhili vsiu nashu sem'iu*).[527] When the children at school laughed at her because she had no food, she decided to start going to the market to steal sustenance. The teasing continued, however, and she eventually began skipping school. When her father received a note from her teacher about her absences and subsequently learned about her thefts, he punished her severely and symbolically, cutting off her long, beautiful braids, the envy of all the school and a symbol of her femininity, instructing her that the family may lack means but it is honest.[528] Her shame about skipping school is now added to her shame about being poor. Praskov'ia's description of finally tiring of the criminal life sounds strangely similar to confessions made during Stalin's purges:

> I wanted a quiet life, I didn't want to steal anymore. I was sick of this life. I was sick of trembling at every step for my freedom and being scared by rustling and knocks. Every rustle made me think, here they are coming again for you. But it is so hard to get off of this road when your life itself is already placed on a slippery path. I found myself on this path again.[529]

The road to crime was often more alluring and unavoidable than the path to socialist labor.

The prisoner Motia Podgorskaia also addresses the specific problems women face in entering the criminal world. Motia lost both of her parents when she was three years old and spent her childhood in an orphanage. It was there, at the age of fourteen, that she met a thirty-year-old officer whose promises of food enticed her back to his apartment, where he fed her and then raped her. When he later asked her to strip and perform tricks for him, she refused, and he chased her away. She had similar experiences with other men until she eventually fell into prostitution:

> Finally, I became what you would call a prostitute. But my soul wanted love. It wanted tenderness and a cozy nook. But it was only dreams, dreams, where is your sweetness?[530] I turned seventeen. To sell one's body at this age? There was no support from anywhere. I didn't hear tender words; I had no one to complain to. And so I reached prison. I looked at the world with contempt. Not a bit of hope or faith. Now I am a person active in social life.[531]

Motia compares the relatively good conditions in prison to those of her previous life, mentioning the availability of sausage, clean sheets, and almost daily baths (Motia's favorable description of camp conditions seems to be exaggerated, as such frequent bathing at a Gulag camp would have been virtually impossible). Yet despite these supposedly favorable conditions, Motia cites the hardships of prison as being the best teacher: "Life in the camps trained you to fight for existence, to believe deeply in your own strength. In the camps your character is forged: resolutely going towards an outlined goal.[532] Motia's rather romantic story of overcoming hardship was exactly the sort of narrative the authorities wanted to cull for inclusion in the biographically-themed *History of the Construction*, and may have been the inspiration for the Sonia character in Pogodin's *The Aristocrats*.

The camp site, though in theory divided by gender, was in reality quite loosely divided. Prisoners were permitted to sleep in different places, and many women slept at the work site rather than returning to their bunks so as to avoid rabid men and the circus-like atmosphere of the noisy barracks.[533] However, they had to deal not only with drunken men, but also with intoxicated women from the criminal population. The philosopher and Belomor prisoner Iuliia Danzas recalls the horrific scene:

> The generally frightening human hodgepodge was burdened with an enormous mass of men, prowling like wolves around our barracks [...] using the greater freedom found here than at Solovki to walk around the entire camp where there are more than 30,000 men crowded together, like us fenced in by barbed wire on this territory. That's why, from the evening and through the length of the night, were brought in tens of drunk women, who sobered up next to us or right above our heads if they got up to the second level of bunk beds.[534]

Women's bodies were most often what brought them into prison (due to prostitution and other sexual crimes), and these same bodies experienced abuse and rape within the camps. Women prisoners' narratives often include corporeal references in addition to a focus on the disgrace inherent in choosing a criminal lifestyle. The shift of focus from radical gender equality in the 1920s to domestic virtues and submission in the 1930s illuminates how particularly shameful it would be for women to find themselves disgraced in terms of their womanhood.[535] The performance of gender was complicated by prison life, which necessarily placed women in a particularly dangerous situation. The mere notion of women as criminals violated the norms of their gender performance, challenging the typical womanly "virtues" of purity and motherhood in the 1930s Soviet Union.

Conclusion: Performance and the Slipperiness of Reality

In 1931, the same year that construction on the White Sea-Baltic Canal began, an architectural competition was announced for the Palace of the Soviets, a grandiose building that was to serve as socialism's temple. Eventually the open competition had to become a closed one, because too many of the submitted plans were modern and modest rather than monumental and monolithic.[536] The final, officially approved design included a soaring tower taller than any other building in the world at the time, which was topped by an enormous statue of Lenin pointing even higher, toward the bright future. Despite years of planning, a specially constructed metro station, an elaborate exhibition about the building at the 1939 New York World's Fair, and the demolition of one of the most famous Orthodox churches in the country to make way for the "Palace," it was never built. The commencement of World War II and the sheer enormity of the project made it difficult to complete, and the foundation pit for the building was transformed instead into the world's largest swimming pool. While the project was abandoned due to lack of resources, the building broadcast the regime's ideals despite not being actually, physically present. Never built, it became larger than life, mythical, monumental. Its image was well known and ubiquitous. It was already so firmly implanted in Soviet citizens' minds that building it was practically unnecessary; it was more familiar to Moscow residents than structures that actually did exist.[537]

The story of the Palace of the Soviets has much in common with Belomor. The waterway was more important for its symbolic value than its practical use. The banks served as advertising space for the budding Soviet Union, a country proud that it could achieve what Tsarism could not. Despite its eventual completion, the canal was built so hastily that it could not be properly used. Like the titular pit in Platonov's *Foundation Pit*, an eerily accurate foreshadowing of the Palace of the Soviets fiasco, Belomor became known more as a graveyard than as a construction site. In a way, this did not matter much to the regime. Belomor—in spite of its poor functionality—was already lodged in the public imagination, so much so that commemorative brands, bands, and baubles exist even to this day, as will be explored in the following chapter. So while it is customary to consider the waterway a failure, I would call it a success: a chilling, sinister success. Belomor was such a cogent summation of Stalinism because it captured its very essence—in the collusion of the artistic with the physical, the creative with the destructive, the project blurred reality and falsehood to such an extreme that what was "true" no longer even mattered. Work reports could be falsified, just as re-forging could be faked. Gender and identity could be performed according to various scripts. Only the fictional creation, the monumental idea, was real. Given the perpetual collapsing of creative and destructive urges in the performance of reality, Stalinism was only possible as simulacra.

Figure 32. A larger-than-life Soviet star prominently displayed on the banks of the White Sea-Baltic Canal. From *Belomorsko-Baltiiskii kanal imeni tov. Stalina*, 1933. Russian State Library, Moscow, Russia.

V
THE MAPPING OF UTOPIA

> In every area,
> There is a war going on,
> We are battling with nature
> Armed with wheelbarrows.
> We are battling with nature
> Armed with labor
> With the powerful weapon of competition [...]
> It is
> Poetry as an order
> And an order as poetry [...]
> The mind on work
> The hand on the trigger. [538]
>
> —Sergei Alymov (1932)

In making the transition to modern Belomor narratives, there is a large and nearly empty gap, punctuated only by Aleksandr Solzhenitsyn's discussion of the canal in his landmark *Gulag Archipelago* (*Arkhipelag GULAG*, 1973-75).[539] The collectively-written *History of the Construction of the White Sea-Baltic Canal* was banned in 1937, and copies of the volume disappeared even from personal libraries as it became apparent that owning the tome could be a liability. The still-extant volumes were often disfigured, as the copy held by the Gulag Museum in Moscow demonstrates—Leopol'd L. Averbakh's name is furiously scribbled out on the title page, visually and physically depicting his violent purge from the upper echelons of the Soviet elite in 1937. What was once a highly visible and lauded Soviet construction project nearly disappeared from public memory. Maps, however, play an essential role in bridging the time from the Belomor construction to contemporary Russia. The map is imperative to the construction project because it is the proof of victory in the war against nature, and the guide to a realized utopia. While Belomor was certainly a dystopia in actuality, it was propagandistically portrayed as a utopia—a self-contained, highly regulated, and ideologically pure world. As demonstrated in Chapter Three, creative techniques such as montage enable the creation of new, fantastical landscapes. The map and the transformation of nature permeate contemporary Belomor narratives more than any other themes do. Cartography also represents an essential link from past to present, thanks to the most unlikely of Belomor products: cigarettes. As references to the White Sea-Baltic Canal slipped from view due to the controversial methods of its construction and its questionable success, the cigarettes named in its honor in 1932 continue in production to this day. The Belomorkanal brand of *papirosy* features a map on its label, and despite many slight changes to the label over the course of the years, the geographical image has remained largely unaltered.[540] This choice is telling, as the Belomor project sought to forever transform the map and to irrevocably place Soviet power upon it. To make the transition to a discussion of modern Belomor narratives, it is essential to first document the signficance of the map in Belomor narratives and link its presence to the larger trope of the war against nature, a key ideological principle in the Soviet Union's radical transformation during Stalin's first Five-Year Plan.

The Map and the War against Nature

Russia sought to make the transition from agrarian society to industrial powerhouse overnight. The transformation came to a head during Stalin's first Five-Year Plan, completed in 4.5 years, from 1928-1932. Given that the industrial revolution had begun in the United States nearly a hundred years earlier, Russia's need for transformation became all the more acute. The harnessing of the physical environment through technology and appropriation soon became known as the "war against nature" (*bor'ba s prirodoi*). The military diction—and the rapidity of the campaign—necessitated a violent, physical upheaval in the natural environment. While such efforts were very often part of modernization programs across the globe, the extremity of the militaristic diction differentiated the Soviet case from others. The battle against nature was to be as violent and aggressive as possible, which introduced a raw physicality into creative works about the new socialist landscape. Yet this overtly militaristic diction was not present only in the war against nature; it was ubiquitous. The violent language endemic to the Bolshevik takeover infused Soviet culture in all arenas.[541] During the Revolution, violence was "articulated and legitimized by a new language of class, and class conflict."[542] Given the violence endemic to the Bolshevik takeover, soon all aspects of life were configured in terms of battles, warfare, and enemies. This approach is echoed in the all-important word *udarnik*, or shock-worker, in which the Russian word "strike" makes up the root. While the word "strike" points to a military allusion, I would also add that the concept carries an inherently violent tone—an *udar* is a strike or blow that implies physical force. The shock-workers were the most productive type of laborer, and the concept originated during the Russian Revolution, when Bolsheviks had to work day and night to forge successfully their vision of a new world.

The war against nature exemplified the desire to wrest wild Karelia, one of the northernmost republics of the Soviet Union, from the primordial grip of nature. The violent rhetoric promoted in the battle against the natural world allowed for the introduction of war-like diction in many Belomor texts. The creation of a new vocabulary highlighted this militaristic approach; perhaps the best example is the fabrication of the word *kanaloarmeets* (canal-army soldier) as the name for a prisoner working on the canal. Prisoners and the regime alike used the ubiquitous and highly popular word *shturm* (assault) for the intense work drive to finish the canal. Authorities encouraged the prisoners to tap into an aggressive, war-like mentality in order to complete the seemingly impossible task of building a 227-kilometer-long canal in only twenty months. Mikhail Prishvin, the writer who visited and wrote about the canal, was also a great lover of Karelian nature (he composed his *In the Land of the Unfrightened Birds* as an homage to the wild beauty of Northern Russia). He felt uneasy about the violent transformation of landscape, even if he could appreciate the creative transformation of people.[543] He notes in his 1933 sketch "Little Spruce Island" ("Elovyi ostrovok") that the very spot where he had met a Karelian elder years before was now drowned by the waters of the White Sea-Baltic Canal, and that where bears once roamed, now there were none.[544]

The creative transformation of individual psyches accompanied the violent transformation of nature. The Belomor prisoner Prokofii Vedernikov writes in his diary that "Consciousness is growing. The Belomor-Baltic Waterway is growing. With it the new man is growing. And Pron'ka Baranenok is also developing at the new construction."[545] Vedernikov understands the changing landscape as running parallel to the changing man. His diary passage moves from the more general to the more specific—from the universal idea of consciousness, to the specificity of the work site, to the individuality of one particular laborer. Sergei Alymov makes a similar move in one of his many Belomor poems: "We are building, comrades / Socialism / High walls— / Fastened with cement / We are building, comrades / A new life ... / For our republic / For millions."[546] In the war against nature, both human beings *and* nature would be radically transformed, and altering one necessarily meant transforming the other. As the caption to the Kostia-like figure pictured in the *USSR in Construction* Belomor issue explains, "Here not only did the area's nature change, but also 'former' (*byvshie*) people transformed into laborers." Or, in the words of Karl Marx, "In changing nature man changes himself."[547] Even outside of Belomor, many Soviet workers expressed radical self-realizations while in the process of work, like a construction worker who wrote to Gorky to elaborate on his delight of remaking himself through building.[548]

Closely connected to the idea of the war against nature is the changing map. Cartography offers proof of the progress made in bending nature to human will. Maps, therefore, are highly prevalent in cultural artifacts regarding the White Sea-Baltic Canal: The *History of the Construction* opens with a map, the commemorative Belomor issue *USSR in Construction* features a map on the cover as well as several others within its pages (see Figures 25 and 26), and the infamous Belomorkanal *papirosy* and vodka use a map on their packaging.

The *History of the Construction* opens with a diagram of the White Sea-Baltic Canal entitled "schematic map" (*skhematicheskaia karta*) and ends with a diagram of the Moscow-Volga Canal, demonstrating how Soviet power will continue transmogrifying future landscapes. The changing of the map in light of the revolutionizing agency of socialist power is particularly highlighted:

> There is an incredible connectedness in our new map. We see how one part of it strives for another, and then they are connected: the Urals and the Kuzbass, Siberia and Turkestan. The map of the future classless country must become a whole, like the map of one city. Its dots, marking villages, strive to be transformed into circles. Its dotted lines will become straight lines.[549]

Figure 33.
Belomorkanal brand
cigarettes (papirosy).
Photograph by author.

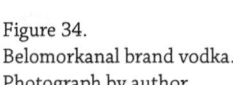

Figure 34.
Belomorkanal brand vodka.
Photograph by author.

Just like the diverse prisoner population[550] is unified into one working mass and the different styles of creative texts[551] are meant to convey a singular message, so will the different areas of the country be pieced together by the people's interacting with nature. As explored in Chapter Three, it is possible to see this geographical project as yet another type of collage—here more like the three-dimensional style of assemblage—in which disparate pieces are connected to form a whole. Yet until the prisoners have finished their work, all of these sections of the canal dwell only in the imagination, "Locks.... Dams.... Dikes.... All of them for now are only on paper!"[552]

The ability of the Soviet Union to change the map and to alter permanently the natural environment was a source of ideological pride because it offered tangible, visible evidence of socialist progress. At a famous October 1932 meeting of Soviet writers (with Stalin in attendance) at Gorky's home (with Stalin in attendance), the alleged "father" of socialist realism makes it clear that Belomor is a great achievement precisely because it redrew the map: "Even geography is changing. Here is the Belomor Canal. This is already a change in geography."[553] Early in the *History of the Construction*, the administrative bosses look at the map and marvel at how all the locks, dams, and dikes are for now only on paper, and dream about how the achievement of the project will be possible.[554] Later, after the canal's completion, Comrade Rapoport gestures to the newly-created map as he underscores the connection between Soviet greatness and the completion of the project: "From time immemorial [it was] conceived, but only socialism could complete the path, newly and widely, through the northern waters in the Baltic."[555] Significantly, the book ends with a map of the Moscow-Volga Canal, the next project that is to carve Soviet domination into the physical landscape, with many former Belomor prisoners and officials present to help complete the task.[556] Despite the integral role of human endeavor in re-configuring the physical environment, the *History of the Construction* at times presents the creation of the White Sea-Baltic Canal in a naturalized manner: "The dikes went down under the water, everything was lodged in place, as if it had always been like this, as if Karelia itself was born with the canal."[557] The canal's very existence—and not just the people who created it—is presented in the organic terms of life and death, those paired yet opposing moments that have a crucial impact on the culture surrounding Belomor, moments that represent creation and destruction.

This Soviet obsession with mapping, of course, was not exclusive to the White Sea-Baltic Canal project. Moscow was the center of the utopian desire to build a new socialist world, with city maps in 1935 depicting projects projected to be finished ten years later rather than already completed structures.[558] In an even broader context, the particularities of the Russian landscape play an important role both literally and metaphorically. The study of Soviet culture has witnessed a recent preoccupation with topography, as demonstrated by numerous scholars: "Understanding Sovietness [...] means understanding the space of Sovietness";[559] "The very history of Russia is the otherness of its geography";[560] "[The Soviet Union] was a country in which [...] the notion of space [...] was imbued with remarkable ideological prominence."[561] Harnessing of the physical environment and winning the war against nature, therefore, had enormous significance. Historically, the space of Russia is often equated with the idea of Russia itself; as the religious philosopher Nikolai Berdiaev contends, "There is that in the Russian soul which corresponds to the immensity, the vagueness, the infinitude of the Russian land: spiritual geography corresponds with physical."[562] The success of the New Man, therefore, was in some ways dependent on his ability to navigate and remake the Soviet landscape, a landscape that would be radically transformed by the war against nature.

In one of his rather rare appearances in the *History of the Construction*, Stalin stands in front of a map, pencil in hand, designating how the marshes will be dried out and the landscape will be transformed by Soviet labor.[563] As Iakov Rapoport gestures to a large diagram of the canal's pathway, it is noted that, despite being conceived from "time immemorial," only under socialism could this grandiose project be performed.[564] These remarks are echoed by the words of Leon Trotsky a decade earlier in his landmark work *Literature and Revolution* (*Literatura i revoliutsiia*, 1924): "The socialist man wants to and will command nature in all its breadth.... He will indicate where the mountains should be, and where they should part. He will change the direction of rivers and will create rules for the oceans."[565] Trotsky goes on to explain that such an aggressive relationship with nature will change the composition of man himself:

> Man will become immeasurably stronger, wiser, and subtler, his voice more musical. The forms of life will

become dynamically dramatic. The average human will rise to the heights of an Aristotle, a Goethe, or a Marx.[566]

Exemplifying the auditory theme discussed previously, Trotsky refers to harmony, rhythm, and music to establish his argument. He does this for reasons similar to those that influenced the other authors to use images of melody—such metaphors aptly capture the notion of a collective body working in harmony, a sonorous orchestra composed of many different instruments. The forms of life are to become "dynamically dramatic," as if life itself were a theatre performance.

In keeping with the "war" against nature, the *History of the Construction* is replete with military diction: people are "collectively organized in the fight against the rocky stubbornness of nature," and they must face "the fight with rock, marsh, and river."[567] Water is described as an "enemy" (*vrag*) that must be "trained" (*rastit'*), since every day this foe becomes more and more dangerous,[568] and nature itself is "cunning" (*khitraia*),[569] just like an enemy would be. The outcome of this battle with nature is an entirely original, subjugated, and rationalized physical environment: 'The result of this new science—planning—changed the understanding of geography while also changing the landscape.... As it is said in prison, we 'mastered nature.'"[570] This trope of war against nature might be traced back to one of the foundational texts of socialist ideology, Karl Marx's *Capital: A Critique of the Political Economy* (1867), in which the relationship between man and nature is described as one of struggle and dominance:

> Labour is, in the first place, a process in which both man and Nature participate, and in which man of his own accord starts, regulates, and controls the material reactions between himself and Nature. He opposes himself to Nature as one of her own forces, setting in motion arms and legs, head and hands, the natural forces of his body, in order to appropriate Nature's productions in a form adapted to his own wants. By thus acting on the external world and changing it, he at the same time changes his own nature.[571]

This connection is clearly made by the editors of the *History of the Construction*, who include the phrase "In changing nature, man changes himself" as the title to a photograph of a stout woman wielding a drill at the construction site.[572]

One of the most significant technical achievements at Belomor—and a source of much pride—was the engineer Maslov's development of all-wood locks. When he first suggested the idea, others noted with incredulity that no such system existed anywhere in the world and thought that his proposal was a joke, yet his design was ultimately accepted because "genuine space for technology and science is possible only under socialism."[573] The Soviet project, therefore, went beyond individual construction sites or new industrial centers; it was intended to recreate all of science, since "under socialism you can work ... and not only work, you can create a new chapter within a new science: socialist hydro-technology."[574] In this example, the White Sea-Baltic Canal was not just a metaphorical laboratory for new experiments, but also a literal, scientific one. Humankind, landscape, culture, industry, science—everything was to be remade under the revolutionary power of socialism, but only at the cost of great destruction.

Water: An Element to Be Tamed

In order for the map to be redrawn and the war against nature to be won, the wild reaches of the Karelian region had to be subdued. A worthy foe in battle, the far northern environment created deep hardships for the project's completion. The authorities, in turn, exploited the unfriendly working conditions as a testament to the success of socialist labor in the face of grave difficulty. In particular, the hard, dense Karelian rock proved extremely challenging to break up and remove, especially since the construction began in the winter—November 1931—when the ground was frozen solid. Yet perhaps the most defining feature of Karelia is water, as the region is famous for the lakes and rivers that cover more than a quarter of its territory. Water has a symbolic value for the region, as an exhibit in the State Museum of Karelia makes clear:

> Water is the single most valuable element. Water is not only a mineral material, it is not only a means for the development of industry and agriculture, it is an effective conductor of culture, it is living blood, which creates life where there was none before.[575]

It is important here that water is portrayed not simply as a chemical compound or element of nature; it is a culture-bearer, closely linked to the blood of life.

Viktor Shklovskii, a participant in the collectively written *History of the Construction*, remembers his visit to Belomor in terms of liquid. He describes how the water levels would rise and fall in the locks (*shliuzy*), and how the earth would drink the water and, in turn, water would overtake the earth. He draws a profound parallel between the phenomenon he observes at Belomor and the role of the Soviet writer, "I think that in Soviet literature, the soil is the writer. He drinks water for a long time, taking a very long time to absorb it, but then the sudden emergence of the writer rises up, and this unexpected high level of the writer is explained by the fact that he has already consumed a large quantity of time."[576] This description sounds not unlike the mechanism by which a canal operates, with water filling a lock's chamber in order to lift a vessel to the next level of the waterway, or, as in Shklovskii's example, the next level of metaphorical understanding.

The water motif is essential in works about Belomor, since the harnessing of water is the project's end goal. Yet water in this context often represents death rather than life, since the prisoners working at the canal, "along with the forested banks and flooded cliffs, also drown [their] past life."[577] In fact, one of the slogans of the canal itself is precisely this idea of "drown[ing] [one's] past in the depths of the canal," as the camp newspaper *Perekovka* makes clear.[578] An exhibit on the White Sea-Baltic Canal in the local history museum in Medvezh'egorsk dramatically portrays the canal's fatality, with a visual representation of the project showing bodies drowning in water. In this reversal, water is no longer something natural that allows for human existence; instead, it is something to be conquered and signifies death. It is crucial to realize that both interpretations of water contain a direct link to the physicality of human existence—water ultimately creates or destroys life; it is the blood associated either with birth pains or with death throes. At the White Sea-Baltic Canal, where thousands of people perished on a landscape already marred by death and cruelty,[579] this violent extremism is part and parcel of the overall physicality of cultural narratives surrounding the canal. Vera Inber, who was mentioned earlier as a member of the writers' brigade that visits the camp and a participant in the collectively-written *History of the Construction*, recounts in her diary just weeks before her visit to Belomor a river outing made frightening due to powerful waves. Despite the fear induced by the water, the incident prompts Inber to think she would like to visit the Mocow-Volga construction site. Fittingly, she begins her post-Belomor visit journal entry with a detailed description of the water and geography, and the connection of lakes and rivers created by the canal, and ends with a mere two-sentence description of the camp itself, mentioning the newspaper and criminal prisoners.[580] Whether Inber's motivations were prompted by the fact that it was simply safer to discuss geography or by a simple desire to focus on the remaking of a watery landscape we can never know, though it is likely a mixture of the two.

One of the most dramatic attempts to control water, master nature, and create the aesthetically beautiful occurred in the eighteenth century with Peter the Great's founding of St. Petersburg. This grandiose project had much in common with the Belomor experience: the struggle to control a wet, natural environment in an isolated and nearly unpopulated northern location; the sacrifice of thousands of lives in the name of a culturally significant project meant to swell national pride; the presence of a great, larger-than-life personality who serves as the construction's namesake; the use of primitive tools to build a grand design; a rationalist, utopian vision applied to a landscape with dramatic consequences. In addition, Peter had already envisioned a waterway along the current route of the Belomor Canal nicknamed the "Tsar's Road" after his land overhaul of ships along this passage. St. Petersburg was designed around a series of canals and employed Karelian granite for its riverbanks, with the end result a composition of "water, stone and sky."[581] Both locations—city and canal—were blank slates for ideology and eventually lodged into the popular imagination as mass graveyards.

Stalin himself had a particular obsession with water, with his favorite film being Grigorii Aleksandrov's 1938 river-based musical *Volga-Volga*.[582] This fascination played itself out in the urban capital of the Soviet Union, since "water was perceived in the 1930s as a sacred and powerful element, as the basis of existence" and "the cult of water could be seen in the numerous ponds and fountains that mushroomed all over Moscow" as well as "in the provision of the General Plan to concentrate major architectural objects on the banks of the Moscow River."[583] In regards to the loss of life at the Moscow-Volga Canal, Stalin downplayed the high fatality rates, claiming that "man after all is mortal" but "the canal would last forever."[584] Water formed a central motif not only in the *History of the Construction*, but in many production novels and stories of the 1920s and 1930s: Andrei Platonov's "The Epiphan Locks" (*Epifanskie shliuzy*, 1927); Leonid Leonov's *Soviet River* (*Sot'*, 1930); Boris Pil'niak's *The Volga Flows into the Caspian Sea* (*Volga vpadaet v Kaspiiskoe more*, 1930); and Marietta Shaginian's *Hydro-central* (*Gidrotsentral'*, 1931). Even the most famous book in all of Gulag literature—Aleksandr Solzhenitysn's *Gulag Archipelago*—employed a water-based metaphor in its conceptualization of the prison camps.

Solzehnitsyn's Gulag masterpiece also serves as the first transitional work to contemporary Belomor narratives. "The Archipelago Metastasizes," in volume III of the capacious work, includes Solovki as well as Belomor. Exceedingly negative and brutally sarcastic, Solzhenitsyn examines the Belomor legacy, including photographs of prisoners and camp administrators as well as a lengthy discussion of the *History of the Construction of the White Sea-Baltic Canal*. Solzhenitsyn was perhaps the first to write creatively about Belomor since the canal's completion, and his stern assessment subsequently prompted additional Russian writers to take up the prison camp as a subject. Now, nearly eighty years after the condemnation of the *History of the Construction*, a panoply of cultural products and scholarly treatises exist concerning the project. It is time to turn directly to the contemporary aesthetic re-interpretations of the Belomor experience through the examples of three artists and writers: Sergei Stratanovskii, Vadim Voinov, and Petr Belov. The war against nature and the mapped landscape, as made evident through the cartographic Belomorkanal brand of cigarettes, play a supporting role in all three instances.

Figure 35.
Poet and bibliographer Sergei Stratanovskii. Photograph by author.

Sergei Stratanovskii:
The "Waterway" to Contemporary Belomor Texts

Sergei Stratanovskii—a contemporary poet, critic, and bibliographer at the National Library in St. Petersburg—never spent any time in the Gulag, yet became fascinated by the topic of Stalin's White Sea-Baltic Canal.[585]

His attraction stems not from lived experience but from an interaction with cultural texts: the chapter on the White Sea-Baltic Canal in Aleksandr Solzhenitsyn's *Gulag Archipelago* and the philosophical writings of Belomor prisoner Aleksandr Meier. Stratanovskii notes the incongruity of the canal project; there is an evident disjuncture between the propaganda advertising the canal and the reality of its mass death. As Stratanovskii notes, both are true—the canal was completed in record time, yet it was a dark moment in Soviet history. Although coming to terms with this anomaly is difficult, the situation is a perfectly appropriate summation of Stalinist culture. The project again serves as an apt case study for Stalinism, distilling contemporary Russian society's approach toward the Soviet past. This conflicted attitude is perhaps one reason for the present-day indifference to the evils of the Gulag, an apathy that Stratanovskii and others note. People smoke Belomorkanal cigarettes without thinking about their potential implications, and many

Russians continue to harbor nostalgia for the Soviet period.[586] Despite the flood of prison memoirs currently available, Stratanovskii claims that people actually knew more about the Gulag during its existence than they do today. Although historical information is now more widely available, contemporary youth in Russia is often simply not interested in exploring these resources.

Stratanovskii's poetic work about the White Sea-Baltic Canal, "Waterway" (*Gidroarteriia*, 1985-1993), is written in the form of an oratorio composed of eleven titled sections, with each section representing a different voice or group within the canal's prisoner population.[587] The work chillingly captures the horrific landscape of the camp, highlighting water particularly. The first section, titled "The Chorus of Prisoners" (*Khor zakliuchennykh*), immediately illuminates the overall vocality of the poem, as the convicts are described as "outcasts" (*otverzhentsy*) on the Soviet land. The collective body is still present, but it has been redefined as negative; the prisoners recognize their identity as a stratum of refuse. As in earlier Belomor texts, the diversity of the prison population is acknowledged—they are "priests, murderers, thieves" (*popy, ubiitsy, vory*)—while they are simultaneously being turned into an indistinguishable mass—they are simply a "collection of voices" (*sobor golosov*). Like in the orchestras, songs, and dramatic productions that came before it, the poem contains a musical performance of identity, but here the chorus demands rather than entertains. Relying on aural participation, the poem cries out "listen, listen to us, listen to us through the shadows,"[588] in a plea that mirrors yet subverts the opening of Aleksandr Lemberg's documentary film *Belomorstroi Reports* (1933), which also demands, "Listen!" repeatedly in its effort to disseminate Belomor propaganda. Even if this ragtag crowd of prisoners may be lonely, lost, and poor, as the poem describes them, there is an element of strength in their collective misery and desire to be heard.

Just as the notion of the collective is infused with a raw physicality informed by the prisoners' recognition of themselves as slaves, so does the motif of *put'*, or pathway, introduce an element of violence. This is the waterway of destruction, the landscape of brutality—the end result of the war against nature. Both the Tsar's Road (in reference to Peter the Great's overland haul of ships) and the canal itself are figured as a road of bones, with the prisoners acknowledging themselves as such:

"My—doroga kostei."[589] The title of the poem, "Gidroarteriia," literally means a hydro-artery, naming the work with a reference to the human body. A waterway is a path that connects larger bodies of water and institutions with one another, just as the veins and arteries of the human body connect to organs in order to allow them to function. This metaphor follows—albeit in a negative way—Alymov's previously cited comparison between the construction site and the beating heart, with the many work collectives and brigades as the organ's arteries. The fact that human bodies have literally become part of the natural landscape makes the leap from industrial construction project to human organic matter less drastic; the physicality of flesh and the materiality of industry have become inseparable.

Selfhood is a prominent theme in the poem, and the seemingly endless attempts of the masses to define themselves borders on obsessive; "We are outcasts of the Soviet land," "We are a chorus of voices," "We are free refuse," "We are an inkblot in history," "We are a road of bones," "We are canal army members," "We are soldiers," "We were wreckers," "We will be victors."[590] The definition is dependent on the theme of the stanza. The first seven classifications come from the first and last verses, both titled "The Chorus of Prisoners" (*Khor zakliuchennykh*) and the last two—rather different—definitions of selfhood come from the section titled simply "Engineer" (*Inzhener*). These self-identifications attest to the need for everyone associated with the canal project to define him- or herself as well as his or her relationship to work, and the desire for a repetitive assertion of selfhood becomes urgent in light of the collectivizing and homogenizing effect of the Stalinist labor camps. The demarcation of subjectivity reaches a feverish pitch—with the help of word play—in the final verse of the oratory that is titled identically to the first ("Chorus of Prisoners"):

> Listen to us—it's us
> Listen, listen to us
> We are from a hole, from shadows
> We speak from the depths of the earth
> We are canal-armymen, soldiers ...
> It's not us, not slaves
> You are not slaves, and neither are we
> Slaves are muter than fish

———————————— CHAPTER FIVE ————————————

And we, as a reward—have graves[591]

The wordplay of *my*, *vy*, *raby*, and *ryby* cannot be captured in the English translation; the rhyming of these words plays with the negligible differences between "us" and "you," between "slaves" and "fish." Despite the earlier classification of self according to profession or social status—for example, engineer or non-political prisoner—here there is a sense of collectivity; all of the speakers are prisoners and ultimately face the same fate.

Issues of identity in the poem also become apparent in the contrast between the (much more common) use of the pronoun "we" and the individualized pronoun "I," the latter occurring most frequently in the stanza entitled "Kulak" (*Raskulachennyi*). Kulaks were the largest portion of the Belomor prisoner population, and in this verse the reader glimpses their tragic fate; the "rapists of the earth" (*nasil'niki zemli*) come to seize the peasants' livestock, confiscate their bread, devastate their homes, and divide their household belongings. Given that kulaks were defined as wealthy, landowning peasants, it is perhaps not surprising that here the individualistic "I" takes precedence over the collective "we," and that the definition of the self is cruel and harsh:

> And since then I am a slave
> And God will not give me even
> A crude grave
> When he finds out that I'm dead
> I am a Belomorkanal *zek*[592]

Untranslatable into English, the verb chosen for "die" in the above passage (*dokhnut'*) is used primarily for animals, underscoring the status of the prisoners as mere expendable livestock. Unapologetic identifications of the self occur in the opening and closing lines of the stanza: "I am a slave" and "I am a *zek*" (*zek* is a word for a Gulag prisoner that comes from the abbreviation z/k, for *zakliuchennyi*). However grim, these declarations of individuality reclaim some type of identity in the name of the lost masses, even if the collective body remains the central focus.

While some of the stanzas have an individual personality at their head—like "poet," "historian," "philosopher," "engineer," or "Chekist"—

others denote a collective group: "Chorus of Prisoners" and "Chorus of Non-Political Prisoners." The collective body formed here is much more misshapen and haphazard than its predecessors, and the group ultimately does not sing in a unified voice. Stratanovskii is hesitant, as many writers are, to offer any clear meaning behind the symbols in his poem, and prefers for readers to draw their own conclusions. Yet when asked about the role of the chorus—which appears to be one of the most important elements of the poem—he offered the idea that the chorus represents a "general consciousness" (*obshchee soznanie*) of the people. The "chorus" of prisoners and "chorus" of non-political prisoners, as well as the definition of the poem as an oratory, underscore the work's musical and performative motifs in the transformation of nature.

The dramatic alteration of the landscape is a key theme in the poem, and it is often related to historical legacy and utopian/dystopian characteristics. Stratanovskii chooses Faust as a vehicle to explicate this change in nature. It is an appropriate selection for a multitude of reasons: the desire to re-shape nature according to man's will in Goethe's *Faust* parallels the efforts at the canal; Faust is mentioned in numerous other works regarding the canal (both those contemporaneous to the Belomor construction and those that come afterwards);[593] and Stratanovskii claims that the work of well-known Russian philosopher Aleksandr Meier on *Faust* is one of the original inspirations for the writing of his poem. Goethe's *Faust* is a rich summation of the issues connected to Belomor, including the desire to organize and control the world by understanding it; the role of aesthetic production in redemption; the innate human desire to strive; the significance of the deed; and the creation of the new man (with the homunculus symbolically paralleling the idea of re-forging).[594]

Goethe's *Faust* contains a grand construction site involving the taming of water revolving around a system of dikes. Like Belomor's, and unlike St. Petersburg's, the dike system in *Faust* is ultimately a failure. Faust believes that the construction project—a reclamation of land from the sea—is being built for him, but in reality it is his own grave, just as the prisoners at Belomor are essentially constructing a road of bones, and the laborers in Platonov's *Foundation Pit* are digging their own tombs rather than a base for the All-Proletarian Home. Even though Faust will find out that "the only way for modern man to transform himself ... is by radically transforming the whole physical and social world he lives in," such efforts and the "great developments he initiates—intellectual, moral, economic, social—turn out to exact great human costs."[595] This fictional predicament succinctly echoes the Belomor experience and explains why *Faust* would be a predominant subtext in canal narratives.

Sergei Stratanovskii's previously discussed poem "Gidroarteriia" uses *Faust* as a cultural touchstone, particularly in the section titled "A Chekist by the Name of Faust" (*Chekist po familii Faustov*). The stanza opens with the assertion that Belomor is "not just the construction of a large waterway—it is the beginning of the great task of re-imagining nature."[596] Alongside this re-creation of nature, men will be re-created. The Chekist arrogantly claims that they will become masters of the natural environment: they will flood the rivers, make the birds unnecessary, and tame nature like a "beast in a cage" (*kak zveria v kletku*)[597] in the name of the Five-Year Plan. The animals will be abolished like the letter "iat'," in a reference to the orthographic reforms following the Russian revolution. While the poem employs the same kind of terminology used in other Belomor texts, here the end result is clearly a dystopian, rather than utopian, vision.

Meier, who served as an inspiration for Stratanovskii and was an important *Faust* critic, worked as a hydro-technical specialist at Belomor. His profession in prison, therefore, echoed his intellectual concerns, both of which were concerned with water. He obtained his favorable technical occupation after completing special courses at the camp, and continued to work on his own intellectual projects while imprisoned at the canal. Released early, he subsequently worked on the Moscow-Volga Canal as a free citizen. Meier wrote very actively in the 1930s, and he called this period a "summing up" (*vremia podvedeniia itogov*) of his work. Some of his most personal works, including *Victim* (*Zhertva*) and *Three Sources* (*Tri istoka*) were written in Medvezh'ia Gora, the capital of the Belomor construction.[598] Meier's commentary on water brings to mind *Faust*'s homunculus:

> The beginning of life is a wet beginning; everything living comes out of moisture, the carrier of the seed hides itself in the form of living existence, is moisture, fertilizing strength, without which the earth would be dry and fruitless. Moisture at the same time resuscitates, makes fresh, rouses what has fallen, is tired or dying.[599]

Meier cites another liquid—blood—as the key to life, and notes that "rhythmic flood" (*ritmicheskii potok*) weakens the spirit.[600] Both Stratanovskii and Meier share a raw physicality in their verse. During a project in which death and suffering was an everyday affair—with the landscape itself functioning as a mass grave—this physicality is unavoidable, yet it is a violence that spurs them to engage in creation.

Alina Mal'tseva, another St. Petersburg poet, also chooses Stalin's White Sea-Baltic Canal as a subject for her verse.[601] Her "Poem about the Belomorkanal" (*Poema o Belomorkanale*, 1995) begins with a mystical, rather than physical, part of the body: "The northern part of my soul / Whispers to me: 'Soon you will write / About freedom…'"[602] Similar to their representation in Stratanovskii's work, the prisoners are related to mute fish, carcasses that have become imbedded in the landscape. There is a "crimson abyss" above the canal that "throws thunder,"[603] and the depths of the new waters are "paved with bones" as well as stones.[604] A hybrid musicality reigns in the poem, with the moans of prisoners juxtaposed with the sounds of the orchestra. Mal'tseva's work, therefore, continues some of the efforts made by Stratanovskii, infusing physicality—including mass death—into the poem as well as exploring the prison camp's landscape.

Vadim Voinov and the Landscape of Collage

Vadim Voinov, a contemporary Russian artist and thinker, employs Gulag—and specifically Belomor—motifs in his many art pieces. Voinov was born into the Party elite; his father served as the director of the Propaganda Center, his cousin studied with Stalin's daughter, and his uncle was a right-hand man to Andrei Zhdanov and eventually became the first secretary of the Leningrad (St. Petersburg) Regional Party Committee. At one point, this uncle was even suggested as a successor to Stalin, although his untimely execution prevented this possibility. Voinov's father was arrested when the artist was nine years old, and eventually passed away in a hospital for veterans wounded in World War II. Despite their closeness to the regime—or precisely because of it—Voinov's family members faced many hardships. Voinov studied art history and architecture and worked as a sailor before becoming involved in the art world in the 1970s. His pieces have complex spatial relationships and profound historical suggestions, demonstrating his parallel interests in architecture and museum studies.

When I met with Vadim Voinov in St. Petersburg at the artistic-cultural center Pushkinskaia 10, which houses his studio as well as a permanent collection of his work, he acknowledged the link between his work and the collage experiments of the 1920s and 1930s. The prison camps serve as a common motif in his works, and he had read the *History of the Construction*, which he called an "anti-book" (*anti-kniga*). He recognized that he had faced difficulties because of the very sensitive, political nature of his collages' themes, yet claimed that what was most important was that he continued to produce artworks and function as an artist.[605] Working in the found object tradition popular in contemporary art, Voinov's works often include everyday objects and are mostly three-dimensional.

In Voinov's constructions, random objects are put together that prompt particular connections in the viewer's mind, not unlike Sergei Eisenstein's theory of filmic montage. These items are replete "with the blood and flesh of existence, creating a Benjaminesque 'aura of authenticity,' and for this reason they pester and importune, demanding the viewer's attention, demanding decipherment."[606] The emphasis on "flesh and blood" in this explication, as well as Voinov's specific choice of everyday objects, injects Voinov's art works with physicality and rawness. Items that have been ripped from their usual contexts, stripped from the mundane world in which they had a home, now become violently transformed into art objects. Not insignificantly, many of Voinov's pieces have sharp or pointed items as part of their composition: spears, swords, axes, razor blades, screwdrivers, shovels, picks, daggers, scissors, bayonets, and even mousetraps are included in his works, creating a palpable sense of danger. Because the items that Voinov chooses for his pieces have such an unbelievably "strong emotional aura,"[607] it is impossible for the viewer not to react, not to enter into dialogue with the works.

Yet the employment of such everyday objects, while offering profound associations, also poses the threat of the "profanization of culture: the loss of the *message* in triviality, its sinkage in mud and garbage."[608] Just as the Belomor prisoners were portrayed as "worthless trash" in Stratanovskii's verse and will be represented as actual refuse in Petr Belov's paintings (to be discussed next), the mundane, ordinary object again rears its head in contemporary culture to provide commentary on the Stalinist past. There is a danger—one that becomes literal with the example of real-life cigarette packs—that the legacy of the Soviet experience will somehow become lost in the garbage dump of history, devoid of meaning and denied of articulation. Nevertheless, the significance in Voinov's works stems not from the objects themselves, but rather from how they are placed in relationship to one another, which frees the assemblages from their individual components.

The importance of the interrelationship between objects often necessitates a certain amount of deciphering. For example, the piece *Wounded Elephant in a Family Album* (*Ranennyi slon v semeinnom al'bome*, 1994) might at first seem to be related to the black elephant figurine that is placed in the center of the assemblage. Yet "elephant" is Russian is *slon*, which is also the acronym for the Solovki Gulag camps (*Solovetskie lageria osobogo naznacheniia*, or SLON). The fractured pieces of photographs from the family album dissect the human figure; a head is upside down, legs are at a forty-five degree angle. The elephant in the center of the work has a hole in the middle of its chest, as if the animal had been shot with a bullet in an execution. The artist renders physical violence pictorially in a similar way in *The Purge* (*Chistka*, 1992), which includes a group photograph of individual, oval-shaped faces that has been torn to pieces, with some visages missing altogether. Such violence can be represented by the selection of material as well as by the inclusion of particular objects; the title of this work itself invokes brutal associations. *Conditioned Reflex* (*Uslovnyi refleks*, 1991) contains the same type of group photographs, and although they are not torn into pieces, the presence of a metal chain encircling the pictures alludes to a sinister brutality. Voinov represents the violence of the Soviet experience with the physical dissection and reformulation of images.

Figure 36. Vadim Voinov collage, *Conditioned Reflex* (*Uslovnyi refleks*, 1991). Reproduced with permission from the artist.

Figure 37. Vadim Voinov collage, *Smoke Break* (*Perekur*, 1990). Reproduced with permission from the artist.

Voinov's works often focus on the aspect of hard, physical labor in the Soviet Union by featuring picks, shovels, and construction projects. *The Difficulties of Growing Up* (*Trudnosti rosta*, 1980-1990) includes a spade and shovel alongside a typical star-shaped communist pin; *Here's Your Shovel* (*Vot Vam lopata*, 2000) has a shovel—as the title indicates—along with a poster titled "The erection of the canal"; *The Pharoah's Profile II* (*Profil' faraona*, 1984) assembles a cast-metal profile image of Stalin along with a pamphlet on the Cult of Personality and a worn, dirt-caked shovel;[609] *We Have Constructed* (*My postroili*, 1991) juxtaposes a poster of the same name with a cardboard container labeled "bricks," a matchbox, and a spade; *Silhouette of a Proletarian* (*Siluet proletariia*, 1991) includes a wrench alongside an image of a factory worker ripped from sort of catalogue or publication; *Record* (*Rekord*, 1992), referring to shock-worker labor, draws together a miniature pick-axe and a 1933 cover of *USSR in Construction* (*SSSR na stroike*); and the list could easily go on. The assemblage that most directly references Stalin's White Sea-Baltic Canal, entitled *Smoking Break* (*Perekur*, 1990) also includes the head of a shovel, in reference to the physical labor undertaken to complete the project. Yet the title of this piece is perhaps even more significant; not only does Voinov use the title *Smoking Break*, but he also includes an empty, crumpled pack of Belomorkanal cigarettes on top of a poster of the dams of the Moscow-Volga Canal. A pack of the infamous *papirosy*—and a crumpled pack, no less, making evident its status as a piece of refuse—becomes the focus of a contemporary art piece regarding Belomor.

The violence of Voinov's art pieces—demonstrated by both the frequent usage of sharp objects and the repeated slicing or cutting of the compositional materials that make up his assemblages—becomes linked to the importance of physical labor in the Soviet Union. Violence irrevocably changes the composition of the human body, just as hard labor physically transforms it. The raw, visceral component of the Soviet experience bleeds through, with individuals presented not as distinct personalities, but rather as so many bits of garbage: forgotten, unwanted, and discarded. If we compare this with the legacy of the Holocaust,[610] it is possible to see differences between the Soviet prison experience and its Nazi counterpart. It is precisely the reclamation of the individual voices and individual lives that forms the most distinctive feature of the recovery of survivors after the Holocaust. Holocaust survivors travel to schools to tell their specific stories; oral histories are laboriously collected at the Yale Fortunoff Video Archives for Holocaust Testimony and Steven Spielberg's Survivors of the Shoah Visual History Foundation; at the Holocaust Memorial Museum in Washington, D.C., visitors are presented with an identity card of a particular Holocaust victim so that they can imagine that individual's personal story and struggle. Soviet memory, on the other hand, is decidedly more collectively oriented.

Voinov's assemblages offer a type of selfhood that is not entirely unrelated to the collective body present in the cultural narratives contemporaneous to the canal's construction. Belomor motifs—the war against nature, utopian/dystopian space, collectivity, musicality—are not rejected but rather re-formulated. Instead of re-claiming the individual or denigrating the project, contemporary works highlight the traumatized collective body and the canal's spatial landscape. This is not a joyful collective working in the name of Soviet labor, but rather an abused and forgotten mass of humanity. This is not the glorious re-creation of the canal landscape through photomontage, but rather the dissection and attenuation of the project's natural environment. Destruction is expressed creatively.

Petr Belov and Belomor Papirosy: Images of a Dystopian Landscape

Like Stratanovskii, the artist Petr Belov did not spend any time in the Gulag, and his family members were not victimized during the Stalinist Terror. In his early career, Belov worked mostly as a set designer and a landscape painter; a spirit of performativity permeates all of his artistic work. In his later life he chose the violence of Soviet rule as a theme for a final, masterful series of paintings. Two of these paintings, *White Sea Canal* (*Belomorkanal*, 1985) and *The Rooks Have Arrived, or April Plenary Session* (*Grachi prileteli, ili aprel'skii plenum*, 1987) will be the focus of the discussion here, since these works continue the contemporary efforts to reclaim the victims of the White Sea-Baltic Canal.[611]

In *Belomorkanal*, Belov uses a modern manifestation of the Belomor legacy—an empty pack of Belomorkanal brand cigarettes—as the centerpiece of his painting. The pack, essentially a piece of garbage, takes up nearly the entire canvas, with a string of barbed wire in the lower left-hand corner reminding the viewer that we are in the landscape of a Gulag camp. From the right-hand side, an indistinguishable mass of prisoners walks into a hole at the top of the cigarette pack; some have wheelbarrows, others hold shovels. The faces of the prisoners are impossible to differentiate. They are one lump, a mass of humanity that eventually melts into a shadow of black on the right side of the canvas. They are walking toward their fate: the empty promise of a construction project called the Belomorkanal, where the scale of life is entirely shifted. The human bodies are only as tall as an empty cigarette pack; people and objects are made equivalent to one another. Both human lives and cigarette packs are disposable, and the painting captures the tragic fate of Belomor victims.

While *Belomorkanal* highlights the collective mass of prisoners, there are some gestures towards individuality in *The Rooks Have Arrived*. In a small, half-frozen stream between two sheets of ice, the individual faces of prisoners can be discerned. This painting visually captures the idea that the canal is a "road of bones," with the victims of its construction permanently submerged under water. The body of water in the painting is not a grandiose canal; instead, it is a tiny stream, mirroring the too-shallow reality of the White Sea-Baltic Canal. On the left bank of the ice stream, which comprises the majority of the painting, there is a collection of garbage that includes squashed cigarette butts, empty cans, newspapers, and a vodka bottle. The refuse heap parallels the prisoners' underwater faces; they are side-by-side in the painting and made equivalent. Once again, the convicts are mere bits of garbage, their eyes closed permanently in the frosty embrace of death, their positioning reminiscent of the *besplatnoe bydlo* (cattle working for free) in Stratanovskii's poem. The White Sea-Baltic Canal is directly referenced by the inclusion of an empty pack of Belomorkanal brand cigarettes in the junk heap, this time crumpled up as a real piece of garbage would be. The painting captures the absurdity endemic to Belomor. Although the faces of the forgotten are permanently inscribed in the depths of the water, spring has arrived, as the title and the arrival of birds foreshadows. Yet even this natural event is coupled with political significance: the return of the rooks accompanies the April Plenary Session.[612]

Belov repeatedly uses Belomorkanal cigarette packs in his paintings. The ongoing availability of this brand of *papirosy* in Russia today has become an embarrassing symbol of the canal project. Contemporary critics often point out derisively that Germany has no cigarette brand named Auschwitz or Dachau.⁶¹³ Yet the very fact that the Belomorkanal brand does exist—and continues to be produced to this day—suggests that the historical conditions surrounding the Gulag are different than those of the Holocaust. The cigarette brand has in some ways become more emblematic of the project than the waterway itself is. While the latter is rarely used because of its too-shallow depth, most Russians are familiar with Belomorkanal cigarettes.⁶¹⁴ The true reality of the canal—an ambitious creation constructed entirely by prisoners—has been displaced by a cigarette brand. There is perhaps no text or material from the White Sea-Baltic Canal experience that captures the notion of absurdity inherent in the project as adeptly as these *papirosy*. The cigarettes' availability in contemporary Russia makes perfect sense as a Belomor symbol precisely because of its irrationality. While it is unclear who designed the original cigarette package (there are several versions of the container, all of which include the all-important map of Karelia), they became available very soon after the canal's completion in what was likely a celebratory gesture in recognition of another "achievement" of Stalin's Five-Year Plan. The newspaper *Red Tobacco* (*Krasnaia tabachnitsa*) already mentions the brand—and the struggle to maintain satisfactory quality—in a March 1934 article.⁶¹⁵

This may explain why the Belomor pack has become a common reference point for numerous artists and filmmakers. Just as Belomor can serve as a synecdoche for the Soviet Union, the image of the cigarette label can be a synecdoche for the entire construction project. The rock group Belomorkanal uses the curved logo of the company on all of their album covers, further ingraining the cigarette brand as an instantly recognizable emblem for the Gulag project. With song titles like "Letter from Prison" (*Pis'mo iz lageria*), "Night before Execution" (*Noch' pered rasstrelom*), "Thief" (*Vor*), "Zek in Freedom" (*Zek na vole*), and "I Am Not Guilty" (*Ia ne vinovat*), all of which appear in their album *Song Frame of Mind* (*Nastroenie shanson*, 2005), the group clearly attempts to address elements of criminal life in their music.

The Mapping of Utopia

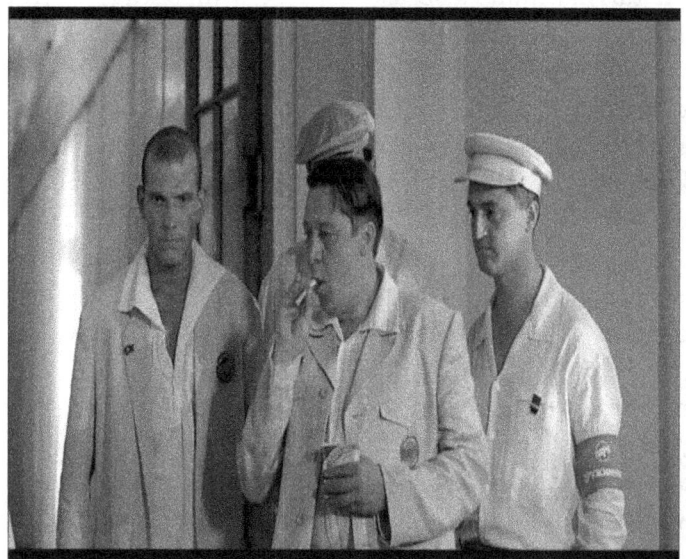

Figure 38. A screen shot from the 2006 Iulii Gusman film *Soviet Park* (*Park sovetskogo perioda*), featuring Belomorkanal cigarettes.

Figure 39. A screen shot from the 2008 Brad Anderson film *Transsiberian*, featuring Belomorkanal cigarettes.

Recent Russian films also use the logo symbolically, with the cigarette label's recognizability allowing the audience to make specific associations. An administrator in Iulii Gusman's 2006 film *Soviet Park* (*Park Sovetskogo perioda*) smokes Belomorkanal cigarettes; given that he's one of the cruelest and most corrupt officials in this Soviet-themed Disneyland, his tobacco habits do not seem coincidental. The recent American film *Transsiberian* (2008) also features Belomorkanal cigarettes. In the opening scene, corrupt Russian detectives investigate a crime scene, most likely gang-related, that includes frozen dead bodies on an abandoned tanker at sea. The chief inspector smokes Belomorkanal *papirosy* in a close-up shot.

In the brand's logo, the word Belomorkanal is sandwiched between two curved arches composed of numerous lines. These archways are akin to rainbows, with the separate lines mimicking the individual colors of a rainbow's composition—a symbol that represents good luck in Russian as well as American culture. The curved arches, given the canal's watery existence, also bring to mind the rounded slopes of currents or waves. The repetition of the arches on either side of the word Belomorkanal could also represent the two banks of the canal, with the text running through the middle as the waterway's content. The logo as pictured on the cigarette and vodka brand also includes a map, referring to the ever-important Soviet alteration of nature (see Figures 33, 34). Significantly, the map does not simply document the area of the White Sea-Baltic Canal itself; instead, it includes multiple cities in a large swath of landscape in order to affirm the existence of Moscow as the "port of five seas." The legacy of Belomor once again reaches beyond itself; not meant to be bound merely to Karelia or to the period of its construction, it instead becomes emblematic of the whirlwind of change occurring in the country more broadly during the Soviet period.

Even in the non-visual realm of jokes, or *anekdoty*, the Belomorkanal brand of cigarettes has made an appearance. This tendency demonstrates the durability of the cigarette brand as an equivalent for the canal; indeed, some claim that the canal is "celebrated, but not famous" because it is known most directly through the brand of cigarettes and not the actual construction, which is too deficient to be used to any extensive degree.[616] One of the most common jokes (*anekdoty*) about Belomor directly references the cigarette pack in an untranslatable pun:

Two pilots with bad hangovers are getting ready to take
off. The captain asks the navigator:
–Did you bring the maps?
–And also two new decks of cards.
–Bah! Again flying by the "Belomor" pack.[617]

Since the word *karty* in Russian means both maps and playing cards, the joke can simultaneously reference the map that is on the cigarette pack as well as card-playing, one of the most common criminal pastimes. Yet perhaps the most common[618] joke regarding the Belomorkanal does not refer to the cigarette pack:

–Do you know who built the Belomorkanal?
–The right bank was built by those who told the joke and
the left by those who heard it.[619]

This joke has more in common with the Russian *anekdot* tradition in the sense that it is self-referential, alluding to the inherent danger of joke telling.

Although the tendency is to point out the absurdity of having the Belomorkanal brand available at all, this odd vehicle of commemoration for the canal project is actually extremely appropriate. Just as grief stemming from the Soviet experience often manifests itself in contemporary literature rather than in open dialogue,[620] so does the historical legacy of the Gulag make an appearance in material culture perhaps more than in formal monuments. Indeed, the lack of the latter in contemporary Russia underscores an ambivalent approach towards the legacy of the Gulag, or at least a different approach to memory.[621] The cigarette brand, therefore, posits an alternative, albeit odd, type of memorialization.

Belov's paintings can help us to understand why the symbol of the Belomorkanal cigarette pack is quite useful in contemporary art. The prisoners at the White Sea-Baltic Canal were, on some level, refuse; they were used as ideological containers and laboring workhorses. The fact that the construction would be memorialized on something as impermanent as a cigarette pack demonstrates the disposability of the prisoners. Cigarette packs—and cigarettes themselves—are nothing of substance; they are broken down immediately into smoke that disappears into the air and cardboard cartons that are crumpled and thrown away in the garbage. In contemporary Belomor works, the disposability of the prisoners, the transformation of the landscape, and the violence of the Gulag are all underscored, regardless of whether the artists have the specific intent of chastising the socialist experiment.

Despite the supposed economic and cultural magnitude of the canal's construction, the impact of the waterway on the Karelian region was much less than the administration expected. The cigarette container itself embodies this disparity: while both the original and current design of the label include the map's permanent transformation of landscape, this achievement is eroded by the very disposability of the pack itself, allowing it to appear as a piece of garbage in numerous contemporary cultural products. Trash itself has more generally become an important component of postmodernist culture. The contemporary critic Mikhail Epstein organized collective discussions in Russia on specified themes—one of which included garbage—for his "laboratory" of contemporary culture.[622]

Contemporary Russian magazines acknowledge that the cigarettes are now more famous than the canal itself.[623] Not only do the cigarettes remain available in spite of their condemnation, but an affordable vodka has been added to the Belomorkanal brand of products. The vodka also uses a map of the canal region for its label and also represents an inexpensive, easily consumed, and hastily disposed product. In Belov's *The Rooks Have Arrived*, a bottle of vodka, although not of the Belomorkanal brand, rests with the crumpled cigarette packs in the refuse pile on the snowy ice patch. It is not insignificant that Belomorkanal would be chosen as a brand name for cigarettes and vodka—two products, detrimental to the health, that are designed for immediate usage followed by disposal. The Belomorkanal cigarettes are notoriously harsh, with very high levels of tar and nicotine. Their main appeal to consumers is their low price. Dangerous and cheap, the cigarettes are an oddly fitting representation of the Gulag project. Yet in 2011 different packs of Belomorkanal *papirosy* were released in specially designed, imprinted metal tins at a higher price, in what could be a subconscious attempt to ameliorate the Belomor legacy.[624] However packaged, the map label of the Belomorkanal brand must remind us that the war against nature was also conducted against humans.

Contemporary artists who employ Belomor as a theme for their work highlight the violence committed against humanity. Artists recognize the changing of the map within the context of thousands of lost lives rather than that of laborers fighting nobly in the war for a new civilization. The irony of creation in the face of destruction is still apparent, perhaps most overtly in the Belomorkanal brand *papirosy* and vodka, thanks to which you can literally ingest the legacy of the canal. The destructive history of the canal has led to the creation of innumerable artistic works, many of which recognize the miserable fate of the prisoners. The Soviet drive to alter the reality of the natural landscape necessitated the use of violence. Artistic texts reiterate this aggression on the levels of both content and form: the environment was destroyed physically but created aesthetically. And in the performative re-imagination of nature, fact and fiction were necessarily muddled.

Conclusion:
The Performance of Violence in Contemporary Works

The repetition inherent in performance connects it to the category of trauma, since trauma itself stems from the repeated suffering of an event, in what Sigmund Freud would call "repetition compulsion."[625] It is not surprising, therefore, that repetition should represent such a prominent feature of Gulag narratives.[626] An artwork, in turn, can often be a type of conscious memorialization, especially when depicting the violence endemic to the Gulag. Yet the viewer of any such piece plays just as important of a role as the one who created it. As Frances Guerin and Roger Halls suggest:

> The act of bearing witness is not the communication of a truth that is already known, but its actual production through this performance act. In this process, the listener becomes a witness to the witness, not only facilitating the very possibility of testimony, but also subsequently sharing its burden. That is to say, the listener assumes responsibility to perpetuate the imperative to bear witness to the historical trauma for the sake of collective memory.[627]

Many of the works here—in particular the contemporary ones—beg commentary from the viewer or reader; they prompt reaction and are not meant to be understood in a vacuum. In addition, while many of these objects can be found in traditional museums—such as Belov's paintings or Voinov's art pieces—they insistently employ the everyday in their constructions, another feature that draws them closer to the earlier cultural narratives from the canal. The prisoners' autobiographies, performance pieces, and fictional works are all examples of the most democratic type of artistic participation, despite the violent context of incarceration.

Contempoary Belomor works share significant characteristics with the narratives produced during the canal's construction. As it did in the 1930s, art today serves as a pathway to understanding the deeply-embedded themes of the project, themes that are mirrored in Stalinist culture and continue to influence the country years after the waterway's completion. While contemporary aesthetic works often highlight the downtrodden prisoners and their miserable fates, it is important to note that the convicts were not simply victims of an all-seeing Panopticon that invisibly governed their every move. Nor were they actors in masks, or subjects completely imprisoned by their political environments. The prisoners were a complicated, diverse group of individuals with varying desires, motivations, and reactions. While one might speculate that the sometimes clear commonalities between the regime's discourse and that of its citizens is due to a normative, oppressive political environment, the situation is in fact more complicated than that. The regime was not effectively organized enough in the early 1930s to enforce its doctrine universally and systematically. Belomor was often poorly managed and poorly controlled, and so it cannot be assumed that the administration could unilaterally inscribe messages into its citizens. Instead, prisoners took up various themes in part because they integrated well with their own personal lived experience—orphans could identify with the state as substitute family, criminals could imagine educators as socialist versions of their thieving mentors, convicts could channel their talents for music and song into different avenues. Despite the horror and difficulty of camp life, prisoners could adapt to Belomor's cultural landscape in numerous ways.

Epilogue

> Man puts up a building—and falls apart himself. Who'll be left to live then?[628]
> –Andrei Platonov, *The Foundation Pit* (1930)

Belomor was a unique prison camp. While it mirrored much of the Soviet experience, it did not necessarily represent a typical example of incarceration. Criminal prisoners were given important ideological and functional posts, and they were directly in charge of overseeing other convicts. There was a relative freedom of motion and a lack of barbed wire and tall fences. Prisoners wrote, read, and performed while building the canal. Both criminals and the regime valued or recognized the importance of performance, the significance of music, and the helpfulness of mentor figures. Many criminal texts—such as the thieves' song "Music Is Playing on the Moldovanka"—incorporated aspects of official ideology just as officially published texts—like *The Aristocrats*—specifically highlighted the criminal realm.

In the face of such seemingly lax policies, there was ubiquitous death. Prisoners were used like expendable livestock in order to achieve a socialist vision. The camp was mired in such paradoxes. The construction site lacked any type of modern equipment, and yet its engineering design was radical and innovative. Political prisoners were treated as outcasts but could stay in local hotels. Criminal prisoners participated in literary competitions but also died by the thousands. The underlying, recurring contradictions between these and so many other narratives on the canal animate the tension between creation and destruction. While there is a danger in interpreting Soviet culture exclusively according to dyads,[629] oppositional pairs do tend to play a role in the Russian imagination: even Orthodoxy has no purgatory; there is no in-between. The Soviet Union had utopian, maximalist tendencies coupled with nihilistic ones, just as pre-revolutionary Russia did.[630]

Creation was represented aesthetically, with the production of autobiographies, musical numbers, and theater performances. Destruction was represented violently, with the annihilation of individual lives and the serenity of nature. This producing/eliminating dialectic meant that nearly all Belomor cultural texts dealt with physicality or aggression, whether in content or in form. The prisoner Mikhail Polokhin captures this physicality—and his esteem for it—in a poem he included in his autobiography, noting "and so we understood that in the work of muscles we are not any worse than in the work of brains needed for our thieving specialties. We can bravely say that:

> We have elastic muscles
> Muscles swollen on our chests
> We won't be scared by work
> On no matter what ground.[631]

Polokhin views the criminal trade as one of the "brains," just as many other thieves understood their craft to be artistic and graceful. Criminals lived their lives as productions; as the Kostia character in Pogodin's play notes, "And, speaking generally, if a thief can't paint life, then it's better for him to go and be a dentist."[632] Art was essential for both political and criminal prisoners at Belomor, but this was not the typical view of penal hierarchies. A 1934 sketch in the magazine *Thirty Days* titled "Conversation in Prison" compares political and criminal prisoners: "So this means reason took a person out of prison, through drawing people went out, passed through the walls. We are just sitting, but they sit—with consciousness!"[633] Although the political and criminal prisoners were long imagined as diametrically opposed groups that had little interaction or interest in one another, Belomor shows us that they often crossed paths.[634]

Art offered escape and could also be a way to ingratiate oneself with the regime. Prisoners themselves were like works of art in progress: their personalities could be crafted, shaped, edited. The *History of the Construction* uses a textual metaphor for identity creation, "Prisons changed the internal contents of people."[635] The conflict between creation and destruction at the camp was so exaggerated that eventually fiction and reality became blurred. It seemed that the only way to truly capture the Belomor experience was through art—music and plays, collage and film, painting and poetry. Not only did the coupling of creation with destruction occlude the distinction between fact and fiction, but it also incorporated art into the everyday, and it mired the camps with messiness and inconsistency. Despite the ubiquitous propaganda and highly ideological messages of Belomor, the regime exhibited much disorganization and had a surprising lack of control over day-to-day matters at the construction site.

The metaphor of performance pulls together creation and destruction, art and labor. Performance is a creative act but one that disappears once performed, a spectacle vanishes and can never be re-created exactly. More than most other art forms, performance necessitates the human body; it includes the corporeal through the physical labor of acting. Performance, in the end, is precisely what accounts for the multiplicity of Belomor narratives, since prisoners could perform a variety of roles at the camp site—devoted laborer, shamed peer, recalcitrant convict, privilege-seeking sycophant. While this does not give us a black-and-white answer about Belomor, the Gulag, or the Soviet experience, that is precisely the point of the book you hold in your hands. The privileged role of art and its fusion with physicality made fictional realities possible. During socialist holidays—such as the aforementioned "Physical Culture Day"—traditional boundaries that "separate work from play, life from the arts, and the spectator from the artist"[636] disappeared in what is a chilling reiteration of Erving Goffman's model of total institutions. This, after all, is the defining feature of prison: the indistinguishable divisions between sleep, work, and play. Perhaps it is no surprise, then, that so many prisoners imagined the space outside of the Gulag camps not as "freedom" but rather as the "bigger prison," as a Russian criminal tattoo demonstrates.

In many ways, therefore, Belomor was a condensation of Soviet tendencies; it underscored the violent physicality—and its uncanny link to the artistic—that was part and parcel of selfhood under Stalin.

Figure 40. © FUEL / Danzig Baldaev.
Criminal tattoo depicting the "big prison" of the Soviet Union, with the words GULAG and NKVD (the Soviet secret police organization from 1934-54). Reproduced with permission from *Russian Criminal Tattoo Encyclopaedia* Volume I, FUEL Publishing, London 2004.

List of Figures

Figure 1.
An entrance to the prison camp at Stalin's White Sea-Baltic Canal. Stalin's portrait hangs at the top of the gate, above slogans concerning political re-education. Photograph reproduced with permission of Iurii Dmitriev.

Figure 2.
A group of prisoners at the construction of the Stalin's White Sea-Baltic Canal. Photograph reproduced with permission of Iurii Dmitriev.

Figure 3.
A 1945 photo exhibit in Moscow that emphasized the importance of promoting physical fitness among youth. Russian Pictorial Collection, Box 29, Hoover Institution Archives.

Figure 4.
Prisoners work with wheelbarrows during the construction of Stalin's White Sea-Baltic Canal. Photograph reproduced with permission of Iurii Dmitriev.

Figure 5.
An example of the wooden construction at Stalin's White Sea-Baltic Canal. Photograph reproduced with permission of Iurii Dmitriev.

Figure 6.
Slogans and banners at the White Sea-Baltic Canal. The banner across the top reads, "The USSR's corrective-labor politics does not punish, but rather corrects on the basis of socially beneficial labor and political re-education." Note also the portrait of Lenin. Photograph reproduced with permission of Iurii Dmitriev.

Figure 7.
A graphic representation of shock-worker output at the canal's construction. Note that even 100% is not ideal—all prisoners should be producing at 130% or higher. Photograph reproduced with permission of Iurii Dmitriev.

Figure 8.
A smattering of visual propaganda at the canal's construction, including announcements of the best workers, collections of local types of rock, administrative orders, and slogans. Photograph reproduced with permission of Iurii Dmitriev.

Figure 9.
Prisoners reading wall newspapers at the White Sea-Baltic Canal. Photograph reproduced with permission of Iurii Dmitriev.

— List of Figures —

Figure 10.
A newspaper kiosk at the White Sea-Baltic Canal. Photograph reproduced with permission of Iurii Dmitriev.

Figure 11.
A collection of Belomor wall newspapers with the slogan above reading, "Every shock-worker is a camp journalist, every camp journalist is a shock-worker. Photograph reproduced with permission of Iurii Dmitriev.

Figure 12.
A page from Sergei Alymov's Belomor journal documenting criminal slang. RGALI, f. 1885, op. 3, d. 30, l. 5.

Figure 13.
An *agitbrigada*, or agitational brigade, performance troupe at the White Sea-Baltic Canal. Photograph reproduced with permission of Iurii Dmitriev.

Figure 14.
A self-portrait of the futurist and Belomor prisoner Igor' Terent'ev from Vladimir Markov's *Russian Futurism: A History*. Reproduced with permission from the Vladimir Markov Trust.

Figure 15. © FUEL / Danzig Baldaev
An anti-Semitic criminal tattoo. Across the forehead reads "Boss of the Gulag" and next to the image is "SLON [Solovetskii camp], Belomorkanal, Bamlag, Dal'stroi. Save thy sinful servant from the regime here, from physical labor and political lessons!"
Reproduced with permission from *Russian Criminal Tattoo Encyclopaedia* Volume I, FUEL Publishing, London 2004.

Figure 16. © FUEL / Danzig Baldaev.
A tattoo of three skeletons digging the White Sea-Baltic Canal. The caption reads, "Dig Deeper, throw further, farting steam. 1931-33. The White Sea-Baltic Canal."
Reproduced with permission from *Russian Criminal Tattoo Encyclopaedia* Volume II, FUEL Publishing, London 2006.

Figure 17. © FUEL / Danzig Baldaev.
A tattoo of a Belomorkanal ration cup. The caption reads, "The extra rations of a convict-hero of socialist labor." The letters on the ration cup are an acronym for the White Sea-Baltic Canal. Reproduced with permission from *Russian Criminal Tattoo Encyclopaedia* Volume II, FUEL Publishing, London 2006.

Figure 18.
Belomor prisoner D. Iansen's "Oratoriia." RGALI, f. 1885, op. 3, d. 35, l. 62

Figure 19.
A scene from the 1935 production of Nikolai Pogodin's play *The Aristocrats* (*Aristokraty*) at the Moscow Realist Theater.

———————————— List of Figures ————————————

Figure 20.
A scene inside the prisoners' barracks from Evgenii Cherviakov's 1936 film *The Prisoners* (*Zakliuchennye*) based on Nikolai Pogodin's play.

Figure 21.
A Kostia-like figure playing an accordion in the Belomor-themed issue of *USSR in Construction* (*SSSR na stroike*). Reproduced with permission of Productive Arts.

Figure 22.
A map-guide to White Sea-Baltic Canal, published in 1934. Russian State Library, Moscow, Russia.

Figure 23.
Images from Photo-Tourist (*Foto-turist*), a small collection of photographs documenting the canal. The bottom right image includes Stalin, Voroshilov, and Kirov. Russian State Library, Moscow, Russia.

Figure 24.
Dmitri Nalbandian painting of Stalin sailing through the White Sea-Baltic Canal. Note the overcoat hanging over the railing, which replaced the then-purged Genrikh Iagoda. Russian Pictorial Collection, Box 29, Hoover Institution Archives.

Figure 25.
The front cover of *USSR in Construction*, featuring an inset map. Reproduced with permission of Productive Arts.

Figure 26.
The back cover of *USSR in Construction*, featuring a map overlay. Reproduced with permission of Productive Arts.

Figure 27.
An image from the publication *BBK and the Polar Region* (*BBK i zapoliar'e*), published in 1936. Russian State Library, Moscow, Russia.

Figure 28.
A chalkboard at the Belomor labor camp noting the output percentages of prisoner labor. Those who underperform are included in the column "our shame," while those who overperform are in a column titled "our pride." Photograph reproduced with permission of Iurii Dmitriev.

Figure 29.
A factory chalkboard documenting workers' production levels that was included in a Moscow photo exhibit in 1945. Russian Pictorial Collection, Box 29, Hoover Institution Archives.

Figure 30.
A performance stage at the Belomor construction site. Photograph reproduced with permission of Iurii Dmitriev.

———————————— List of Figures ————————————

Figure 31.
An agitational brigade's performance for spectators at the Belomor labor camp. Photograph reproduced with permission of Iurii Dmitriev.

Figure 32.
A larger-than-life Soviet star prominently displayed on the banks of the White Sea-Baltic Canal. From *Belomorsko-Baltiiskii kanal imeni tov. Stalina*, 1933. Russian State Library, Moscow, Russia.

Figure 33.
Belomorkanal brand cigarettes (*papirosy*). Photograph by author.

Figure 34.
Belomorkanal brand vodka. Photograph by author.

Figure 35.
Poet and bibliographer Sergei Stratanovskii. Photograph by author.

Figure 36.
Vadim Voinov collage, *Conditioned Reflex* (*Uslovnyi refleks*, 1991). Reproduced with permission from the artist.

Figure 37.
Vadim Voinov collage, *Smoke Break* (*Perekur*, 1990). Reproduced with permission from the artist.

Figure 38.
A screen shot from the 2006 Iulii Gusman film *Soviet Park* (*Park sovetskogo perioda*), featuring Belomorkanal cigarettes.

Figure 39.
A screen shot from the 2008 Brad Anderson film *Transsiberian*, featuring Belomorkanal cigarettes.

Figure 40. © FUEL / Danzig Baldaev.
Criminal tattoo depicting the "big prison" of the Soviet Union, with the words GULAG and NKVD (the Soviet secret police organization from 1934-54). Reproduced with permission from *Russian Criminal Tattoo Encyclopaedia* Volume I, FUEL Publishing, London 2004.

ENDNOTES

PREFACE

1. RGALI, f. 1885, op. 3, d. 34, l. 100.
2. Anne Applebaum, ed., *Gulag Voices: An Anthology* (New Haven: Yale University Press, 2011), 10.
3. D. S. Likhachev, "Cherty pervobytnogo primitivizma vorovskoi rechi," *Iazyk i myshlenie*, 3-4 (1935): 54.
4. There are numerous examples of such an explanation in histories of the Soviet Union, such as in Robert Service, *A History of Modern Russia* (Cambridge, MA: Harvard University Press, 2009).
5. The archival sources in this book come from the RGALI and GARF archives, both located in Moscow. The former provided materials related to Sergei Alymov and his role as Belomor poet at the camp, and the latter provided materials related to the *Istoriia stroitel'stva* volume.
6. There are, of course, several notable exceptions, most prominent among them Cynthia Ruder's groundbreaking work on the topic, *Making History for Stalin: The Story of the Belomor Canal* (Gainesville, FL: University Press of Florida, 1998).
7. Sheila Fitzpatrick, *Everyday Stalinism: Ordinary Life in Extraordinary Times: Soviet Russia in the 1930s* (New York: Oxford University Press, 2000), 75.
8. Ruth Wilson Gilmore, *Golden Gulag: Prisons, Surplus, Crisis, and Opposition in Globalizing California* (Berkeley: University of California Press, 2007), 5.
9. Ibid.

PROLOGUE

10. Fedor Gladkov, *Cement*, trans. A. S. Arther and C. Ashleigh (Evanston, IL: Northwestern University Press, 1980), 229.
11. RGALI, f. 1885, op. 3, d. 38, l. 146.
12. The *Glavnoe upravlenie lagerei* or GULAG was officially organized as the camp administration in 1930, although the foundations of the system were laid much earlier. See Oleg V. Khlevniuk, *The History of the Gulag: From Collectivization to the Great Terror* (New Haven: Yale University Press, 2004), 2, 28.
13. For an economic treatment of the Gulag, see Paul R. Gregory and Valery Lazarev, eds., *The Economics of Forced Labor: The Soviet Gulag* (Stanford: Hoover Institution Press, 2003). For an understanding of the Gulag as a political tool of oppression, see Dariusz Tolczyk, *See No Evil: Literary Cover-Ups and Discoveries of the Soviet Camp Experience* (New Haven: Yale University Press, 1999). The debate as to the primary function of the Gulag continues among scholars; it was a key topic of debate at the 2006 "Conference on the Soviet Gulag: Its History and Legacy" at Harvard University.
14. Erving Goffman, *Asylums: Essays on the Social Situation of Mental Patients and Other*

Inmates (Chicago: Aldine, 1961), 4.

15 The shrinking of space in the prison context has other implications. According to the Bakhtinian chronotope, when space contracts time expands. Time, of course, often seems endless to prisoners as they serve out their sentences. I would argue that this expansion of time allows prisoners to re-configure their physical space in unusual ways. In her Gulag memoir, Irina Zalmanovna Tsurkova notes the intimate connection between time and space felt in prison: "I did not notice the flight of time, not only because we had no clock or watch in the cell but also because time, which only a month ago had tortured me with the necessity of filling it, somehow had suddenly picked up speed and was galloping away. [...] My next discovery was that time could take the place of space. I was surprised that the cell had seemed so small to me before. It housed so many things to do, so many ideas and conversations; and it seemed to me that when I stood in the middle of the cell with my arms spread and palms turned toward the walls, the walls moved apart." Veronica Shapovalov, ed. and trans., *Remembering the Darkness: Women in Soviet Prisons* (Lanham, MD: Rowman and Littlefield, 2001), 179.

16 Not only do prisoners make up stories about their pasts, but story-telling itself is often linked to survival, specifically within the Gulag context. Since prisoners who could tell entertaining yarns alleviated boredom and entertained the criminal population, they were able to earn favors and esteem. For more on this topic, see the chapter "The Art of Crime."

17 Jochen Hellbeck, *Revolution on My Mind: Writing a Diary under Stalin* (Cambridge, MA: Harvard University Press, 2006); Irina Paperno, *Stories of the Soviet Experience: Memoirs, Diaries, Dreams* (Ithaca, NY: Cornell University Press, 2009); Thomas Lahusen, *How Life Writes the Book: Real Socialism and Socialist Realism in Stalin's Russia* (Ithaca, NY: Cornell University Press, 1997); Igal Halfin, *Terror in My Soul: Communist Autobiographies on Trial* (Cambridge, MA: Harvard University Press, 2003); Steven A. Barnes, *Death and Redemption: The Gulag and the Shaping of Soviet Society* (Princeton: Princeton University Press, 2011).

18 Jochen Hellbeck, "Working, Struggling, Becoming: Stalin-Era Autobiographical Texts" *Russian Review* (July 2001): 341. See also his *Revolution on My Mind: Writing a Diary under Stalin* (Cambridge, MA: Harvard University Press, 2006).

19 Mike O'Mahony, *Sport in the USSR: Physical Culture—Visual Culture* (London: Reaktion, 2006), 59.

20 While Soviet bodies were depicted as healthy, strong, and young, they were often deformed by prison camps, war experiences, and the difficulties of living in the Soviet Union. See, for example, Khans Giunter, "O krasote, kotoraia ne smogla spasti sotsializm," *Novoe literaturnoe obozrenie* 101 (2010): 13-31 and Lilya Kaganovsky, *How the Soviet Man Was Unmade: Cultural Fantasy and Male Subjectivity under Stalin* (Pittsburgh: University of Pittsburgh Press, 2008).

21 Igal Halfin, *Terror in My Soul: Communist Autobiographies on Trial* (Cambridge, MA: Harvard University Press, 2003), 19.

22 John Freccero, "Autobiography and Narrative," *Reconstructing Individualism: Autonomy, Individuality, and the Self in Western Thought*, eds. Thomas C. Heller, Morton Sosna, and David E. Wellbery (Stanford: Stanford University Press, 1986), 16-29.

23 Halfin, *Terror in My Soul*.

24 Goffman, *Asylums*, 84.

25 While Soviet authors like Maxim Gorky stressed the dignity of physical labor, the import of the laboring body also had significance in pre-revolutionary Russia. Lev Tolstoy

believed that exercise was essential for mental stimulation, and the physical capabilities of Nikolai Chernyshevskii's Rakhmetov in *What Is to Be Done?* served as a precursor to the Soviet New Man. See Mike O'Mahony, *Sport in the USSR* (London: Reaktion, 2006) and James Riordan, *Sport in Soviet Society* (Cambridge: Cambridge University Press, 1977).

26 Andrei Siniavskii, "Dostoevskii i katorga," *Sintaksis* 9 (1981): 108-11.
27 RGALI, f. 1604, op. 1, d. 21, 1. 30.
28 Goffman, *Asylums*, 7.
29 This system is often cited as the backbone of cruelty in the Gulag. Since a prisoner's food ration was dependent on the amount of work he produced, a weak, sickly prisoner received less nourishment, which subsequently made it more difficult to work, beginning a potentially deadly cycle.
30 Such was the case with Semen Firin, who was chief of the construction at Belomor but was later arrested and executed in 1937.
31 Leon Trotsky, "Leninism and Workers' Clubs," 17 July 1924, from *Pravda* 23 July 1924, translation from *Seventeen Moments in Soviet History*, www.soviethistory.org.
32 For an in-depth treatment of this topic, see Rolf Hellebust, *From Flesh to Metal: Soviet Literature and the Alchemy of the Revolution* (Ithaca, NY: Cornell University Press, 2003).
33 The prisoners, in fact, do become part of the physical landscape, with the waterway often referred to as the "road of bones" (*doroga na kostiakh*).
34 See the prisoner Vasilii Atiasov's statement in "The Factory of Life."
35 Editors' introduction, *Ab Imperio* 3 (2002): 211.
36 This line of thinking is followed in Aleksandr Etkind, "Soviet Subjectivity: Torture for the Sake of Salvation?" *Kritika* (Winter 2005): 171-86. Yet I would also disagree with Etkind on several points: on his assertion of the monologicity of the Soviet experience, on his claim that the diarists Hellbeck cites were "sincere," and on his attenuated role for religious and ritualistic elements of Soviet ideology. While I agree that the ur-source should be shifted to Nietzsche rather than Foucault, it is important to bear in mind that Nietzsche's work was to fill the vacuum left by the statement "God is dead," and so necessarily infers and picks up a conversation with God and religiosity. For other contestations of Hellbeck, see Svetlana Boym, *Ab Imperio* 3 (2002).
37 Jerrold Siegel, *The Idea of the Self: Thought and Experience in Western Europe since the Seventeenth Century* (Cambridge: Cambridge University Press, 2005), 630.
38 Alexander Nehamas, *Nietzsche: Life as Literature* (Cambridge, MA: Harvard University Press, 1985), 7, 154.
39 Qtd. Anna Lisa Crone, "Nietzschean, All Too Nietzschean? Rozanov's Anti-Christian Critique," *Nietzsche in Russia*, ed. Bernice Glatzer Rosenthal (Princeton: Princeton University Press, 1986), 111.
40 Nehamas, *Nietzsche*, 181.
41 Friedrich Nietzsche, *Thus Spake Zarathustra*, *The Portable Nietzsche*, ed. and trans. Walter Kaufmann (New York: Penguin, 1968), 146.
42 Varlam Shalamov, "Tishina," *Sobranie sochinenii*, vol. 2 (Moscow: Khudozhestvennaia literatura, 1998), 114.
43 An interesting literary exploration of the physicality of prisoners' bodies is Franz Kafka's 1919 short story "The Penal Colony," in which criminals' sentences are tattooed onto their bodies as a type of torture device.
44 Liuba Iurgenson, "Kozha—Metafora teksta v lagernoi proze Varlama Shalamova," *Telo v russkoi kul'ture* (Moscow: Novoe literaturnoe obozrenie, 2005), 340.

45 Goldovskaia, Marina, dir. *Vlast' Solovetskaia*. Mosfil'm, 1988.
46 Irina Ratushinskaia, *Seryi—tsvet nadezhdy* (London: Overseas Publications Interchange, 1989), 10.
47 W W. E. B. DuBois, *The Souls of Black Folk* (New York: Simon and Schuster, 2005), 7.
48 Friedrich Nietzsche, *On the Genealogy of Morals*, trans. Walter Kaufmann (New York: Vintage, 1967), 86.
49 V. I. Lenin, *Selected Works in Two Volumes* (Moscow: Foreign Language Publishing House, 1952), vol. 2, 316-17.
50 While Lenin denounced god-building as heresy, it was popular among many other Bolsheviks for the practical function it could fulfill in replacing Orthodoxy. Katerina Clark even claims that god-building served as a subtext for High Stalinism. Katerina Clark, *The Soviet Novel: History as Ritual* (Bloomington, IN: Indiana University Press, 2000), 152.
51 As R. Lanier Anderson notes, "Nietzsche remains surprisingly dependent on character-istically *religious* and even quasi-*Christian*, materials in forging new comforts for life." "Nietzsche on Redemption and Transfiguration," 226.
52 Friedrich Nietzsche, *The Gay Science* (New York: Random House, 1974), 181.
53 Katerina Clark, *The Soviet Novel*, 55.
54 At first, the mother is horrified by her son's criticism of religion, claiming it is all she has in the world. Yet the mother experiences a gradual, transformative journey regarding religion, and the first step in the her disillusionment occurs when she notices all the silver and gold in church and wonders why God would need such riches. She later shifts her devotion from God to Christ, believing that the latter represents the sacrifices of her metaphorical, revolutionary children.
55 Maxim Gorky, *Mother*, trans. Isidor Schneider (New York: Citadel, 1947), 38.
56 Maksim Gor'kii, "Rech' na Pervom vsesoiuznom s"ezde sovetskikh pisatelei 22 avgusta 1934 goda." *O literature* (Moscow: GOSIZDAT khudozhestvennoi literatury, 1961), 445.
57 Gorky was a vocal promoter of the transformative potential of prisoner labor at Belomor and other labor camps. He wrote glowingly of the Solovki labor camp in the journal *Our Achievements* [*Nashi dostizheniia*] and served as the chief editor of the official "history" of the White Sea-Baltic Canal, a volume written collectively by thirty-six prominent Soviet authors.
58 Maxim Gor'kii, *Nesvoevremmenye mysli*, 28.
59 For example, see Irwin Weil, *Gorky: His Literary Development and Influence on Soviet Intellectual Life* (New York: Random House, 1966), 166.
60 Maxim Gor'kii, "O tom, kak ia uchilsia pisat'," 128.
61 Jay Bergman, "Valerii Chkalov: Soviet Pilot as New Soviet Man," *Journal of Contemporary History* 33 (1998): 135-52.
62 Scott W. Palmer, "Peasants into Pilots: Soviet Air-Mindedness as an Ideology of Dominance" *Technology and Culture* 41 (2000): 21.
63 While many dismiss this volume out of hand as the greatest apologia to slave labor ever written, it is nevertheless a complex and fascinating book that is coauthored by some of the most famous Soviet writers, such as Maxim Gorky, Mikhail Zoshchenko, Valentin Kataev, and Viktor Shklovskii. I will not a conduct a sustained analysis of the monograph here, as other scholars have already carried out this work and the focus here is on unpublished, criminal narratives. For an excellent treatment of the volume, see Cynthia A. Ruder, *Making History for Stalin: The Story of the Belomor Canal* (Gainesville:

University Press of Florida, 1998).
64 It is significant that this concept is not just any road, but rather the word *put'* in Russian, which implies movement towards a goal, unlike the more common word for road in Russian, *doroga*. The concept of *put'* is discussed at length in the chapter "The Factory of Life."
65 Nietzsche is unequivocal in his condemnation of the state: "State is the name of the coldest of all cold monsters." *Thus Spake Zarathustra*, 160.
66 Nehamas, *Nietzsche*, 8.
67 For example, Communist Party members were required to write autobiographies for their files, texts that could be revised many times over the course of their careers, demonstrating the potential to literally re-write one's life as the political atmosphere necessitated. For an in-depth treatment of this topic, see Igal Halfin, *Terror in My Soul: Communist Autobiographies on Trial* (Cambridge, MA: Harvard University Press, 2003).
68 Thomas Lahusen, *How Life Writes the Book: Real Socialism and Socialist Realism in Stalin's Russia* (Ithaca, NY: Cornell University Press, 1997), 2.
69 Miriam Dobson, *Khrushchev's Cold Summer: Gulag Returnees, Crime, and the Fate of Reform after Stalin* (Ithaca, NY: Cornell University Press, 2009).
70 Nick Baron, "Conflict and Complicity: The Expansion of the Karelian Gulag, 1932-33" *Cahiers du Monde Russe* 42 (2001): 636.
71 T. S. Willan, *The Early History of the Russia Company* (New York: Augustus M. Kelley, 1956), 48-49, 67.
72 Konstantin Gnetnev, *Kanal: Belomorsko-Baltiiskii Kanal 1933-2003* (Petrozavodsk: PetroPress, 2003), 6-10.
73 Chukhin, *Kanaloarmeitsy*, 9.
74 Gnetnev, 11-16.
75 The *Belomorsko-Baltiiskii Vodnyi Put'* project is shown at the Paris Exposition n in 1900, where it wins a gold medal. Gnetnev, 17.
76 Ibid, 18.
77 Baron, "Conflict and Complicity," 639.
78 A. I. Kokurin and Iu. N. Morkurov, eds., *Stalinskie stroiki GULAGA 1930-1953* (Moscow: Materik, 2005), 30-31.
79 This is a disastrous amendment to the plans for the canal's construction, as the completed waterway is only deep enough to allow the passage of barges and tourist boats, severely limiting the economic capabilities of the canal.
80 Kokurin and Morkurov, eds., 32.
81 Baron, "Conflict and Complicity," 641-43. Baron's article provides an excellent overview of the numbers debate.
82 Kokurin and Morkurov, eds., 35.
83 Ibid.
84 Gnetnev, 13.
85 Kokurin and Morkurov, eds., 36.
86 Baron, 637.
87 L. Averbakh, S. Firin, and M. Gor'kii, eds., *Istoriia stroitel'stva*, 291.
88 After the completion of the canal, there was interest in building a second, deeper canal that would parallel the White Sea-Baltic Canal's route exactly 1 km to the east, but the project was never pursued, most likely out of embarrassment. Gregory and Lazarev, eds., *The Economics of Forced Labor: The Soviet Gulag* (Stanford: Hoover Institute Press, 2003), 167.

89 Konstantin Gnetnev, conversation with author, 28 March 2007.
90 Gnetnev, 30, 33.
91 Mikhail Morukov, "The White Sea-Baltic Canal," in *The Economics of Forced Labor: The Soviet Gulag*, ed. Paul R. Gregory and Valery Lazarev (Stanford: Hoover Institute Press, 2003), 151-62, 160.
92 Morukov, "The White Sea-Baltic Canal," 162.
93 Ronald Suny, "Ambiguous Categories: States, Empires, and Nations," *Post-Soviet Affairs* 11 (1995): 185-96; Emil' Pain, "Rossiia mezhdu imperiiei i natsiiei," *Pro et Contra* (May-June 2007): 42-59; Terry Martin, "The Soviet Union as Empire: Salvaging a Dubious Analytical Category," *Ab Imperio* 2 (2002): 103.
94 Sergei Stratanovskii's Belomor poetry, discussed in Chapter Five, connects the project with ancient Egypt and Babylon. Lev Losev also makes such a connection in his memoirs (*Zhizn*, 303). The *History of the Construction* also makes numerous comparisons between the project and Egypt, also referencing ancient history in an attempt to create an epic backdrop for the waterway.
95 Viktor Shklovksii, *Tret'ia fabrika* (Moscow: Krug, 1926), 137.

CHAPTER ONE

96 Pogodin, 10, and Wixley and Carr, 186.
97 Pogodin, 64, and Wixley and Carr, 268.
98 Erving Goffman, *The Presentation of the Self in Everyday Life* (New York: Anchor, 1959), 41.
99 The predecessor of the KGB, the acronym OGPU stands for *Ob"edinennoe gosudarstvennoe politcheskoe upravlenie*, or Unified State Political directorate. The OGPU was the administrative body in charge of the Belomorkanal's construction.
100 The very complex subject of belief will temporarily be set aside. Since we cannot gain access to what a prisoner "truly" thought, it is impossible to assess for certain whether prisoners participated in *perekovka* only for material advantages or whether they actually considered themselves reformed, although I would claim evidence exists for both arguments. Instead, the performative aspect of the endeavor will take prominence here; just as prisoners could perform various beliefs for a variety of reasons, so could their performances of such beliefs eventually alter their own as well as others' perceptions about their attitudes.
101 The autobiographies were most likely collected as raw material for the *History of the Construction*, since most of them are housed along with draft manuscripts of the publication. The holdings associated with Sergei Alymov, editor of camp newspaper *Perekovka*, were also consulted for this research. While some of the criminal autobiographies echo what is published in the Gorky volume, it is very difficult to make one-to-one correspondences, and the autobiographies collected here were never officially published.
102 Sergei Alymov, a Belomor prisoner, describes the voyage in his notebooks: "The scariest trip that was ever made on earth. Hell on wheels. Without any of Dante's poetry. Night and its horrors—thefts, stuffiness. Bodies on bodies. Cries: 'Oh, my sugar was taken ... my basket was ripped." ... Thieves scurry like rats." RGALI, f. 1885, op. 3, d. 23, l. 1.
103 Katerina Clark, *The Soviet Novel: History as Ritual* (Bloomington, IN: Indiana University Press, 2000), 256.

104 Jeffrey Brooks, *How Russia Learned to Read: Literacy and Popular Literature 1861-1917* (Princeton: Princeton University Press, 1989), 188.
105 Igal Halfin, *Terror in My Soul: Communist Autobiographies on Trial* (Cambridge, MA: Harvard University Press, 2003).
106 For more on the trope of criminal educator, see Julie Draskoczy, "The Put' of Perekovka: Transforming Lives at Stalin's White Sea-Baltic Canal," *The Russian Review* 71 (2012): 30-48.
107 I. L. Averbakh, *Ot prestupleniia k trudu* (Moscow: OGIZ, 1936), 58, 60, 73, 75.
108 Ibid., 45.
109 Anna Iankovskaia, a criminal on the White-Baltic Sea Canal, attributes her transformation specifically to the fact that a fellow prisoner coerced her into starting to work. See the English translation of her story in the collection *In the Shadow of the Revolution: Life Stories of Russian Women from 1917 to the Second World War*, ed. Sheila Fitzpatrick and Yuri Slezkine (Princeton: Princeton University Press, 2000), 282-85.
110 Dmitrii Vitkovskii, "Polzhizni," *Znamia* 6 (1991): 110.
111 I. L. Averbakh, *Ot prestupleniia k trudu*, 27.
112 Ibid., 4.
113 This concept finds a precedent in French socialist thought, in particular the utopian philosophy of Charles Fourier (referenced numerous times in Fedor Dostoevskii's 1872 novel *The Possessed*), and the anarchist thought of Pierre-Joseph Proudhon ("all property is theft").
114 Michael Jakobson, *Origins of the Gulag: The Soviet Prison Camp System 1917-34* (Lexington, KY: University Press of Kentucky, 1993), 5.
115 Stephen A. Barnes, "In a Manner Befitting Soviet Citizens: An Uprising in the Post-Stalin Gulag," *Slavic Review* 4 (2005): 840.
116 Valery Chaldize, *Criminal Russia: Essays on Crime in the Soviet Union* (NY: Random House, 1977), 4-6, 22-24.
117 David R. Shearer, "Crime and Social Disorder in Stalin's Russia. A Reassessment of the Great Retreat and the Origins of Mass Repression," *Cahiers du Monde russe* 39 (1998): 119-48.
118 I. L. Averbakh, *Ot prestupleniia k trudu*, 14.
119 Ibid., 8.
120 Ibid., 21.
121 "Труд в СССР, дело чести, дело славы, дело доблести и геройства".
122 The debate concerning the feasibility of a comparison between Nazi concentration camps and the Soviet Gulag continues to the present day. See Paul R. Gregory and Valery Lazarev, eds., *The Economics of Forced Labor: The Soviet Gulag* (Stanford: Hoover Institution Press, 2003), 191. For a discussion of Soviet labor camps and Nazi concentration camps in the same context, see Terrence Des Pres, *The Survivor: An Anatomy of Life in the Death Camps* (New York: Oxford University Press, 1976). For a recent monograph comparing the Soviet and Nazi experiences, see Sheila Fitzpatrick and Michael Geyer, eds., *Beyond Totalitariansim: Stalinism and Nazism Compared* (Cambridge: Cambridge University Press, 2009).
123 Sheila Fitzpatrick and Michael Geyer, eds., *Beyond Totalitarianism*, 25, 34.
124 The topic of art in the Nazi camps has been widely and thoroughly researched; I will name just a few resources here: Janet Blatter and Sybil Milton, *Art of the Holocaust* (New York: Rutledge, 1981); Gerald Green, *The Artists of Terezin* (New York: Hawthorn, 1969); Joseph P. Czarnecki and Chaim Potok, *Last Traces: The Lost Art of Auschwitz* (New York: Atheneum, 1989).

125 Elena Makarova, *Freidl Dicker-Brandeis: The Artist Who Inspired the Children's Drawings of Terezin* (Los Angeles: Tallfellow and the Simon Wiesenthal Center, 2001), 43.
126 Anne D. Dutlinger, ed., *Art, Music and Education as Strategies for Survival: Theresienstadt: 1941-45* (New York: Herodias, 2001); Miriam Novitch, ed., *Spiritual Resistance: Art from Concentration Camps* (Philadelphia: Jewish Publication Society of America, 1981).
127 Shirli Gilbert, *Music in the Holocaust: Confronting Life in the Nazi Ghettos and Camps* (Oxford: Oxford University Press, 2005), 7-8.
128 Sharon A. Kowalsky, *Deviant Women: Female Crime and Criminology in Revolutionary Russia 1880-1930* (DeKalb, IL: Northern Illinois University Press, 2009), 55.
129 M. N. Gernet, *Prestupnyi mir Moskvy* (Moscow: MKhO, 1991).
130 Gernet, *Prestupnyi mir*, xli.
131 Richard Stites, *Russian Popular Culture: Entertainment and Society since 1900* (Cambridge: Cambridge University Press, 1992); various articles in the Soviet monthly magazine *30 dnei*.
132 Kowalsky, *Deviant Women*, 13.
133 David R. Shearer, "Crime and Social Disorder in Stalin's Russia," 120-21.
134 Khlevniuk, *History of the Gulag*, 217-18.
135 I. L. Averbakh, *Ot prestupleniia k trudu*, 29.
136 Ibid., 36.
137 Stephen Kotkin, *Magnitogorsk: Stalinism as Civilization* (Berkeley: University of California Press, 1997).
138 I. L. Averbakh, *Ot prestupleniia k trudu*, 36.
139 Ibid., 35.
140 Michael Jakobson, *Origins of the Gulag*, 96.
141 I. L. Averbakh, 52.
142 A. I. Solzhenitsyn, *Odin den' Ivana Denisovicha* (Moscow: Slovo, 2001), 46. Translation based on H. T. Willetts 1991: 48, with modifications by the author.
143 *Karelo-Murmanskii krai* 5-6 (1933): 27.
144 Kokurin and Morkurov, eds., 34.
145 V. G. Makurov, *GULag v Karelii. Sbornik dokumentov i materialov 1930-1941* (Petrozavodsk: RAN, 1992), 14.
146 I. L. Averbakh, 72.
147 A. I. Kokurin and Iu. N. Morkurov, eds., 34.
148 J. Otto Pohl, *The Stalinist Penal System* (Jefferson, NC: McFarland, 1997), 13.
149 L. Averbakh, S. Firin, and M. Gor'kii, eds., *Belomorsko-Baltiiskii Kanal imeni Stalina: Istoriia stroitel'stva* (OGIZ, 1934), 523.
150 Ibid., 12.
151 Ibid., 609.
152 Rufus W. Mathewson, Jr., *The Positive Hero in Russian Literature* (Stanford: Stanford University Press, 1975), 152.
153 Jerrold Seigel, *The Idea of the Self: Thought and Experience in Western Europe since the Seventeenth Century* (Cambridge: Cambridge University Press, 2005).
154 See the prisoner-written essay of the same name, RGALI, f. 1885, op. 3, d. 33, l. 134.
155 L. Averbakh, S. Firin, and M. Gor'kii, eds., *Istoriia stroitel'stva*, 180.
156 Ibid., 177.
157 Ibid., 185, 187, 197, 231, 132, 263, 197, 197, 390, 390.
158 Mircea Eliade, *Rites and Symbols of Initiation: The Mysteries of Birth and Rebirth* (Woodstock, CT: Spring, 1958), xiii.

159 Mikhail Prishvin, *V kraiu nepuganykh ptits* (Moscow: Gosudarstvennoe izdatel'stvo khudozhestvennoi literatury, 1934), 28.
160 Quoted in Irina Paperno, *Stories of the Soviet Experience: Memoirs, Diaries, Dreams* (Ithaca, NY: Cornell University Press, 2009), 175.
161 L. Averbakh, S. Firin, and M. Gor'kii, eds., *Istoriia stroitel'stva*, 161.
162 Ibid., 342.
163 For example, the new word *kanaloarmeets*, or Canal Army Solider, is reportedly created during the canal project. Ibid., 209.
164 Ibid., 542.
165 Ibid., 177.
166 RGALI, f. 1885, op. 3, d. 33, l. 134.
167 RGALI, f. 1885, op. 33, d. 3, l. 285.
168 Hans Günther, "Der Bau des Weißmeerkanals als Laboratorium des neuen Menschen," *Bücher haben ihre Geschichte*, eds. Petra Josting and Jan Wirrer (Hildesheim: Olms, 1996), 63.
169 Many prisoner-written texts liken the birth of the canal to the re-birth of humanity. Alymov makes such a comparison in his notebooks during the canal's opening celebration (RGALI, f. 1885, op. 5, d. 22, l. 5), and a prisoner-submitted short story for a literary competition, entitled "The Birth of the Canal" (*Rozhdenie kanala*) makes the same analogy (RGALI, f. 1885, op. 3, d. 33, l. 222).
170 Mircea Eliade, *Rites and Symbols*, xiv.
171 L. Averbakh, S. Firin, and M. Gor'kii, eds., *Istoriia stroitel'stva*, 542. See also Katerina Clark's treatment of this moment in "Little Heroes, Big Deeds," in *Cultural Revolution in Russia 1928-1931*, ed. Sheila Fitzpatrick (Bloomington, IN: Indiana University Press, 1978), 192-93.
172 This turn of phrase emerges from the Freemason movement, which spread rapidly in eighteenth-century Russia, and asserts that people could smooth the roughness of their passions just as a stone setter hews rock. See Thomas Smith, *Working the Rough Stone: Freemasonry and Society in Eighteenth-Century Russia* (DeKalb, IL: Northern Illinois University Press, 1999).
173 L. Averbakh, S. Firin, and M. Gor'kii, eds., *Istoriia stroitel'stva*, 342. Note also that the Russian word *tvorchestvo* used here also refers to creativity as well as creation, beautifully capturing the artistic-industrial hybridity inherent in the canal's construction.
174 Ibid., 85-86, 111, 125, 494-524, 342, 467, 324, 166, 173, 366.
175 Il'in, 9.
176 Harriet Bourland, *Soviet Literary Theory and Practice during the First Five-Year Plan 1928-1932* (New York: King's Crown Press, 1950), 62.
177 "Istoria fabrik i zavoda," *Bol'shaia Sovetskaia Entsiklopediia*, 1959.
178 BMS is an acronym for the canal construction, *Belomorstroi*.
179 GARF, f. 7952, op. 7, d. 30, l. 9.
180 Atiasov's statement echoes the previously discussed phenomenon of *besprizornye*, in which allegiance to the state was substituted for familial love. For a further treatment of this topic, see Alan M. Ball, *Now My Soul Is Hardened: Abandoned Children in Soviet Russia 1918-1930* (Berkeley: University of California Press, 1994). Interestingly, the phrase Atiasov uses to describe his transformative trajectory, "putevka v zhizn'," is identical to the name of Nikolai Ekk's 1931 film, in which young delinquents are brought to a special camp in order to be reformed (*Road to Life*).
181 The idea of the New Man, however, does not begin with Stalin; for example, Leon

Trotsky mentions the concept at the end of his seminal essay "Art and Revolution."
182 Katerina Clark, *The Soviet Novel: History as Ritual* (Bloomington, IN: Indiana University Press, 1981), 167-76.
183 Clark uses this terminology in her breakdown of the socialist realist master plot, 257.
184 Clark, *The Soviet Novel*, 45.
185 Rufus Mathewson's early work on the positive hero analyzes the tendency of Russian literature to focus on symbolic literary heroes, from the *bogatyr* to the peasant fool, from Onegin to Pechorin. What separates these figures from literary heroes in other traditions, as Mathewson argues, is the fact that hero-centered Russian literature focuses on the "beneficent," not the "terrible or pitiable," in the main character. See Rufus Mathewson, *The Positive Hero in Russian Literature*, 2nd ed. (Stanford: Stanford University Press, 1975).
186 Clark, *The Soviet Novel*, 47.
187 This process could also be likened to the performance of last rites, a final confession of one's soul. In both instances, a previous way of life—or life itself—is abolished to make possible a higher, more ideological existence.
188 Vladimir Shlyakhov and Eve Adler, eds., *Russian Slang and Colloquial Expressions* (New York: Barron's, 1999), 104.
189 RGALI, f. 1885, op. 3, d. 33, l. 65.
190 The importance of dialogue in the conversion of prisoners, it should be noted, also highlights the important role of oral phenomena (like songs and music) at Belomor.
191 Another example of the transformative power of dreams occurs in the short story "Bura," in which the main character, during his "sleepless" (*bezsonnye*) nights, remembers all of his past crimes and criminal life in general, thinking about how all of his friends had forgotten him. Books, newspapers, and education facilitate his transformation, making it appropriate that he would define his conversion in enlightenment terms, saying that he went "from the darkness to the light," (*iz mraka k svetu*). RGALI, f. 1885, op. 3, d. 33, l. 119-23.
192 RGALI, f. 1885, op. 3, d. 38, l. 30.
193 In addition to the function of facilitating *perekovka* and life examination, dreams also act as an escape from the prisoner's everyday reality, a realm in which one is truly free.
194 Likhachev, "Cherty," 56.
195 RGALI, f. 1885, op. 3, d. 33, l. 65.
196 Ibid., l. 66.
197 Likhachev, "Cherty," 61.
198 RGALI, f. 1885, op. 3, d. 33, l. 66.
199 The issue of how to address prisoners is discussed at length in the *History of the Construction* (see the chapter entitled "Kanaloarmeitsy"). While it was decided that "prisoner" was too ignominious a term for the incarcerated at Belomor, it was also unthinkable to call them comrades—and so a compromise was struck: *kanaloarmeits* (canal-army-soldier).
200 GARF, f. 7952, d. 7, op. 30, l. 133.
201 Emma Widdis, "To Explore or Conquer? Mobile Perspectives on the Soviet Cultural Revolution," in *The Landscape of Stalinism: The Art and Ideology of Soviet Space*, ed. Evgeny Dobrenko and Eric Naiman (Seattle: University of Washington Press, 2003), 235.
202 The ubiquity of family problems in criminal autobiographies perhaps affords a certain appeal to the notion that the state could serve as a substitute for biological relatives.
203 RGALI, f. 1885, op. 3, d. 38, l. 105.

204 RGALI, f. 1885, op. 3, d. 38, l. 107.
205 RGALI, f. 1885, op. 3, d. 38, l. 108.
206 RGALI, f. 1885, op. 3, d. 33, l. 143-44.
207 In Russian, a railroad engineer is not simply a train employee; rather, he is a *puteets*, one whose profession stems from the idea of *put'*.
208 GARF, f. 7952, op. 7, d. 30, l. 58.
209 RGALI, f. 1885, op. 38, d. 3, l. 70.
210 RGALI, f. 1885, op. 38, d. 3, l. 72.
211 RGALI, f. 1885, op. 3, d. 38, l. 73.
212 RGALI, f. 1885, op. 3, d. 38, l. 221.
213 GARF, f. 7952, op. 7, d. 30, l.112.
214 RGALI, f. 1885, op. 3, d. 38, l. 304.
215 GARF, f. 7952, op. 7, d. 30, l. 19.
216 This is an acronym for the *Kul'turno-vospitatel'naia chast'*, or cultural-educational division, which is an organizational sub-division of the KVO, or *Kul'turno-vospitatel'nyi otdel*, or cultural-educational department.
217 GARF, f. 7952, op. 7, d. 30, l. 25.
218 This last name, literally meaning "sleepless" in Russian, could very well be a pseudonym. This seems all the more likely given his potentially controversial narrative about life at the canal. His choice of surnames, if it is indeed assumed, relates back to the earlier discussion of sleep and dreams on the canal, the lack of which caused constant difficulties and the presence of which assured an escape from the harsh reality of camp life.
219 The prisoner Iurii Margolin, who served time at the White Sea-Baltic Canal after its completion, also notes the impossibility of keeping secrets in prison: "В лагере нет ни одиночества, ни возможности охранить надолго секреты." Iurii Margolin, *Puteshestvie v stranu ze-ka* (New York: Izd. Chekhova, 1952), 139.
220 GARF, f. 7952, op. 7, d. 31, l. 48.
221 Ibid.
222 GARF, f. 7952, op. 7, d. 30, l. 3.
223 Ibid, l. 4.
224 RGALI, f. 1885, op. 3, d. 47, l. 104. The specific infractions and even percentages are given in the documentation of the proverka of the labor collectives. Prisoners were excluded for the following reasons: counter-revolutionary crimes (278 prisoners, 29.6%), the violation of rules (222 prisoners, 25.2%), bad relationship to production (210 prisoners, 23%), and the violation of camp order (220 prisoners, 22.2%).
225 Wixley and Carr, *The Aristocrats*, 202.
226 For a more general treatment of the problem of homeless children in newly industrialized countries, including the attempt to substitute the family with the state, see Hugh Cunningham, *Children and Childhood in Western Society since 1500* (Harlow: Pearson, 2005). For an excellent treatment of the Russian situation specifically, see Catriona Kelly, *Children's World: Growing Up in Russia 1890-1991* (New Haven: Yale University Press, 2007).
227 Marina Balina and Larissa Rudova, "Introduction: Russian Children's Literature—Changing Paradigms," *Slavic and East European Journal* 49 (2005): 193.
228 Interestingly, Andrei Platonov also wrote a short story entitled "The Sluices [Locks] of Epiphany" ("Epifanskie shliuzy," 1927), which focuses on Peter the Great's attempt to build a waterway connecting the Baltic, Black, and Caspian seas. The title page of the short story was on display in the Gor'kii House-Museum during a 2007 visit.

229 Balina and Rudova, "Introduction," 190.
230 Evgeny Dobrenko, "The School Tale in Children's Literature of Socialist Realism," *Russian Children's Literature and Culture*, ed. Marina Balina and Larissa Rudova (New York: Routledge, 2008), 43-66.
231 Ibid., 191-92.
232 Marina Balina, "Troubled Lives: The Legacy of Childhood in Soviet Literature" *Slavic and East European Journal* 49 (2005): 249.
233 Ibid., 251.
234 A parallel could also be drawn between the trajectory of the prisoners' or children's transformations and that of saints: in the sacred tradition of hagiography, a future saint undergoes a period of trial and separation in which he is outcast from society and/or family members. Eventually, however, the gifted one goes through a type of re-forging in the monastery setting, where a new life and family is adopted. One example of such a *zhitie* would be the life of the Saint Theodosius, written by the monk Nestor.
235 Mikhail Nikolaev, *Detdom* (New York: Russica, 1985), 89.
236 In addition, the criminal and childhood experiences at times directly overlap; for example, Nikolai Ekk's famous 1931 film *Putevka v zhizn'* (*Road to Life*) deals specifically with delinquent children trying to forge a new path for themselves.
237 NARK, f. 36651, op. 1, d. 12, l. 1.
238 A. S. Makarenko, *Pedagogicheskaia poema* (Moscow: ITRK, 2003), 16. Anton Makarenko, *The Road to Life*, trans. Ivy and Tatiana Litvinov (New York: Oriole, 1973), 4.
239 Litvinov, 20, 43, and Makarenko, 24, 35.
240 Litvinov, 7, and Makarenko, 17.
241 Litvinov, 321, and Makarenko, 170.
242 Litvinov, 15, 317, 319, and Makarenko, 21, 162, 169.
243 Litvinov, 135-36, and Makarenko, 79.
244 Makarenko, 381.
245 This attempt to transform not just the working ethic but also the everyday life and culture of the prisoners resonates with the overall scheme of Cultural Revolution in Stalin's Russia from 1928-1932.
246 Anton Makarenko, "Opyt metodiki raboty detskoi trudovoi kolonii," *Sochineniia*, vol. 5 (Moscow: Akademiia pedagogicheskikh nauk, 1951), 339-463, 441. Translation mine.
247 Jakobson, *Origins of the Gulag*, 123.
248 RGALI, f. 1885, op. 3, d. 39, l. 10.
249 Pilgrimage studies as a discipline has witnessed a recent shift from concentrating on the fixed characteristics of pilgrimage to the particular features of an individual pilgrim's experience. See, for example, Marysia Galbraith, "On the Way to Częstochowa: Rhetoric and Experience on a Polish Pilgrimage," *Anthropological Quarterly* 73 (April 2000): 61-73.

CHAPTER TWO

250 Abram Terts/Andrei Siniavskii, *Golos iz khora. Sobranie sochinenii*, vol. 2 (Moscow: Start, 1992), 543. English translation from Abram Tertz (Andrei Sinyavsky), *A Voice from the Chorus*, trans. Kyril Fitzlyon and Max Hayward (New York: Farrar, Straus, and Giroux, 1976), 147.

251 Valerii Frid, *58 ½: Zapiski lagernogo pridurka* (Moscow: Rusanova, 1996), 114.
252 For these and other criminal slang definitions, see Dantsik Baldaev et al, eds., *Slovar' tiuremno-lagerno-blatnogo zhargona* (Moscow: Kraia Moskvy, 1992).
253 GARF, f. 7952, op. 7, d. 31, l. 35.
254 RGALI, f. 1885, op. 3, d. 38, l. 275.
255 Ibid., l. 277.
256 Qtd., Abram Terts (Andrei Siniavskii), "Progulki s Pushkinym," *Oktiabr'* 4 (1989): 199.
257 Jeffrey Brooks, *When Russia Learned to Read: Literacy and Popular Literature: 1861-1917* (Princeton: Princeton University Press, 1985), 169.
258 Brooks, *When Russia Learned to Read*, 188-198.
259 Andrei Sinyavsky, *Ivan the Fool: Russian Folk Belief A Cultural History* (Moscow: Glas, 2007), 45-50.
260 Z. Khatsrevin, "Bandit," *30 dnei* 3 (1934): 18-24.
261 See *Karelo-Murmanskii krai* 5-6 (1933): 30, for an article on the projected role for art as an inspirational and motivational tool at the camp site.
262 RGALI, f. 1885, op. 3, d. 47, l. 101.
263 Given that the mechanisms of oppression were so stringent and pervasive during Stalinism, it should be noted that citizens would also engage in self-censorship even within the more private realms of diaries and letters.
264 Konstantin Gnetnev, conversation with author, 28 March 2007.
265 *Perekovka* 96-97 (22-24 October 1932).
266 Only one issue of the newspaper was ever published. Anna Lawton, ed., *Russian Futurism through its Manifestoes, 1912-1928* (Ithaca: Cornell University Press, 1988), 177.
267 Elizabeth Astrid Papazian, *Manufacturing Truth: The Documentary Moment in Early Soviet Culture* (DeKalb, IL: Northern Illinois University Press, 2009), 8.
268 Sergei Tret'iakov, "Novyi Lev Tolstoi," *Literatura fakta*, ed. N. Chuzak (Munich: Wilhelm Fink, 1972), 31-33.
269 Papazian, *Manufacturing Truth*, 6.
270 *Perekovka* 40 (11 June 1932), 7.
271 Alla Gorcheva, *Pressa GULaga* (Moscow: Izd. Moskovskogo universiteta, 1996), 42-49.
272 On the back of a stylized portrait of Alymov, there is written the caption: "Belomorskii kanal. Poet velikoi stroiki." (Belomor Canal. Poet of the grand construction.). RGALI, f. 1885, op. 1, d. 160, l.7.
273 RGALI, f. 1185, op. 3, d. 33, l. 109-10.
274 Alymov's collection of criminal slang shows his predilection for linguistics. Alymov makes notations about criminal language in a highly organized manner, including word variations, roots, and examples of usage in sentences as well as entire conversations in thieves' jargon.
275 RGALI, f. 1885, op. 3, d. 25.
276 RGALI, f. 1885, d. 1, op, 1, 1-2.
277 Gorcheva, 43.
278 RGALI, f. 1885, op. 3, d. 18, l. 1-2 and d. 21, l. 135.
279 RGALI, f. 1885, op. 3, d. 33, l. 306.
280 RGALI, f. 1885, op. 3, d. 38, l. 155.
281 RGAKFD, No. 3878, *Port piati morei*, dir. Aleksandr Lemberg, 1932-33. "Un des machines les plus importantes, pour transformer les gens." The fact that the film's subtitles are entirely in French indicates that this film was intended for an international

audience and shows how the publicity campaign in the name of the White Sea-Baltic Canal was not limited to the Soviet Union but was meant to captivate and woo the world.

282 The use of the pronoun "svoi" here emphasizes that the cultural institutions at the camp site belong to the prisoners themselves. SSSR *na stroike* 12 (1933): 18, 25-26.
283 The poems from the collection *Moria soedinim!*, "Perekovka"(41); "Lagkoram" (43); insertion of citations from *Perekovka* (44), Belmorstroi: 1932.
284 GARF, f. 7952, op. 7, d. 72, l. 1, 42.
285 GARF, f. 7952, op. 7, d. 51, l. 6.
286 Again, the use of the pronoun "svoi" makes it apparent that the newspaper belongs to the prisoners themselves. *Perekovka* 96-97 (22-24 October 1932).
287 RGALI, f. 1885, op. 3, d. 38, 1. 142.
288 Since in the Russian language it is required, not optional, to write in cursive while handwriting, those who attempt to write in the normally printed block letters are exhibiting their unfamiliarity with literacy. RGALI, f. 1885, op. 3, d. 39, l. 5-10.
289 *Perekovka* 40 (11 June 1932): 7.
290 The "living newspaper" is an unusual and interesting form of Soviet agitational theater that requires further definition. In order to keep illiterate audiences apprised of news events, these acting performances included short sketches on current events, with the actors having highly visible props to identify their characters: a large top hat for a capitalist, a big red pencil for a bureaucrat. The performances also often included song and dance, and given their primitive design, were highly mobile. Lynn Mally, "Exporting Soviet Culture: The Case of Agitprop Theater," *Slavic Review* 2 (2003): 324-42, 325-26.
291 *Perekovka* 40 (11 June 1932): 6.
292 RGALI, f. 1885, op. 3, d. 28, l. 6.
293 Alymov, one of the main editors of the newspaper, definitely understood English. His notebooks and diaries contain vocabulary lists of English words and notes about works he is reading in English. Some of the words included in Alymov's vocabulary list for reading the play *City of the Plague* are: weaklings, subtle, suave, mild, desperate, defeat, fear, gild, and glut. RGALI, f. 1885, op. 3, d. 21, l. 118.
294 RGALI, f. 1885, op. 3, d. 33, l. 298.
295 RGALI, f. 1885, op. 3, d. 33, l. 98.
296 Ibid.
297 See the discussion of dreams in Chapter One.
298 RGALI, f. 1885, op. 3, d. 33, l. 120.
299 This is most likely a *klichka*, or nickname for the English first name Andy. Criminal prisoners often assumed nicknames that were proper names in foreign languages.
300 RGALI, f. 1885, op. 3, d. 33, l. 285.
301 Platonov, trans. Robert Chandler and Geoffrey Smith, 54.
302 RGALI, f. 1885, op. 3, d. 33, l. 285.
303 Ibid.
304 RGALI, f. 1885, op. 3, d. 47, 1. 101.
305 See earlier commentary on page 000 on the importance of dreams and sleep in prison.
306 RGALI, f. 1885, op. 3, d. 33, l. 99.
307 RGALI, f. 1885, op. 3, d. 33, l. 100.
308 Ibid.
309 RGALI, f. 1885, op. 3, d. 33, l. 99.
310 RGALI, f. 1885, op. 3, d. 33, l. 100.

311 RGALI, f. 1885, op. 5, d. 22, l. 16.
312 Terent'ev, *Sobranie sochinenii*, 72.
313 Vladimir Markov, *Russian Futurism: A History* (Washington, DC: New Academia Publishing, 2006), 338.
314 Boris Groys, *The Total Art of Stalinism*, trans. Charles Rougle (Princeton: Princeton University Press, 1992).
315 "Manifesto of the 41°," *Russian Futurism through Its Manifestoes, 1912-1928*, trans. and eds. Anna Lawton and Herbert Eagle (Ithaca: Cornell University Press, 1988), 177.
316 Markov, 339.
317 Markov, 358.
318 Gerald Janecek, *Zaum: The Transrational Poetry of Russian Futurism* (San Diego: San Diego University Press, 1996), 1, 3.
319 Lawton and Eagle, 182-83.
320 Markov, 345.
321 Konstantin Rudnitskii, *Russian and Soviet Theatre: Tradition and the Avant-Garde*, trans. Roxane Permar (London: Thames and Hudson, 1988), 201.
322 Rudnitskii, 202-3.
323 Markov, 318.
324 Markov, 348.
325 The futurists adapted the symbolist notion of art as the creation of life (*tvorchestvo zhizni*) to the idea of life-building (*zhiznestroenie*), infusing technical connotations into an aesthetic, utopian vision of the world and the "new man" who will inhabit it. For more on the topic of *zhiznestroenie*, see Chapter One and also Irina Paperno and Joan Delaney Grossman, eds., *Creating Life: The Aesthetic Utopia of Russian Modernism* (Stanford: Stanford University Press, 1994).
326 Terent'ev, *Sobranie sochinenii*, 331.
327 Terent'ev, *Sobranie sochinenii*, fn 17, p. 547.
328 Terent'ev, *Sobranie sochinenii*, fn 1, p. 501.
329 Tat'iana Terent'eva, "Moi otets Igor' Terent'ev," *Zaumnyi futurizm i dadizm v russkoi kul'ture*, ed. Luigi Magarotto, Marco Marciaduri, and Daniela Rizzi (Bern: Peter Lang, 1991), 358.
330 "Iskusstvo na sluzhbe perekovki cheloveka na stroitel'stve BBVP," *Karelo-Murmanskii krai* 5-6 (1933).
331 Terent'eva, "Moi otets," 358.
332 Ibid.
333 For a further treatment of this discussion (the emphasis on Nazi and Gulag concentration camps rather than the much more deadly phenomena of mobile killing squads and forced famine and collectivization), see Timothy Snyder, "Holocaust: The Ignored Reality," *New York Times Review of Books* 12 (16 July 2009): 14-16.
334 Igor' Terent'ev, *Moi pokhorony* (Moscow: Gileia, 1993), 51, 60.
335 Terent'ev, 357.
336 D. S. Likhachev, "Cherty," 62.
337 Aleksandr Solzhenitsyn, ed., *Voices from the Gulag*, and Anne Applebaum, *Gulag*, 387.
338 Qtd., Roshanna P. Sylvester, *Tales from Old Odessa: Crime and Civility in a City of Thieves* (DeKalb: Northern Illinois University Press, 2005), 56.
339 Odessa, importantly, is also known for its long association with satire and comic literature.
340 Roshanna P. Sylvester, *Tales from Old Odessa*, 48.

341 Ibid.

342 In a second version, Masha threatens to turn all of the criminals in to the police for wanting to kill Ios'ka because she too has learned to swear allegiance to the Belomorkanal, a change of heart which leads to her being murdered by the gang first. See Robert A. Rothstein, "How It Was Sung in Odessa: At the Intersection of Russian and Yiddish Folk Culture," *Slavic Review* 4 (Winter 2002): 781-801, 794.

343 Maikl and Lidiia Dzhekobson, *Pesennyi folk'lor GULAGa kak istoricheskii istochnik 1917-39* (Moscow: Sovremennyi gumanitarnyi universitet, 1998), 335-38.

344 Likhachev, "Cherty," 60.

345 Varlam Shalamov, in his essays on the criminal world, notes how mothers are the most important people in criminals' lives and supersede all loyalty to other family members, including wives and children.

346 The Zionist leader Vladimir Jabotinsky offers an interesting description of the specifically Jewish thieving culture in Odessa, his native city: "The Jewish characterization of my fellow residents was an insult: 'A thieving city.' But this must be understood philosophically [...] The word 'thief' in Yiddish ('*ganev*') has a much deeper meaning. It characterized a person who could fool you before you could fool him—in short, experienced, shrewd, a trickster, a manipulator, a maneuverer, a man of ingenuity, a screamer, an exaggerator, a speculator—but I said 'in short.'" *The Golden Tradition: Jewish Life and Thought in Eastern Europe*, ed. Lucy S. Dawidowicz (Syracuse: Syracuse University Press, 1996), 397-98. For fictional representations of Jewish criminal life in Odessa, see Isaak Babel''s short story collection *Odessa Tales* (*Odesskie rasskazy*, 1931), in particular "How It Was Done in Odessa," which highlights the gangster character Benya Krik.

347 Yuri Slezkine, *The Jewish Century* (Princeton: Princeton University Press, 2004), 199.

348 Alice Nakhimovsky, *Russian-Jewish Literature and Identity: Jabotinsky, Babel, Grossman, Galich, Roziner, Markish* (Baltimore: John Hopkins University Press, 1992), 21.

349 Danzig Baldaev, *Tatuirovki zakliuchennykh* (St. Petersburg: Limbus, 2006), 38.

350 Baldaev, *Taturirovki*, 93 and others, see also Dobson, *Khrushchev's Cold Summer*, 113-15.

351 Nikki Sullivan, *Tattooed Bodies: Subjectivity, Textuality, Ethics, and Pleasure* (Westport: Praeger, 2001), 16.

352 Nancy Condee, "Body Graphics: Tattooing the Fall of Communism," *Consuming Russia*, ed. Adele Marie Barker (Durham, NC: Duke University Press, 1999), 350.

353 Alix Lambert, *Russian Prison Tattoos* (Atglen, PA: Schiffer, 2003), 40.

354 RGALI, f. 1885, op. 3, d. 34, l. 30-31.

355 Dmitri Likhachev, "Kartezhnye igry ugolovnikov," *Stat'i rannikh let* (Tver': Tverskoe oblastnoe otdelenie rossiiskogo fonda kul'tury, 1993), 45-53, 46.

356 Likhachev, "Cherty," 56.

357 Ibid, 46-52.

358 RGALI, f. 1185, op. 3, d. 33, l. 104.

359 Another example comes from the manuscript draft of the *Istoriia stroitel'stva*: "Агитбригадник Володька-Кузнецов, в прошлом отъявленна [sic] шпана, рассказывает:
— У нас у всех глаз юркий, воровской, особенный глаз, зрачком вкось: все видит. Сегодня, к примеру, я узнаю, что возят торф, а тачки у них спальные, – значит меньшего размера, для скалы, которые. Это все равно что воду рюмками пить, тьфу. Разве это не вредительство? И кто мне этот материал сообщил? Свой, бывший жулик, и на кого? На десятника, который тоже из уголовнового мира." f. 7952, op. 7, d. 73 (XI глава, 2 вариант), l. 30. (This section was crossed out by editors).

360 For an elaboration on the specifically Russian connotation of the term in the 1920s-

1930s, when the term cultural person collapsed "all differential descriptions," see Mikhail N. Epstein, *Transcultural Experiments: Russian and American Models of Creative Communication* (NY: St. Martin's, 1999), 36.
361 See, for example, Sheila Fitzpatrick, ed., *Cultural Revolution in Russia* (Bloomington: Indiana University Press, 1978).
362 *Perekovka* 40 (11 June 1932), 10.
363 RGALI, f. 1885, op. 3, d. 33, l. 148.
364 RGALI, f. 1885, op. 3, d. 21, l. 101.
365 For a further treatment of the Cultural Revolution and its moral dictates, see Sheila Fitzpatrick, ed., *Cultural Revolution in Russia 1928-1931* (Bloomington: Indiana University Press, 1978), and Kate Transchel, *Under the Influence: Working Class Drinking, Temperance and Cultural Revolution in Russia 1895-1932* (Pittsburgh: University of Pittsburgh Press, 2006).
366 Nadya Peterson, "Dirty Women: Cultural Connotations of Cleanliness in Soviet Russia," *Russia, Women, Culture*, ed. Helena Goscilo and Beth Holmgren (Bloomington: Indiana University Press, 1996), 178.
367 Joan Neuberger, *Hooliganism: Crime, Culture, and Power in St. Petersburg 1900-1914* (Berkeley: University of California Press, 1993), 3-5.
368 Neuberger, 5.
369 For example, see *Karelo-Murmanskii krai* 5-6 (20 July 1933): 25.
370 For example, the popular illustrated magazine *Thirty Days (30 dnei)* often includes short stories and articles about the criminal world in its issues from the early 1930s. Stories such as "Bandit" (18-24) and "Razgovor v tiurme" (61-62) are a few examples, from the March 1934 issue of the magazine.
371 L. Averbakh, S. Firin, and M. Gor'kii, eds., *Istoriia stroitel'stva*, 187, 188, 234, 253-55, 356, 366.
372 Vera Inber, *Stranitsy dnei perebiraia* (Moscow: Sovetskii pisatel', 1967), 18.
373 Neuberger, 12.

CHAPTER THREE

374 Richard Stites, *Revolutionary Dreams: Utopian Vision and the Experimental Life in the Russian Revolution* (New York: Oxford University Press, 1988), 135-40.
375 For more on the interconnections between collage, montage, and photomontage in the Russian context, see the first chapter of Katherine Hoffman, *Collage: Criticial Views* (Ann Arbor: University of Michigan Press, 1989).
376 Ol'ga Velichkina, "Muzykal'nyi instrument i chelovecheskoe telo (na material russkogo fol'klora)," *Telo v russkoi kul'ture: sbornik statei* (Moscow: Novoe literaturnoe obozrenie, 2005), 161-76.
377 Vera Inber, *Za mnogo let* (Moscow: Sovetskii pisatel', 1964), 170-71.
378 Aleksandr Solzhenitysn, ed., *Voices from the Gulag*, trans. Kenneth Lantz (Evanston, IL: Northwestern University Press, 2010), 233-34.
379 Veronica Shapovalov, ed. and trans., *Remembering the Darkness: Women in Soviet Prisons* (Lanham, MD: Rowman and Littlefield, 2001), 215.
380 Anne Applebaum, ed., *Gulag Voices: An Anthology* (New Haven: Yale University Press, 2011), 54.

381 Alexander Dolgun and Patrick Watson, *Alexander Dolgun's Story: An American in the Gulag* (New York: Knopf, 1975), 164. Emphasis in original.
382 Tofik Shakhverdiev, dir., *Stalin s nami?*, 1989.
383 RGALI, f. 1885, op. 3, d. 21, l. 21.
384 This is also the title of a 1907 short story collection by Mikhail Prishvin, who goes on to write the *Tsar's Road*, a 1957 work about Peter the Great's overland haul of ships that is full of parallels with the construction of the White Sea-Baltic Canal.
385 RGALI, f. 1885, op. 3, d. 21, l. 24.
386 RGALI, f. 1885, op. 3, d. 21, l. 72.
387 The prisoner V. Mironov writes at length about the sounds at the canal in his short story "Triumf ozera Vygy." RGALI, f. 1885, op. 3, d. 33, 1. 172-73.
388 RGALI, f. 1885, op. 3, d. 33, l. 149.
389 RGALI, f. 1885, op. 3, d. 33, l. 148.
390 For a further treatment of avant-realism, see Julie Draskoczy, "A Body of Work: Building Self and Society at Stalin's White Sea-Baltic Canal," doctoral dissertation, 2010.
391 RGALI, f. 1885, op. 3, d. 33, l. 143.
392 Interestingly, the idea of "unity through diversity" is one that holds an important position in the Russian Orthodox Church. Rather than seeing unity and diversity as two opposing constructs, church doctrine argues that the diversity of the autocephalous structure of the church is unified through the singular message of the church's teaching and traditions, allowing what are two contrasting notions to become complementary ones. See Timothy Ware, *The Orthodox Church* (New York: Penguin, 1997). The idea of unity through diversity is an important one to this research, and it will continue to be explored throughout the dissertation.
393 RGALI, f. 1885, op. 3, d. 33, l. 286-88.
394 For further clarification, see the discussion of Terent'ev and "lito-montazh."
395 RGALI, f. 1885, op. 3, d. 35.
396 This piece echoes the structure of the contemporary poet Sergei Stratanovskii's work, to be discussed in Chapter Five.
397 Interestingly, the word "montage" (*montazh*) in Russian refers to both the literary device and the assembly of machinery or editing of a film or literary work.
398 Terent'ev, *Sobranie sochinenii*, 299.
399 Leah Dickerman, ed., *Building the Collective: Soviet Graphic Design 1917-37* (Princeton: Architectural Press, 1996), 12, 28.
400 Diane Waldman, *Collage, Assemblage, and the Found Object* (New York: Harry Abrams, 1992), 76.
401 Ibid., 85, 88-92.
402 Terent'ev, *Sobranie sochinenii*, 299.
403 Ibid., 332.
404 Ibid.
405 Fedor Gladkov, *Cement*, trans. A. S. Arthr and C. Ashleigh (Evanston, IL: Northwestern University Press, 1980), 53.
406 Valerii Frid, *58 1/2: Zapiski lagernogo pridurka* (Moscow: Rusanova, 1996), 13.
407 V. Zaleskii, "Sovetskaia p'esa," *Sovetskii teatr* 1 (1935): 7.
408 Given the film's similarity to Pogodin's play, it will not be discussed in detail here, as the work essentially follows the same story line as *The Aristocrats*.
409 Wixley and Carr, trans., *The Aristocrats*, 304.
410 Ibid., 302-303.

411 Ibid., 303.
412 Ibid., 274.
413 RGALI, f. 1885, op. 3, d. 21, l. 25.
414 Collage can also serve as an apt metaphor for the construction of biography; for more on this topic, see Cristina Vatulescu's interpretation of secret police files as examples of collage and montage, "Arresting Biographies: The Secret Police File in the Soviet Union and Romania," *Comparative Literature* 3 (2004): 243-61.
415 D. Burliuk, Alexander Kruchenykh, V. Mayakovsky, Victor Khlebnikov, "Slap in the Face of Public Taste," *Russian Futurism through its Manifestoes, 1912-1928*, ed. Anna Lawton and Herbert Eagle (Ithaca: Cornell University Press, 1988), 51.
416 Karen A. McCauley, "Production Literature and the Industrial Imagination," *The Slavic and East European Journal* 42 (1998): 444-66, 456.
417 Katherine Hoffman, ed., *Collage: Critical Views* (Ann Arbor: University of Michigan Research Press, 1989), 3.
418 Hoffman, 4.
419 Ibid, 5, 7.
420 Ibid, 171, 177, 184.
421 GARF, f. 7952, op. 7, d. 72, l. 1, 26. In both of these instances, poems from the newspaper *Perekovka* are cut out and literally glued into the margins of the original manuscript of the *Istoriia stroitel'stva*.
422 Hoffman, 220.
423 Ibid., 221.
424 Ibid., 63.
425 Ibid., 60-61.
426 Pierre Nora, "Between Memory and History: Les Lieux de Mémoire," *Representations* 26 (1989): 7-24, 23.
427 Perhaps such artworks—which have the guise of reality but are clearly artistic fictions—can actually more accurately represent a particular reality as a type of *lieu de mémoire*. The current obsession with the documentary fragment and archival trace, as Pierre Nora would argue, demonstrates that all representations of memory are mere fabrications.
428 I. L. Averbakh, 31.
429 This phenomenon becomes especially clear when working with the original copies of the book in GARF. There you can see paragraphs cut and pasted together (montage) as well as poetry cut out from the *Perekovka* newspaper and pasted into the margins (collage). See also Cynthia Ruder's article on collage and Belomor, "Modernist in Form, Socialist in Content: *The History of the Construction of the Stalin White Sea-Baltic Canal*," *Russian Literature* 44 (1998): 469-84.
430 My thanks to Mikhail Dankov of the Karelian History Museum in Petrozavodsk, Russia, for this insight.
431 In Kafka's story, this method allows for many gaps in the wall, and the announcement of the completion of the project comes before it has actually been finished. What was meant to be the primary purpose of the wall—protection—is undermined by the fact that the wall is full of uncompleted sections. Art, indeed, imitates life, since the canal was also not built properly for its intended purpose. Franz Kafka, "The Great Wall of China," *The Great Wall of China: Stories and Reflections* (New York: Shocken Books, 1970), 83-97.
432 Morukov, "The White Sea-Baltic Canal," 161.

433 The designation *natsmeny*, which is an abbreviation for *natsional'nye men'shinstva*, or national minorities, merited its own specific attention during the construction of the canal and GARF holds archival documents relating specifically to the challenges this group faced at the work site.
434 Makurov, ed., *Gulag v Karelii*, 22.
435 Teodor Shumovskii, conversation with author, 18 February 2007.
436 I. L. Averbakh, *Ot prestupleniia k trudu*, 77.
437 Official documents pertaining to the White Sea-Baltic Canal note a rise in criminal activity and banditry, a phenomenon that is partially blamed on the darkness of Karelian nights. In addition, the prisoners' refusal to work and obstinate behavior are blamed on the lack of prison guards. Makurov, ed., *Gulag v Karelii*, documents 3, 6. and documents 11, 14, respectively.
438 *Karelo-Murmanskii krai* 5-6 (1933): 28.
439 RGALI, f. 1885, op. 3, d. 36, l. 2.
440 NARK, f. 365, op. 1, d. 12, 5. The tenacity of the slogan also became apparent in my interview with Teodor Shumovskii, who emphatically repeated the phrase several times during our conversation together.
441 Thomas Lahusen, *How Life Writes the Book*, 46.
442 Oksana Bulgakowa and David Bordwell, "The Ear against the Eye: Vertov's 'Symphony,'" *Monatshefte* 2 (2006): 219-43.
443 Leah Dickerman, *Building the Collective*, 33.
444 *Belomorsko-Baltiiskii Kanal imeni tov. Stalina: Karta-putevoditel'* (Moscow: TsS Osvod, 1934), 1.
445 Ibid.
446 Peter Nisbet, "El Lissitzky circa 1935: Two Propaganda Projects Reconsidered." In *Situating El Lissitzky: Vitebsk, Berlin, Moscow*, ed. Nancy Perloff and Brian Reed, 211-34. Los Angeles: Getty, 2003.
447 Margarita Tupitsyn, "From the Politics of Montage to the Montage of Politics: Soviet Practice 1919 through 1937," in *Montage and Modern Life 1919-1942*, ed. Matthew Teitelbaum (Cambridge: MIT Press, 1992), 82-127, 88.
448 Tupitsyn, 96.
449 Groys, 22, 29.
450 Erika Wolf, "The Visual Economy of Forced Labor: Alexander Rodchenko and the White Sea-Baltic Canal," in *Picturing Russia: Explorations in Visual Culture*, ed. Valerie A. Kivelson and Joan Neuberger (New Haven: Yale University Press, 2008), 170.
451 L. Volkov-Lannit, *Aleksandr Rodchenko risuet, fotografiruet, sporit* (Moscow: Iskusstvo, 1968), 125.
452 Leah Bendavid-Val, *Propaganda and Dreams: Photographing the 1930s in the USSR and the US* (Zurich: Stemmle, 1999), 65.
453 Wolf, "The Visual Economy," 173.
454 Leah Dickerman, "The Propagandizing of Things," *Aleksandr Rodchenko* (New York: Museum of Modern Art, 1998), 90.
455 Ibid., 96.
456 Peter Kenez, *The Birth of the Propaganda State: Soviet Methods of Mass Mobilization, 1917-1929* (Cambridge: Cambridge University Press, 1985), 254-55.
457 J. B. Harley, "Maps, Knowledge, and Power," in *The Iconography of Landscape: Essays on the Symbolic Representation, Design, and Use of Past Environments*, ed. Denis Cosgrove and Stephen Daniels (Cambridge: Cambridge University Press, 1988), 277-312, 278.

458 "For all our reliance on Figures, we never quite believe in their revelations. Despite the privilege given to the authority and presence of the Figure, it is, after all, just a Figure, a picture. It might be manipulated, biased in perspective: it does not fully reveal the truth of what it claims to represent." Introduction by Guerin and Hallas for *The Figure and the Witness: Trauma, Memory and Visual Culture*, ed. Frances Guerin and Roger Hallas (London: Wallflower Press, 2007), 1-2.
459 Iutkevich, 232.
460 Sergei Eisenstein, *Selected Works*, vol. 1: Writings 1922-34, ed. and trans. Richard Taylor (London and Bloomington: BFI and Indiana University Press, 1988), 185-86.
461 Eisenstein, 190.
462 Ibid., 191. Emphasis in original.
463 Oksana Bulgakowa, "Spatial Figures in Soviet Cinema of the 1930s," in *The Landscape of Stalinism: The Art and Ideology of Soviet Space*, ed. Evgeny Dobrenko and Eric Naiman (Seattle: University of Washington Press), 53.
464 Lev Mil'ianenkov, *Po tu storonu zakona: Entsiklopediia prestupnogo mira* (Saint Petersburg: Damy i gospoda, 1992), 14, 183.
465 Like the slogans of "five in four" for the first Five-Year Plan and "quickly and cheaply" for the construction of the White Sea-Baltic Canal, the idea of Moscow being the "port of five seas" was a particularly contagious catchphrase. In my interview with Tedor Shumovskii, a prisoner who worked in the forests of the canal, he mentioned the phrase numerous times as the ultimate goal of the project, imagining the larger, loftier goal of the administration rather than limiting his commentary to only a discussion of the White Sea-Baltic Canal.
466 Richard Stites, *Russian Popular Culture: Entertainment and Society since 1900* (Cambridge: Cambridge University Press, 1992), 46.
467 Andrey Platonov, *The Foundation Pit* (London: Harvill, 1996), 8.
468 RGALI f. 1885, op. 5, d. 22, l. 4.
469 RGALI, f. 1885, op. 3, d. 21, l. 24.
470 GARF, f. 7952, op. 7, d. 30, l. 152.
471 Stalin famously made this statement in regard to the creation of the 1936 constitution, which was supposed to promise the Soviet citizen a better life. Some five years earlier, the prisoner's statement eerily prefigures what is to become a kind of national slogan.
472 Prishvin, *V kraiu*, 41-42.

CHAPTER FOUR

473 Goffman, *The Presentation of Self*, 17.
474 RGALI, f. 1604, op. 1, d. 21, l. 30.
475 Agitational theater was even exported to capitalist countries in an effort to spread Soviet propaganda; in May 1933 the International Olympiad of Revolutionary Theaters organized its first and only convention of agitprop theater in Moscow, at which capitalist-country participants could learn about the latest techniques in use in Russia. See Lynn Mally, "Exporting Soviet Culture: The Case of Agitprop Theater," *Slavic Review* 2 (2003): 324-42.
476 Vladimir Mayakovksky, "The Backbone Flute," in *The Bedbug and Selected Poetry*, trans. Max Hayward and George Reavey (Bloomington, IN: Indiana University Press, 1960), 111.

477 *Karelo-Murmanskii krai* 5-6 (20 July 1933): 30.
478 Dvorzhetskii, 84.
479 The predominance of theater is especially apparent in the context of the Holocaust, the prisoners of which remember their theatrical productions as singular moments of happiness in a world of pain. Gerda Wiessmann Klein remembers the skits she performed in Nazi concentration camps as a source of genuine joy in an otherwise horrific environment: "I was urged to arrange more performances for Sundays. I spent many a night writing in the washroom. I loved every bit of it. I loved the applause in my ears. I loved the single light burning on our improvised stage when the rest of the room was in darkness. I loved that light falling upon me and illuminating my figure. I loved to hear my voice in the hushed silence. But best of all I loved those upturned faces between the bunks, the smiles and sudden laughter, the knowledge that it was in my power to bring them an hour of fun, to help them forget." *All But My Life* (New York: Hill and Wang, 1995), 141.
480 For an analysis of the collapsing worlds of art and reality in Shalamov's work, see Sarah J. Young, "Criminalizing Creativity: Language, Performance, and the Representation of Convicts in Imperial and Soviet Era Prisons and Penal Colonies," forthcoming in *Acta Universitatis Upsaliensis, Eastern Europe Series*.
481 W. E. B. DuBois, *The Souls of Black Folk* (New York: Penguin, 1989), 5.
482 Wixley and Carr, trans., *The Aristocrats*, 279.
483 RGALI, f. 1885, op. 3, d. 38, l. 276.
484 Likhachev, "Cherty," 58, 64, 78.
485 Likhachev, 64.
486 Qtd., Ioakhim Klein, "Belomorkanal: Literatura i propaganda v stalinskoe vremia" *Novoe literaturnoe obozrenie* 71 (2005): 231-62, 248.
487 Fedor Dostoevskii, *Zapiski iz podpol'ia, Polnoe sobranie sochinenii*, vol. 5 (Leningrad: Nauka, 1973), 99-179.
488 Sona Stephen Hoisington, "'Ever Higher': The Evolution of the Project for the Palace of the Soviets," *Slavic Review* 1 (2003): 46.
489 The first *udarnik* brigades were in the Donbas coal mining region in 1926-27. N. V. Primush, *Udarnichestvo: Mif i real'nost'* (Donetsk: Donbas, 1990), 11.
490 L. Averbakh, S. Firin, and M. Gor'kii, eds., 123.
491 Ibid., 124.
492 Ibid., 81.
493 Balina, "Literatura puteshestvii," 904.
494 Regine Robin, "Stalinism and Popular Culture," in *The Culture of the Stalin Period*, ed. Hans Günther (London: Macmillan, 1990), 33.
495 Rosalinde Sartori, "Stalinism and Carnival: Organisation and Aesthetics of Political Holidays," in *The Culture of the Stalin Period*, ed. Hans Günter (London: Macmillan, 1990): 41.
496 Jon McKenzie, *Perform or Else: From Discipline to Performance* (London: Routledge, 2011), 55-57, 73, 87.
497 Robert Edelman, *Serious Fun: A History of Spectator Sports in the USSR* (New York: Oxford University Press, 1993), 41-43.
498 Edelman, 35.
499 Gorsuch, *Youth in Revolutionary Russia*, 16.
500 *Perekovka* 101 (7 November 1932): 17.
501 Soren Kierkegaard, *Repetition: An Essay in Experimental Psyshology* (New York: Harper, 1941).

502 Pogodin, 29.
503 Gilles Deleuze, *Différence et* Répétition (Paris: Presses Universitaires de Paris, 1968), 7.
504 B. G. Panteleimonov, *U podnozhiia promyshlennoi piatiletki "udarnichestvo"* (Paris: Soiuz Sovetskikh Patriotov, 1945), 31.
505 Emphasis in original. Mikhail Bakhtin, *The Dialogic Imagination: Four Essays*, ed. Michael Holquist, trans. Caryl Emerson and Michael Holquist (Austin: University of Texas Press, 1981), 122.
506 Vatslav Dvorzhetskii, *Puti bol'shikh etapov* (Moscow: Vozvrashchenie, 1994), 7.
507 Dvorzhetskii., 78.
508 Ibid., 84.
509 Ibid., 83.
510 Ibid., 79.
511 According to the Karelian journal *Karelo-Murmanskii krai*, 12,484 prisoners were released early and 59,516 had their sentences reduced. *Karelo-Murmanskii krai* 5-6 (1933): 10.
512 Dvorzhetskii, 81-82.
513 Losev, *Zhizn': Povesti, rasskazy, pis'ma*, 334.
514 Edwin Ware Hullinger, *The Reforging of Russia* (New York: Dutton, 1925), 319.
515 Ibid.
516 Anne E. Gorsuch, *Youth in Revolutionary Russia: Enthusiasts, Bohemians, Delinquents* (Bloomington: Indiana University Press, 2000), 121.
517 Gorsuch, *Youth in Revolutionary Russia*, 323.
518 Anne E. Gorsuch, "Flappers and Foxtrotters: Soviet Youth in the 'Roaring Twenties'," *Carl Beck Papers* 1102 (1994): 1-33, 12.
519 V. V. Maiakovskii, *Klop* (Moscow: Slovo, 1999), 462-506, 497.
520 "TsK profsoiuza rabotnikov iskusstva. Protokol soveshchaniia ot 28 avgusta 1935 g. Po voprosu o zapadnykh tantsakh," http://archive.svoboda.org/programs/hd/2005/hd.010105.asp, 8 March 2010.
521 Judith Butler, *Gender Trouble* (New York: Routledge, 2006).
522 Kowalsky, *Deviant Women*, 84, 97.
523 *Karelo-murmanskii krai* 5-6 (1933), 26.
524 RGALI, f. 1885, op. 3, d. 38, l. 50.
525 The influence of friends in the criminal world is often cited by both male and female prisoners as a reason for remaining in this realm. Although women seem to acknowledge the psychological aspects more, men tend to attribute their behavior to outside influences. A male account of such peer pressure explains how it was only the influence of friends that brought him back to a life of crime after he had already tried to go straight: RGALI, f. 1885, op. 3, d. 38, l. 63.
526 Ibid.
527 RGALI, f. 1885, op. 3, d. 38, l. 271.
528 RGALI, f. 1885, op. 3, d. 38, l. 272.
529 RGALI, f. 1885, op. 3, d. 38, l. 276.
530 This phrase (*mechty, mechty, gde vasha sladost'*) comes from Aleksandr Pushkin's 1816 poem "Probuzhdenie."
531 GARF, f. 7952, op. 7, d. 32, l. 7.
532 Ibid.
533 GARF, f. 7952, op. 7, d. 32, 112.
534 Iuliia Danzas, *Krasnaia katorga* excerpt in Losev, *Radost' na veki*, 203.

535 Nadya L. Peterson, "Dirty Women," 186.
536 Sona Stephen Hoisington, "'Ever Higher': The Evolution of the Project for the Palace of the Soviets" *Slavic Review* 1 (2003): 41-68.
537 Sheila Fitzpatrick, *Everyday Stalinism, Ordinary Life in Extraordinary Times: Soviet Russia in the 1930s* (New York: Oxford University Press, 1999), 69.

CHAPTER FIVE

538 RGALI, f. 1885, op. 3, d. 19, l. 12, 29.
539 Although written in the 1950s and 60s, this classic Gulag tome was not published in the West until 1973 and not in the Soviet Union until 1989, although bits and pieces of it circulated earlier in *samizdat*, the underground publishing network in the Soviet Union.
540 For a pictorial history of the Belomokanal cigarette label, see the online respository of images at http://www.rucig.ru/pap_belomorkanal.htm.
541 Orlando Figes, *A People's Tragedy: The Russian Revolution 1891-1924* (New York: Penguin, 1996), 522.
542 Figes, *A People's Tragedy*, 522.
543 Irina Paperno, *Stories of the Soviet Experience*, 175.
544 Mikhail Prishvin, *V kraiu nepuganykh ptits* (Moscow: gosudarstvennoe izdatel'stvo khudozhestvennoi literatury, 1934), 26.
545 RGALI, f. 1885, op. 3, d. 38, l. 29.
546 RGALI, f. 1885, op. 3, d. 19, l. 13.
547 This quotation also serves as a caption to a photograph of a female laborer wielding a jackhammer in the *History of the Construction*.
548 Sheila Fitzpatrick, *Everyday Stalinism*, 75.
549 L. Averbakh, S. Firin, and M. Gor'kii, eds., 25.
550 In highlighting the varying religions, professions, ethnic backgrounds, and languages among the prisoners at the canal, the volume points to the great diversity of the camp population.
551 The volume contains an incredible amount of narrative styles, including *skaz*, reportage, theatrical, novelistic, direct address of reader, repetition as a device, as well as dramatic shifts in tone, turning abruptly from a short, punctuated style to a more lyrical one, from addressing the general to the specific, and from discussing history to contemporary reality. Part of this great mélange of styles may be due to the fact that the book is collectively written; in the end, its style is not homogeneously modified into a seamless whole.
552 L. Averbakh, S. Firin, and M. Gor'kii, eds., 181.
553 RGALI, f. 1604, op. 1, d. 21, l. 21.
554 L. Averbakh, S. Firin, and M. Gor'kii, eds. ,181.
555 Ibid., 554.
556 Ibid,, 593.
557 Ibid., 542.
558 Orlanda Figes, *The Whisperers: Private Life in Stalin's Russia* (New York: Picador, 2008), 189.
559 Emma Widdis, *Visions of a New Land: Soviet Film from the Revolution to the Second World*

War (New Haven: Yale University Press, 2003), 2.
560 Mikhail Epstein, "Russo-Soviet Topoi," in *The Landscape of Stalinism: The Art and Ideology of Soviet Space*, Eds. Evgeny Dobrenko and Eric Naiman (Seattle: University of Washington Press, 2003), 277-306.
561 Eric Naiman, Introduction, *The Landscape of Stalinism*, xi.
562 Nicolas Berdyaev, *The Russian Idea* (Boston: Beacon, 1962), 2.
563 Ibid., 552.
564 Ibid., 554.
565 Lev Trotskii, *Literatura i revoliutsiia* (Moscow: Izdatel'stvo politicheskoi literatury, 1991), 194. English translation, Evgenii Dobrenko, *Aesthetics of Alienation: Reassessment of Early Soviet Cultural Theories*, trans. Jesse M. Savage (Evanston, IL: Northwestern University Press), 2005, 111.
566 Trotskii, 197. English Translation, Rose Strunsky, *Literature and Revolution* (Ann Arbor: University of Michigan Press, 1970), 256.
567 L. Averbakh, S. Firin, and M. Gor'kii, eds., 14, 15.
568 Ibid., 94.
569 Ibid., 145.
570 Ibid., 358.
571 Karl Marx, *Capital: A Critique of Political Economy*, Trans. Samuel Moore (New York: International Publishers, 1970), 177.
572 L. Averbakh, S. Firin, and M. Gor'kii, eds., 318.
573 Ibid., 115.
574 Ibid.
575 (A. P. Kaprinskii). From exhibit on water in the State Museum of Karelia.
576 Viktor Shklovskii, *Sovetskaia literatura na novom etape* (Moscow: Sovetskaia literatura, 1933), 169. Sincere thanks to Sasha Senderovich for his assistance with this translation.
577 L. Averbakh, S. Firin, and M. Gor'kii, eds., 536.
578 *Perekovka*, 5 June 1934.
579 Although this is not the present aim of the current research, approximate mortality rates at the White Sea-Baltic Canal have been attempted by several scholars. Nick Baron estimates a death rate of 25,025 deaths among the total 175,000 prisoners. Baron, 643. Others break down the death rates by year, with 1931 and 1932 having approximately 2% death rates, and 1933 having more than a 10% death rate. Kokurin and Morkurov, eds., 34.
580 Vera Inber, *Stranitsy*, 16-18.
581 Orlando Figes, *Natasha's Dance: A Cultural History of Russia* (New York: Picador, 2002), 8.
582 Andrew Horton, *Inside Soviet Film Satire: Laughter with a Lash* (Cambridge: Cambridge University Press, 1993), 75. Beyond just mere film preferences, Paperny also argues for the connection between Stalin and water.
583 V. Paperny, "Moscow in the 1930s and the Emergence of a New City," in *The Culture of the Stalin Period*, ed. Hans Günther (New York: St. Martin's P, 1990), 229-39, 232.
584 Martin McCauley, *The Soviet Union 1917-1991* (London: Longman, 1993), 106.
585 From an interview with the author. 7 February 2007, MEMORIAL human rights organization, St. Petersburg.
586 From an interview with the author. 8 February 2007, MEMORIAL human rights organization, St. Petersburg.
587 Sergei Stratanovskii, "Gidroarteriia," *Zvezda* 2 (1994): 75-77.

588 Ibid., 75.
589 "We are a road of bones," ibid., 77.
590 Ibid., 75-77.
591 Ibid., 77. Interestingly, nearly this exact phrasing (*my ne raby, raby ne my*) appears in a propagandistic documentary film on Solovki, as a teacher writes the words on a blackboard in what looks like a classroom. This demonstrates how contemporary works draw from official, ideological ones to create cultural commentary.
592 Ibid., 77.
593 The connection of *Faust* with various personalities involved in the White Sea-Baltic Canal is deep and complex. Gorky himself expressed a desire to write a version of *Faust* in 1906-07; see Nina Berberova, *Moura: The Dangerous Life of Baroness Budberg* (New York: NYRB, 1998), 96. Vera Inber, one of the authors of the *History of the Construction*, writes quotations from Goethe in her diary in 1933, just at the time she would be participating in the Canal project. The philosopher and Belomorkanal prisoner Aleksandr Meier, as already noted, writes at length about *Faust*. Lev Losev also mentions *Faust* (*Zhizn'* 312).
594 The homunculus is created in a laboratory from liquid vapors from the sea, offering more connections with the present research. Alchemy, the premiere science of the eighteenth century, held promise of discovering new formulas and creating new chemical experiments. The idea of re-forging, or the smelting of metals, is itself a type of chemical process. There is, however, a key difference between the homunculus and the re-forged prisoner; the former is all mind and spirit in search of a body, whereas the latter is privileged precisely because of the physical body's ability to produce labor, with the thinking mind downplayed.
595 Marshall Berman, "Faust as Developer," in *Faust*, trans. Walter Arndt, ed. Cyrus Hamlin (New York: Norton, 2001), 717.
596 Stratanovskii, 76.
597 Ibid.
598 Aleksandr Meier, *Filosoficheskie sochinenia* (Paris: La Presse Libre, 1982), 20.
599 Meier, 143.
600 Ibid., 145.
601 Despite her St. Petersburg location and the recent publication of her poetry, it was not possible to locate Mal'tseva for an interview, and none of my contacts at the St. Petersburg branch of MEMORIAL knew of her whereabouts.
602 Alina Mal'tseva, " Poema o Belomorkanale" (St. Petersburg: Real, 1995), 3.
603 Mal'tseva, 7.
604 Ibid., 8.
605 From an interview with the author at 53 Ligovskii Prospekt, 10 March 2007.
606 Emphasis in original. Aleksey Kurbanovsky, "The Struggle with Emptiness," in Vadim Voinov, *A Convoluted Monograph*, 30.
607 Ibid.
608 Emphasis in original. Ibid.
609 It is worth noting that in this piece Stalin is described as "pharaoh." It is not the first time a reference to ancient Egypt is made in works regarding the White Sea-Baltic Canal; both prisoner-written (i.e., Stratanovskii's verse) and non-prisoner-written texts (i.e., the *History of the Construction*) make parallels between the construction of the canal and the erection of the pyramids.
610 For a treatment of contemporary art related to the Holocaust, see Dora Apel, *Memory*

Effects: The Holocaust and the Art of Secondary Witnessing (New Brunswick: Rutgers University Press, 1995).

611 For paintings and biographical information, see *Petr Belov: 1929-1988* (Moscow, 1989), with an introduction written by Anatolii Smelianskii.

612 The work also clearly references the 1871 painting *Grachi prileteli* by Aleksei Savrasov, which Russians know as both a beautiful work and a symbolic harbinger of spring.

613 *Tvorchesto i byt GULAGa* (Moscow: Zven'ia, 1998), Introduction. See also L. Rubinshtein, *Domashnee muzitsirovanie* (Moscow: Novoe literaturnoe obozrenie, 2000), 222.

614 *Vokrug sveta*, http://www.vokrugsveta.com/body/zemla/belomor.htm, 7 February 2010.

615 "K rabochim bumazhnoi fabriki im. Gor'kogo, f-ki "Spartak" i litografii Lentabtresta," *Krasnaia tabachnitsa* (3 March 1934).

616 Ibid.

617 http://myabris.ru/page.php?id=139&PHPSESSID=b3f05700ad9153addd9a0ca50 9b51640, 16 February 2010.

618 I make this claim after informally surveying former Gulag survivors and others familiar with Soviet culture. When I asked them about the existence of jokes regarding the Belomorkanal, this joke was the most commonly told, with the one regarding the pilots as a close second.

619 As told to me by former Gulag prisoner Viacheslav Dalinin.

620 Lipovetskii and Etkind, 176.

621 For a sustained analysis of historical amnesia in contemporary Russia, see Dina Khapaeva, "Historical Memory in Post-Soviet Gothic Society," *Social Research* 76 (2009): 359-94.

622 Epstein, *Transcultural Experiments*, 52.

623 *Vokrug sveta*, http://www.vokrugsveta.com/body/zemla/belomor.htm, 9 February 2009.

624 http://lenta.ru/news/2011/08/24/bel/, 30 June 2013.

625 Calvin S. Hall, *A Primer of Freudian Psychology* (New York: Signet, 1954), 38.

626 Sarah J. Young, "Recalling the Dead: Repetition, Identity, and the Witness in Varlam Shalamov's *Kolymskie rasskazy*" *Slavic Review* 2 (2011): 353-72.

627 Frances Guerin and Roger Hallas, eds., *The Figure and the Witness*, 11.

EPILOGUE

628 Andrey Platonov, *The Foundation Pit*, trans. Robert and Elizabeth Chandler and Olga Meerson (New York: NYRB, 2009), 9.

629 In his recent book *Everything was Forever, Until It Was No More* (Princeton: Princeton University Press, 2006), Alexei Yurchak successfully disassembles and refutes many of the dyads typically used for understanding Soviet reality.

630 Richard Stites, *Utopian Vision*, 3-4, 41.

631 RGALI, f. 1885, op. 3, d. 38, l. 223.

632 Nikolai Pogodin, *Aristokraty* (Moscow: Iskusstvo, 1936), 59.

633 Note that the Russian verb "to sit" in Russian also means serving time in prison. "Razgovor v tiur'me," *30 dnei* 3 (1934): 61-62.

634 This is not true just of Belomor. The Gulag prisoner Valerii Frid, for example, notes his

fascination with the criminal realm and his many interactions with thieves as a type of anthropological experience.
635 L. Averbakh, S. Firin, and M. Gor'kii, eds., 582.
636 Qtd., Rosalinde Sartorti, "Stalinism and Carnival: Organisation and Aesthetics of Political Holidays," in *The Culture of the Stalin Period*, ed. Hans Gunther (London: Macmillan, 1990), 63.

BIBLIOGRAPHY

Archives
GARF, *Gosudarstvennyi arkhiv Rossiiskoi Federatsii*, Moscow, Russia.
NARK, *Natsional'nyi arkhiv respubliki Kareliia*, Petrozavodsk, Russia.
RGAKFD, *Rossiiskii gosudarstvennyi arkhiv kinofotodokumentov*, Krasnogorsk, Russia.
RGALI, *Rossiiskii gosudarstvennyi arkhiv literatury i iskusstva*, Moscow, Russia.

Books and Articles
Anderson, R. Lanier. "Nietzsche on Redemption and Transfiguration." In *The Re-enchantment of the World: Secular Magic in a Rational Age*, edited by Joshua Landy and Michael Saler, 225-58. Stanford: Stanford University Press, 2009.
Antsiferov, N. P. *Iz dum o bylom. Vospominaniia*. Moscow: Feniks, 1992.
Apel, Dora. *Memory Effects: The Holocaust and the Art of Secondary Witnessing*. New Brunswick: Rutgers University Press, 1995.
Applebaum, Anne. *Gulag: A History*. New York: Doubleday, 2003.
------, ed. *Gulag Voices: An Anthology*. New Haven: Yale University Press, 2011.
Avdeenko, Aleksander. "Otluchenie." *Znamia* 3 (1989): 5-73.
Averbakh, I. L. *Ot prestupleniia k trudu*. Moscow: OGIZ, 1936.
Averbakh, L., Firin, S., and M. Gor'kii, eds. *Belomorsko-Baltiiskii Kanal imeni Stalina: Istoriia stroitel'stva*. OGIZ, 1934.

Bakhtin, Mikhail. *The Dialogic Imagination: Four Essays*. Edited by Michael Holquist, translated by Caryl Emerson and Michael Holquist. Austin: University of Texas Press, 1981.
Baldaev, Dantsik et al, eds. *Slovar' tiuremno-lagerno-blatnogo zhargona*. Moscow: Kraia Moskvy, 1992.
------. *Tatuirovki zakliuchennykh*. St. Petersburg: Limbus, 2006.
Balina, Marina. "Literatura puteshestvii." In *Sotsrealisticheskii kanon*, edited by Hans Giunter and Evgenii Dobrenko, 896-909. St. Petersburg: Akademicheskii proekt, 2000.
------. "Troubled Lives: The Legacy of Childhood in Soviet Literature." *Slavic and East European Journal* 49.2 (2005): 249-65.
------, Marina, and Larissa Rudova. "Introduction, Russian Children's Literature: Changing Paradigms." *Slavic and East European Journal* 49 (2005): 186-98.
Ball, Alan M. *Now My Soul Is Hardened: Abandoned Children in Soviet Russia 1918-1930*. Berkeley: University of California Press, 1994.
Barenberg, Alan. "From Prison Camp to Mining Town: The Gulag and Its Legacy in Vorkuta, 1938-65." PhD diss., U of Chicago, 2007.
Barnes, Stephen A. "'In a Manner Befitting Soviet Citizens': An Uprising in the Post-Stalin Gulag." *Slavic Review* 64 (2005): 823-50.
------. *Death and Redemption: The Gulag and the Shaping of Soviet Society*. Princeton: Princeton University Press, 2011.

Baron, Nick. "Conflict and Complicity: The Expansion of the Karelian Gulag, 1923-1933." *Cahiers du Monde Russe* 42 (2001): 615-48.
Basinskii, Pavel. *Gor'kii*. Moscow: Molodaia gvardiia, 2005.
Bauer, Raymond A. *The New Man in Soviet Psychology*. Cambridge, MA: Harvard University Press, 1952.
Belomorsko-Baltiiskii kanal imeni tov. Stalina. Belomorstroi: Postanovlenie SNK SSSR, 1933.
Belomorsko-Baltiiskii Kanal imeni tov. Stalina: Karta-putevoditel'. Moscow: TsS Osvod, 1934.
Belov, Petr. *Petr Belov 1929-1988*. Moscow, 1989.
Bendavid-Val, Leah. *Propaganda and Dreams: Photographing the 1930s in the USSR and the US*. Zurich: Stemmle, 1999.
Berberova, Nina. *Moura: The Dangerous Life of Baroness Budberg*. New York: New York Review Book Classics, 1998.
Berdyaev, Nicolas. *The Russian Idea*. Boston: Beacon, 1962.
Bergman, Jay. "Valerii Chkalov: Soviet Pilot as New Soviet Man." *Journal of Contemporary History* 33 (1998): 135-52.
Berman, Marshall. "Faust as Developer." In *Faust*, edited by Cyrus Hamlin, translated by Walter Arndt, 715-28. New York: Norton, 2001.
Bourland, Harriet. *Soviet Literary Theory and Practice during the First Five-Year Plan 1928-1932*. New York: King's Crown Press, 1950.
Bown, Matthew Cullerne. *Art under Stalin*. Oxford: Phaidon, 1991.
Brooks, Jeffrey. *How Russia Learned to Read: Literacy and Popular Literature 1861-1917*. Princeton: Princeton University Press, 1989.
Brown, Edward. *Russian Literature since the Revolution*. Cambridge, MA: Harvard University Press, 1982.
Bulgakov, Mikhail. *The Master and Margarita*. Translated by Diana Burgin and Katherine Tiernan O'Connor. New York: Vintage, 1996.
------. *Master i Margarita*. Moscow: Slovo, 2000.
Bulgakowa, Oksana, and David Bordwell. "The Ear against the Eye: Vertov's 'Symphony.'" *Monatshefte* 2 (2006): 219-43.
------. "Spatial Figures in Soviet Cinema of the 1930s." In *The Landscape of Stalinism: The Art and Ideology of Soviet Space*, edited by Evgeny Dobrenko and Eric Naiman, 51-76. Seattle: University of Washington Press.
Butler, Judith. *Gender Trouble: Feminism and the Subversion of Identity*. New York: Routledge, 1999.

Camus, Albert. *Le mythe de Sisyphe*. Paris: Gallimard, 1942.
Chaldize, Valery. *Criminal Russia: Essays on Crime in the Soviet Union*. New York: Random House, 1977.
Chukhin, Ivan. *Kanaloarmeitsy*. Petrozavodsk: Kareliia, 1990.
Chuzak, N. F. "Pod znakom zhiznestroeniia." *Lef* 1 (1923).
------, ed. *Literatura fakta*. Munich: Wilhelm Fink, 1972.
Clark, Katerina. "Little Heroes, Big Deeds." In *Cultural Revolution in Russia 1928-1931*, edited by Sheila Fitzpatrick, 189-97. Bloomington: Indiana University Press, 1978.
------. *The Soviet Novel: History as Ritual*. Bloomington: Indiana University Press, 1981.
Condee, Nancy. "Body Graphics: Tattooing the Fall of Communism." In *Consuming Russia*, edited by Adele Marie Barker, 339-61. Durham, NC: Duke University Press, 1999.
Crone, Anna Lisa. "Nietzschean, All Too Nietzschean? Rozanov's Anti-Christian Critique."

In *Nietzsche in Russia*, edited by Bernice Glatzer Rosenthal. Princeton: Princeton University Press, 1986.
Cunningham, Hugh. *Children and Childhood in Western Society since 1500*. Harlow, England: Pearson Longman, 2005.

Daniel', Aleksandr. "Tema GULAGa. Znachimoe otsutstvie." *Iskusstvo kino* 5 (2007): 5-14.
Dawidowicz, Lucy S., ed. *The Golden Tradition: Jewish Life and Thought in Eastern Europe*. Syracuse: Syracuse University Press, 1996.
Deleuze, Gilles. *Différence et Répétition*. Paris: Presses Universitaires de Paris, 1968.
Des Pres, Terrence. *The Survivor: An Anatomy of Life in the Death Camps*. New York: Oxford University Press, 1976.
Dickerman, Leah, ed. *Building the Collective: Soviet Graphic Design 1917-37*. Princeton: Architectural Press, 1996.
Dikavskii, S., and Aleksandr Rodchenko. "Strana meniaet svoiu geografiiu." *30 dnei* 7 (1933): 32-42.
Dmitriev, Iurii. *Belomorsko-Baltiiskii vodnyi put'. Ot zamyslov do voploshcheniia*. Petrozavodsk: Akademiia sotsial'no-Pravovoi zashchity, 2003.
Dobrenko, Evgenii. *The Making of the State Writer*. Translated by Jesse M. Savage. Stanford: Stanford University Press, 2001.
------. *Aesthetics of Alienation: Reassessment of Early Soviet Cultural Theories*. Translated by Jesse M. Savage. Evanston, IL: Northwestern University Press, 2005.
------. "The School Tale in Children's Literature of Socialist Realism." In *Russian Children's Literature and Culture*, edited by Marina Balina and Larissa Rudova, 43-66. New York: Routledge, 2008.
Dobrenko, Evgeny, and Eric Naiman, eds. *The Landscape of Stalinism: The Art and Ideology of Soviet Space*. Seattle: University of Washington Press, 2003.
Dobroliubov, Nikolai. "Chto takoe oblomovshchina." In *Sobranie sochinenii*, edited by B. I Bursov, 307-43, vol. 4. Moscow: Khudozhestvennaia literatura, 1962.
Dobson, Miriam. *Khrushchev's Cold Summer: Gulag Returnees, Crime, and the Fate of Reform after Stalin*. Ithaca, NY: Cornell University Press, 2009.
Dolgun, Alexander, and Patrick Watson. *Alexander Dolgun's Story: An American in the Gulag*. New York: Knopf, 1975.
Dostoevskii, Fedor. *Zapiski iz podpol'ia, Polnoe sobranie sochinenii*, vol. 5. Leningrad: Nauka, 1973.
Draskoczy, Julie. "A Body of Work: Building Self and Society at Stalin's White Sea-Baltic Canal," PhD diss., University of Pittsburgh, 2010.
------. "The *Put'* of *Perekovka*: Transforming Lives at Stalin's White Sea-Baltic Canal." *The Russian Review* 71 (2012): 30-48.
DuBois, W. E. B. *The Souls of Black Folk*. New York: Simon and Schuster, 2005.
Dutlinger, Anne D., ed. *Art, Music and Education as Strategies for Survival: Theresienstadt: 1941-45*. New York: Herodias, 2001.
Dvorzhetskii, Vatslav. *Puti bol'shikh etapov*. Moscow: Vozvrashchenie, 1994.
Dzhekobson, Maikl and Lidiia. *Pesennyi fol'klor GULAGa kak istoricheskii istochnik (1917-1939)*. Moscow: Sovremennyi gumanitarnyi universitet, 1998.

Edelman, Robert. *Serious Fun: A History of Spectator Sports in the USSR*. New York: Oxford University Press, 1993.
Eisenstein, Sergei. *Selected Works, Vol. 1: Writings 1922-34*. Edited and translated by

Richard Taylor. Bloomington, IN: BFI and Indiana University Press, 1988.
Eliade, Mircea. *Rites and Symbols of Initiation: The Mysteries of Birth and Rebirth.* Woodstock, CT: Spring, 1958.
Epstein, Mikhail. *After the Future: The Paradoxes of Postmodernism and Contemporary Russian Culture.* Translated by Anesa Miller-Pogacar. Amherst, MA: University of Massachusetts Press, 1995.
------. "Russo-Soviet Topoi." In *The Landscape of Stalinism: The Art and Ideology of Soviet Space*, edited by Evgeny Dobrenko and Eric Naiman, 277-306. Seattle: University of Washington Press, 2003.
Epstein, Mikhail, and Ellen Berry. *Transcultural Experiments: Russian and American Models of Creative Communication.* New York: St. Martin's Press, 1999.
Etkind, Aleksandr. "Soviet Subjectivity: Torture for the Sake of Salvation?" *Kritika* (Winter 2005): 171-86.
Figes, Orlando. *Natasha's Dance: A Cultural History of Russia.* New York: Picador, 2002.
------. *The Whisperers: Private Life in Stalin's Russia.* New York: Picador, 2007.
Fitzpatrick, Sheila. *Everyday Stalinism. Ordinary Life in Extraordinary Times: Soviet Russia in the 1930s.* New York: Oxford University Press, 1999.
------, ed. *Cultural Revolution in Russia 1928-1931.* Bloomington: Indiana University Press, 1978.
------, ed. *Stalinism: New Directions.* London: Routledge, 2000.
------, and Michael Geyer, eds. *Beyond Totalitarianism: Stalinism and Nazism Compared.* Cambridge: Cambridge University Press, 2009.
------, and Yuri Slezkine, eds. *In the Shadow of the Revolution: Life Stories of Russian Women from 1917 to the Second World War.* Princeton: Princeton University Press, 2000.
Foucault, Michel. *Discipline and Punish.* New York: Random House, 1977.
------. *Power/Knowledge: Selected Interviews and Other Writings 1972-1977.* Edited and translated by Colin Gordon. New York: Pantheon, 1980.
Foulkes, A. P. *Literature and Propaganda.* London: Methuen, 1983.
Freccero, John. "Autobiography and Narrative." In *Reconstructing Individualism: Autonomy, Individuality, and the Self in Western Thought*, edited by Thomas C. Heller, Morton Sosna, and David E. Wellbery, 16-29. Stanford: Stanford University Press, 1986.
Frid, Valerii. *58 ½: Zapiski lagernogo pridurka.* Moscow: Rusanova, 1996.

Galbraith, Marysia. "On the Way to Czestochowa: Rhetoric and Experience on a Polish Pilgrimage." *Anthropological Quarterly* 73 (April 2000): 61-73.
Geller, Mikhail. *Kontsetratsionyi mir i sovetskaia literatura.* Moscow: MIK, 1996.
Gernet, M. N. *Prestupnyi mir Moskvy.* Moscow: MKhO, 1991.
Getty, J. Arch, Gabor T. Ritterspoon, and Viktor N. Zemskov. "Victims of the Soviet Penal System in the Pre-War Years: A First Approach on the Basis of Archival Evidence." *American Historical Review* 98.4 (1993): 1017-49.
Gilbert, Shirli. *Music in the Holocaust: Confronting Life in the Nazi Ghettos and Camps.* Oxford: Clarendon, 2005.
Gilmore, Ruth Wilson. *Golden Gulag: Prisons, Surplus, Crisis, and Opposition in Globalizing California.* Berkeley: University of California P, 2007.
Gladkov, Fedor. *Cement.* Translated by A. S. Arther and C. Ashleigh. Evanston, IL: Northwestern University Press, 1980.
Gnetnev, Konstantin. *Kanal: Belomorsko-Baltiiskii kanal 1933-2003.* Petrozavodsk: PetroPress, 2003.

Goethe, Johann Wolfgang von. *Faust: A Tragedy*. Translated by Walter Arndt. New York: Norton, 2001.
Goffmann, Erving. *The Presentation of the Self in Everyday Life*. New York: Anchor, 1959.
------. *Asylums: Essays on the Social Situation of Mental Patients and Other Inmates*. Chicago: Aldine, 1961.
Gorcheva, Alla. *Pressa GULAGa*. Moscow: Izd. Moskovskogo universiteta, 1996.
Gorsuch, Anne E. "Flappers and Foxtrotters: Soviet Yoth in the 'Roaring Twenties.'" *Carl BeckPapers* 1102 (1994): 1-33.
------. *Youth in Revolutionary Russia: Enthusiasts, Bohemians, Delinquents*. Bloomington, IN: Indiana University Press, 2000.
Gor'kii, Maksim. *Detsvtvo*. Moscow: Slovo, 2000.
------. *Nashi dostizheniia*. Moscow: Zhurnalnoe-gazetnoe ob"edinenie, 1929.
------. *Nesvoevremennye mysli*. Paris: Éditions de la Seine, 1971.
------. "O tom, kak ia uchilsia pisat'." *O literature*. Moscow: Gos. Izd. Kh. Lit., 1961. 127-154.
------. *Perepiska M. Gor'kogo*. Ed. N. K. Gei, et al. Moscow: Khudozhestvennaia literatura, 1986.
------. *Rasskazy i ocherki*. Moscow: Slovo, 2000. 17-126.
------. "Sovetskaia literatura." *Doklad na Pervom vsesoiuznom s"ezde sovetskikh pisatelei 17 avgusta 1934 goda. O literature*. Moscow: Gos. izdat. khudozhestvennoi literatury, 1961. 416-44.
------. *Zametki iz dnevnika*. Moscow: Slovo, 2000. 521-634.
------. *Zhizn' Klima Samgina*. Moscow: Khudozhestvennaia literatura, 1987.
------. *Zhizn' Matveia Kozhemiakina*. Moscow: Gos. izd. kh. literatury, 1937.
Gorky, Maxim. *Mother*. Translated by Isidor Schneider. New York: Citadel, 1947.
Gregory, Paul R. and Valary Lazarev, eds. *The Economics of Forced Labor: The Soviet Gulag*. Stanford: Hoover Institution Press, 2003.
Grodzenskii, Sergei. *Lubianskii gambit*. Moscow: Olimpiia, 2004.
Groys, Boris. *The Total Art of Stalinism: Avant-Garde, Aesthetic Dictatorship and Beyond*. Translated by Charles Rougle. Princeton: Princeton University Press, 1992.
Guerin, Frances, and Roger Hallas, eds. *The Figure and the Witness: Trauma, Memory, and Visual Culture*. London: Wallflower, 2007.
Günther, Hans. "Der Bau des Weißmeerkanals als Laboratorium des neuen Menschen." In *Bücher haben ihre Geschichte*, edited by Petra Josting and Jan Wirrer, 62-68. Hildesheim: Olms, 1996.
------, ed. *The Culture of the Stalin Period*. New York: St. Martin's Press, 1990.
------. "Zhiznestroenie." *Russian Literature* 20 (1986).
Gutkin, Irina. "From Futurism to Socialist Realism." In *Creating Life: The Aesthetic Utopia of Russian Modernism*, edited by Irina Paperno and Joan Delaney Grossman, 167-98. Stanford: Stanford University Press, 1994.

Halfin, Igal. *Terror in My Soul: Communist Autobiographies on Trial*. Cambridge, MA: Harvard University Press, 2003.
Hall, Calvin S. *A Primer of Freudian Psychology*. New York: Signet, 1954.
Harley, J. B. "Maps, Knowledge, and Power." In *The Iconography of Landscape: Essays on the Symbolic Representation, Design, and Use of Past Environments*, edited by Denis Cosgrove and Stephen Daniels, 277-312. Cambridge: Cambridge University Press, 1988.
Hellbeck, Jochen. "Fashioning the Stalinist Soul: The Diary of Stepan Podlubnyi, 1931-

9." In *Stalinism: New Directions*, edited by Sheila Fitzpatrick, 77-116. London: Routledge, 2000.

------. *Revolution on My Mind: Writing a Diary under Stalin*. Cambridge: Harvard University Press, 2006.

Hellebust, Rolf. *From Flesh to Metal: Soviet Literature and the Alchemy of the Revolution*. Ithaca: Cornell University Press, 2003.

Hoffman, Katherine, ed. *Collage: Critical Views*. Ann Arbor: University of Michigan Press, 1989.

Hoisington, Sona Stephen. "'Ever Higher': The Evolution of the Project for the Palace of the Soviets." *Slavic Review* 1 (2003): 41-68.

Horton, Andrew. *Inside Soviet Film Satire: Laughter with a Lash*. Cambridge: Cambridge University Press, 1993.

Hullinger, Edwin Ware. *The Reforging of Russia*. New York: Dutton, 1925.

Il'in, Iakov. *Liudi Stalingradskogo traktornogo*. Moscow: OGIZ, 1934.

Inber, Vera. *Za mnogo let*. Moscow: Sovetskii pisatel', 1964.

------. *Stranitsy dnei perebiraia*. Moscow: Sovetskii pisatel', 1967.

Iurgenson, Liuba. "Kozha—Metafora teksta v lagernoi proze Varlama Shalamova." In *Telo v russkoi kul'ture*, edited by G. I. Kabakova and F. Kont, 340-46. Moscow: Novoe literaturnoe obozrenie, 2005.

Iutkevich, S. I., ed. "Lemberg, Aleksandr Grigor'evich." *Kino: Entsiklopedicheskii slovar'*. Moscow: Sovetskaia entsiklopediia, 1987, 232.

Ivanova, Galina Mikhailovna. *Gulag v sisteme totalitarnogo gosudarstva*. Moscow: Moskovskii obshchstvennyi nauchnyi fond, 1997.

------. *Labor Camp Socialism: The Gulag in the Totalitarian System*. Translated by Carol Flath. Armonk, NY: M. E. Sharpe, 2000.

Izvestiia TsK KPSS 304 (1990): 217-18.

Jakobson, Michael. *Origins of the Gulag: The Soviet Prison Camp System 1917-1934*. Lexington: University Press of Kentucky, 1993.

Jameson, Fredric. *Archaeologies of the Future: The Desire Called Utopia and Other Science Fictions*. London: Verso, 2005.

Janecek, Gerald. *Zaum: The Transrational Poetry of Russian Futurism*. San Diego: San Diego University Press, 1996.

Joyce, Christopher. "The Gulag in Karelia." In *The Economics of Forced Labor: The Soviet Gulag*, edited by Paul R. Gregory and Valery Lazarev, 163-87. Stanford: Hoover Institute Press, 2003.

Kafka, Franz. "The Great Wall of China." In *The Great Wall of China: Stories and Reflections*. New York: Shocken Books, 1970. 83-97.

Karas, Joza. *Music in Terezin 1941-1945*. New York: Beaufort, 1985.

Kataev, Valentin. *Vremia, vpered!* Moscow: Tekst, 2004.

Kelly, Catriona. *Children's World: Growing up in Russia 1890-1991*. New Haven: Yale University Press, 2007.

Kenez, Peter. *The Birth of the Propaganda State: Soviet Methods of Mass Mobilization, 1917-1929*. Cambridge: Cambridge University Press, 1985.

Khapaeva, Dina. *Goticheskoe obshchestvo: morfologiia koshmara*. Moscow: Novoe Literaturnoe Obozrenie, 2007.

------. "Historical Memory in Post-Soviet Gothic Society." *Social Research* 76 (Spring 2009): 359-94.

Khlevniuk, Oleg V. *The History of the Gulag: From Collectivization to the Great Terror*. New Haven: Yale University Press, 2004.

Khodasevich, Valentina. "Takim ia znala Gor'kogo." *Novyi mir* 3 (1968): 11-66.

Kholodov, Efim. *P'esy i gody: Dramaturgiia Nikolaia Pogodina*. Moscow: Sovetskii pisatel', 1967.

Kierkegaard, Soren. *Repetition: An Essay in Experimental Psychology*. New York: Harper, 1941.

Klein, Gerda Wiessman. *All but My Life*. New York: Hill and Wang, 1995.

Klein, Ioakhim. "Belomorkanal: Literatura i propaganda v stalinskoe vremia." *Novoe literaturnoe obozrenie* 71 (2005): 231-62.

Kokurin, A. I., and Ia. N. Mokurov, eds. *Stalinskie stroiki GULAGa*. Moscow: Materik, 2005.

Kotkin, Stephen. *Magnetic Mountain: Stalinism as Civilization*. Berkeley: University of California Press, 1995.

Kowalsky, Sharon A. *Deviant Women: Female Crime and Criminology in Revolutionary Russia 1880-1930*. DeKalb, IL: Northern Illinois University Press, 2009.

LaCapra, Dominick. *Writing History, Writing Trauma*. Baltimore: Johns Hopkins University Press, 2001.

Lahusen, Thomas. *How Life Writes the Book: Real Socialism and Socialist Realism in Stalin's Russia*. Ithaca, NY: Cornell University Press, 1997.

Lambert, Alix. *Russian Prison Tattoos*. Atglen, PA: Schiffer, 2003.

Lawton, Anna and Herbert Eagle, eds. *Russian Futurism through Its Manifestoes, 1912-1928*. Ithaca, NY: Cornell University Press, 1988.

Lenin, V. I. *Selected Works in Two Volumes*. Moscow: Foreign Language Publishing House, 1952.

Likhachev, D. S. "Cherty pervobytnogo primitivizma vorovskoi rechi." *Iazyk i myshlenie*, 3-4 (1935): 47-100.

------. *Ia vospominaiu*. Moscow: Progress, 1991.

------. "Kartezhnye igry ugolovnikov." In *Stat'i rannikh let*, 45-53. Tver': Tverskoe oblastnoe otdelenie rossiiskogo fonda kul'tury, 1993.

Lipovetskii, Mark and Aleksandr Etkind. "Vozvrashchenie triton: Sovetskaia katastrofa i postsovetskii roman." *Novoe literaturnoe obozrenie* 94 (2008): 174-206.

Loe, Mary Louise. "Maksim Gor'kii and the Sreda Circle: 1899-1905." *Slavic Review* 44 (1985): 49-66.

Losev, Aleksei. *Zhizn'. Povesti, rasskazy, pis'ma*. St. Petersburg: AO Komplekt, 1993.

------. *Radost' na veki*. Moscow: Russkii Put', 2005.

Lotman, Iurii. *Struktura khudozhestvennogo teksta*. Moscow: Iskusstvo, 1970.

Lotman, Yuri M. *Universe of the Mind: A Semiotic Theory of Culture*. Translated by Ann Shukman. Bloomington, IN: Indiana University Press, 1990.

Maiakovskii, V. V. *Klop*. Moscow: Slovo, 1999, 462-506.

Makarenko, Anton S. *Pedagogicheskaia poema*. Moscow: ITRK, 2003.

------. *The Road to Life*. Translated by Ivy and Tatiana Litvinov. New York: Oriole, 1973.

------. *Sochineniia*. Vol. 5. Moscow: Akademiia pedagogicheskikh nauk, 1951.

Makurov, V. G., ed. *Gulag v Karelii. Sbornik dokumentov i materialov 1930-41*. Petrozavodsk: RAN, 1992.

Mally, Lynn. Exporting Soviet Culture: The Case of Agitprop Theater." *Slavic Review* 2 (2003): 324-42.

Mal'tseva, Alina. "Poema o Belomorkanale." St. Petersburg: Real, 1995.

Margolin, Iulii. *Puteshestvie v stranu ze-ka*. New York: Izd. Chekhova, 1952.

Markov, Vladimir. *Russian Futurism: A History*. Washington, DC: New Academia, 2006.

Martin, Terry. "The Soviet Union as Empire: Salvaging a Dubious Analytical Category," *Ab Imperio* 2 (2002): 91-105.

Marx, Karl. *Capital: A Critique of Political Economy*. Translated by Samuel Moore. New York: International Publishers, 1970.

Mathewson, Jr., Rufus W. *The Positive Hero in Russian Literature*. Stanford: Stanford University Press, 1975.

Mayakovksky, Vladimir. "The Backbone Flute." *The Bedbug and Selected Poetry*. Translated by Max Hayward and George Reavey. Bloomington, IN: Indiana University Press, 1960.

McCauley, Karen A. "Production Literature and the Industrial Imagination." *The Slavic and East European Journal* 42 (1998): 444-66.

McCauley, Martin. *The Soviet Union 1917-1991*. London: Longman, 1993.

McKenzie, Jon. *Perform or Else: From Discipline to Performance*. London: Routledge, 2011.

Meier, A. A. *Filosofskie sochineniia*. Paris: La Presse Libre, 1982.

Miller, Frank. *Folklore for Stalin: Russian Folklore and Pseudofolklore of the Stalin Era*. Armonk, NY: M. E. Sharpe, 1990.

Mil'ianenkov, Lev. *Po tu storonu zakona: Entsiklopediia prestupnogo mira*. Saint Petersburg: Damy i gospoda, 1992.

Morukov, Mikhail. "The White-Baltic Sea Canal." In *The Economics of Forced Labor: The Soviet Gulag*, edited by Paul R. Gregory and Valery Lazarev, 151-62. Stanford: Hoover Institute Press, 2003.

Nakhimovsky, Alice. *Russian-Jewish Literature and Identity: Jabotinsky, Babel, Grossman, Galich, Roziner, Markish*. Baltimore: Johns Hopkins University Press, 1992.

Nehamas, Alexander. *Nietzsche: Life as Literature*. Cambridge, MA: Harvard University Press, 1985.

Neuberger, Joan. *Hooliganism: Crime, Culture, and Power in St. Petersburg 1900-1914*. Berkeley: University of California Press, 1993.

Nikolaev, Mikhail. *Detdom*. New York: Russica, 1985.

Nietzsche, Friedrich. *On the Genealogy of Morals*. Translated by Walter Kaufmann. New York: Vintage, 1967.

------. *Thus Spake Zarathustra. The Portable Nietzsche*. Edited and translated by Walter Kaufmann. New York: Penguin, 1968.

------. *The Gay Science*. Translated by Walter Kaufmann. New York: Random House, 1974.

Nisbet, Peter. "El Lissitzky circa 1935: Two Propaganda Projects Reconsidered." In *Situating El Lissitzky: Vitebsk, Berlin, Moscow*, eds. Nancy Perloff and Brian Reed, 211-34. Los Angeles: Getty, 2003.

Nora, Pierre. "Between Memory and History: Les Lieux de Mémoire." *Representations* 26 (1989): 7-24.

Novitch, Miriam, ed. *Spiritual Resistance: Art from Concentration Camps*. Philadelphia: Jewish Publication Society of America, 1981.

O'Mahony, Mike. *Sport in the USSR: Physical Culture—Visual Culture*. London: Reaktion,

2006.

Orttung, Robert W. and Anthony Latta, eds. *Russia's Battle with Crime, Corruption, and Terrorism*. London: Routledge, 2008.

Pain, Emil'. "Rossiia mezhdu imperiiei i natsiiei," *Pro et Contra* (May-June 2007): 42-59.

Palmer, Scott W. "Peasants into Pilots: Soviet Air-Mindedness as an Ideology of Dominance." *Technology and Culture* 41 (2000): 1-26.

Panteleimonov, B. G. *U podnozhiia promyshlennoi piatiletki „udarnichestvo."* Paris: Soiuz Sovetskikh Patriotov, 1945.

Papazian, Elizabeth Astrid. *Manufacturing Truth: The Documentary Moment in Early Soviet Culture*. DeKalb, IL: Northern Illinois University Press, 2009.

Paperno, Irina. *Stories of the Soviet Experience: Memoirs, Diaries, Dreams*. Ithaca, NY: Cornell University Press, 2009.

Paperno, Irina, and Joan Delaney Grossman. *Creating Life: The Aesthetic Utopia of Russian Modernism*. Stanford: Stanford University Press, 1994.

Paperny, V. "Moscow in the 1930s and the Emergence of a New City." In *The Culture of the Stalin Period*, edited by Hans Günther, 229-39. New York: St. Martin's Press, 1990.

Park, Robert E. *On Social Control and Collective Behavior*. Edited by Ralph H. Turner. Chicago: University of Chicago Press, 1967.

Parrott, Ray J., Jr. "Questions of Art, Face, and Genre in Mikhail Prishvin." *Slavic Review* 3 (1997): 465-74.

Peterson, Nadya L. "Dirty Women: Cultural Connotations of Cleanliness in Soviet Russia." In *Russia, Women, Culture*, edited by Helena Goscilo and Beth Holmgren, 180-97. Bloomington, IN: Indiana University Press, 1996.

Pil'niak, Boris. "Povest' nepogashennoi luny." *Tret'ia stolitsa*. Moscow: Russkaia kniga, 1992, 275-307.

------. *Volga vpadaet v Kaspinskoe more*. Moscow: Knizhnaia palata, 1989, 130-344.

Platonov, Andrei. *The Foundation Pit*. Translated by Robert Chandler and Geoffrey Smith. London: Harvill Press, 1973.

------. *Kotlovan*. St. Petersburg: Azbuka-klassika, 2004.

Pogodin, Nikolai. *Aristocrats*. Translated by Anthony Wixley and Robert S. Carr. New York: International Publishers, 1937.

------. *Aristokraty*. Moscow: Iskusstvo, 1936.

Pohl, J. Otto. *The Stalinist Penal System*. Jefferson, NC: McFarland, 1997.

Primush, N. V. *Udarnichestvo: Mif i real'nost'*. Donetsk: Donbas, 1990.

Prishvin, Mikhail. *V kraiu nepuganykh ptits*. Moscow: Gosudarstvennoe izdatel'stvo khudozhestvennoi literatury, 1934.

------. *Osudareva doroga*. *Sobranie sochinenii*, vol. 3. Moscow: Terra-Knizhnyi Klub, 2006, 227-460.

Presdee, Mike. *Cultural Criminology and the Carnival of Crime*. New York: Routledge, 2000.

Ratushinskaia, Irina. *Seryi—tsvet nadezhdy*. London: Overseas Publications Interchange, 1989.

Robin, Regine. "Stalinism and Popular Culture." In *The Culture of the Stalin Period*, edited by Hans Günther, 15-40. London: Macmillan, 1990.

Rossi, Zhak. *Spravochnik po GULagu*. London: Overseas Publications, 1987.

Rothstein, Robert A. "How It Was Sung in Odessa: At the Intersection of Russian and

Yiddish Folk Culture." *Slavic Review* 4 (Winter 2002): 781-801.
Rubinshtein, L. *Domashnee muzitsirovanie*. Moscow: Novoe literaturnoe obozrenie, 2000.
Ruder, Cynthia A. *Making History for Stalin: The Story of the Belomor Canal*. Gainesville: University Press of Florida, 1998.
------. "Modernist in Form, Socialist in Content: The History of the Construction of the Stalin White Sea-Baltic Canal." *Russian Literature* 44 (1998): 469-84.
Rudnitskii, K. *Portrety dramaturgov*. Moscow: Sovetskii pisatel', 1961.
------. *Russian and Soviet Theatre: Tradition and the Avant-Garde*. Translated by Roxanne Permar. London: Thames and Hudson, 1988.

Sartori, Rosalinde. "Stalinism and Carnival: Organisation and Aesthetics of Political Holidays." In *The Culture of the Stalin Period*, edited by Hans Günter, 41-77. London: Macmillan, 1990.
Scherr, Barry. "Gor'kij's Childhood: The Autobiography as Fiction." *Slavic and East European Journal* 23 (1979): 333-45.
Service, Robert. *A History of Modern Russia*. Cambridge, MA: Harvard University Press, 2009.
Shalamov, Varlam. "Tishina," *Sobranie sochinenii*, vol. 2. Moscow: Khudozhestvennaia literatura, 1998.
Shapovalov, Veronica, ed. and trans. *Remembering the Darkness: Women in Soviet Prisons*. Lanham, MD: Rowman and Littlefield, 2001.
Shearer, David R. "Crime and Social Disorder in Stalin's Russia. A Reassessment of the Great Retreat and the Origins of Mass Repression." *Cahiers du Monde russe* 39 (1998): 119-48.
Shklovskii, Viktor. *Tret'ia fabrika*. Moscow: Krug, 1926.
------. *Sovetskaia literatura na novom etape*. Moscow: Sovetskaia literatura, 1933.
Shklovsky, Viktor. *Third Factory*. Translated by Richard Sheldon. Ann Arbor: Ardis, 1977.
Shlyakhov, Vladimir and Eve Adler, eds. *Russian Slang and Colloquial Expressions*. New York: Barron's, 1999.
Seigel, Jerrold. *The Idea of the Self: Thought and Experience in Western Europe since the Seventeenth Century*. Cambridge: Cambridge University Press, 2005.
Simonov, Konstantin. "Belomorskie stikhi." In *Sbornik molodykh poetov*, 57-62. Moscow: Khudozhestvennaia literatura, 1935.
Siniavskii, Andrei. "Dostoevskii i katorga." *Sintaksis* 9 (1981): 108-11.
------. *Golos iz khora. Sobranie sochinenii*, vol. 2. Moscow: Start, 1992.
Sinyavsky, Andrei. *Ivan the Fool: Russian Folk Belief A Cultural History*. Moscow: Glas, 2007.
Skitalets, Petrov. *Povesti i rasskazy. Vospominaniia*. Moscow: Moskovskii rabochii, 1960.
Slezkine, Yuri. *The Jewish Century*. Princeton: Princeton University Press, 2004.
Smith, Joseph. *Working the Rough Stone: Freemasonry and Society in Eighteenth-Century Russia*. DeKalb: Northern Illinois University Press, 1999.
Smith, Neil. *Uneven Development: Nature, Capital, and the Production of Space*. Athens, GA: University of Georgia Press, 2008.
Snyder, Timothy. "Holocaust: The Ignored Reality." *New York Times Review of Books* 12 (16 July 2009): 14-16.
Solzhenitsyn, Aleksandr. *Arkhipelag GULag 1918-1956: opyt khudozhestvennogo issledovaniia. III-IV*. Paris: YMCA Press, 1974.
------. *Odin den' Ivana Denisovicha*. Moscow: Slovo, 2001.
Sovetskaia literatura na novom etape. Moscow: Sovetskaia literatura, 1933.

Spiridonova, Lidiia. "Gorky and Stalin (According to New Materials from A. M. Gorky's Archive)." *Russian Review* 54 (1995): 413-23.

------, ed. *Gor'kii i ego korrespondenty*. Moscow: IMLI RAN, 2005.

Stites, Richard. *Revolutionary Dreams: Utopian Vision and the Experimental Life in the Russian Revolution*. New York: Oxford University Press, 1988.

Stratanovskii, Sergei. "Gidroarteriia." *Zvezda* 2 (1994): 75-77.

Sullivan, Nikki. *Tattooed Bodies: Subjectivity, Textuality, Ethics, and Pleasure*. Westport: Praeger, 2001.

Suny, Ronald. "Ambiguous Categories: States, Empires, and Nations." *Post-Soviet Affairs* 11 (1995): 185-96.

Sylvester, Roshanna P. *Tales from Old Odessa: Crime and Civility in a City of Thieves*. DeKalb, IL: Northern Illinois University Press, 2005.

Teitelbaum, Matthew, ed. *Montage and Modern Life 1919-1942*. Cambridge: MIT Press, 1992.

"Tema GULAGa. Znachimoe otsutstvie." *Iskusstvo kino* 5 (2007): 5-14.

Terent'ev, Igor'. *Moi pokhorony: Stikhi. Pis'ma. Sledstvennye pokazaniia. Dokumenty*. Moscow: GILEIA, 1993.

------. *Sobranie sochinenii*. Eurasiatica. Bologna: S. Francesco, 1988.

Terent'eva, Tat'iana. "Moi otets Igor' Terent'ev." *Zaumnyi futurism i dadism v russkoi kul'ture*. Eds. Luigi Magarotto, Marco Marciaduri and Daniela Rizzi. Bern: Peter Lang, 1991, 353-60.

Terts, Abram. *Golos iz khora. Sobranie sochinenii*. Vol. 1. Moscow: Start, 1992, 437-669.

Tertz, Abram. *A Voice from the Chorus*. Translated by Kyril Fitzlyon and Max Hayward. New York: Farrar, Straus, and Giroux, 1976.

Tolczyk, Dariusz. *See No Evil: Literary Cover-Ups and Discoveries of the Soviet Camp Experience*. New Haven: Yale University Press, 2004.

Transchel, Kate. *Under the Influence: Working Class Drinking, Temperance and Cultural Revolution in Russia 1895-1932*. Pittsburgh: University of Pittsburgh Press, 2006.

Tret'iakov, Sergei. "Novyi Lev Tolstoi." *Literatura fakta*. Ed. N. Chuzak. Munich: Wilhelm Fink, 1972.

Trotskii, Lev. *Literatura i revoliutsiia*. Moscow: Izdatel'stvo politicheskoi literatury, 1991.

------. *Literature and Revolution*. Translated by Rose Strunsky. Ann Arbor: University of Michigan Press, 1970.

Tsygankov, Anatolii. *Ikh nazyvali KR: Represii v Karelii 20-30-x godov*. Petrozavodsk: Kareliia, 1992.

Tupitsyn, Margarita. "From the Politics of Montage to the Montage of Politics: Soviet Practice 1919 through 1937." In *Montage and Modern Life 1919-1942*, edited by Matthew Teitelbaum, 82-127. Cambridge: MIT Press, 1992.

Tvorchestvo i byt GULAGa. Moscow: Zven'ia, 1998.

Vatulescu, Cristina. "Arresting Biographies: The Secret Police File in the Soviet Union and Romania." *Comparative Literature* 3 (2004): 243-61.

Vitkovskii, Dmitrii. "Polzhizni." *Znamia* 6 (1991): 107-16.

Voinov, Vadim. *Pons per styx. Most cherez stiks*. St. Petersburg: Dean, 1994.

------. *A Convoluted Monograph*. St. Petersburg: Dean, 2002.

Volkov-Lannit, L. *Aleksandr Rodchenko risuet, fotografiruet, sporit*. Moscow: Iskusstvo, 1968.

Waldman, Diane. *Collage, Assemblage, and the Found Object*. New York: Harry Abrams, 1992.
Ware, Timothy. *The Orthodox Church*. New York: Penguin, 1997.
Weil, Irwin. *Gorky: His Literary Development and Influence on Soviet Intellectual Life*. New York: Random House, 1966.
Weinberg, Robert. *Stalin's Forgotten Zion: Birobidzhan and the Making of a Soviet Jewish Homeland*. Berkeley: University of California Press, 1998.
Weisstein, Ulrich. "Collage, Montage, and Related Terms: Their Literal and Figurative Use in and Application to Techniques and Forms in Various Arts." *Comparative Literature Studies* 15 (1978): 124-39.
Widdis, Emma. "To Explore or Conquer? Mobile Perspectives on the Soviet Cultural Revolution." In *The Landscape of Stalinism: The Art and Ideology of Soviet Space*, edited by Evgeny Dobrenko and Eric Naiman, 219-40. Seattle: University of Washington Press, 2003.
------. *Visions of a New Land: Soviet Film from the Revolution to the Second World War*. New Haven: Yale University Press, 2003.
Willan, T. S. *The Early History of the Russia Company*. New York: Augustus M. Kelley, 1956.
Wolf, Erika. "The Visual Economy of Forced Labor: Alexander Rodchenko and the White Sea-Baltic Canal." In *Picturing Russia: Explorations in Visual Culture*, edited by Valerie A. Kivelson and Joan Neuberger, 168-74. New Haven: Yale University Press, 2008.
Weil, Irwin. *Gorky: His Literary Development and Influence on Soviet Intellectual Life*. New York: Random House, 1966.

Yedlin, Tovah. *Maxim Gorky: A Political Biography*. Westport, CT: Praeger, 1999.
Young, James. "The Counter-Monument: Memory against Itself in Germany Today." *Critical Inquiry* 18 (1992): 267-96.
Young, Sarah J. "Recalling the Dead: Repetition, Identity, and the Witness in Varlam Shalamov's *Kolymskie rasskazy*." *Slavic Review* 2 (2011): 353-72.
------. "Criminializing Creativity: Language, Performance, and the Representation of Convicts in Imperial and Soviet Era Prisons and Penal Colonies." Forthcoming in: *Acta Universitatis Upsaliensis, Eastern Europe Series*.
Yurchak, Alexei. *Everything Was Forever, Until It Was No More*. Princeton: Princeton University Press, 2006.

Zaitsev, N. *Nikolai Fedorovich Pogodin*. Leningrad: Iskusstvo, 1958.
Zaleskii, V. "Sovetskaia p'esa." *Sovetskii teatr* 1 (1935): 7.
Zamiatin, Evgenii. *Litsa*. NY: Mezhdunarodnoe literaturnoe sodruzhestvo, 1967.
------. *My. Sochineniia*. Moscow: Kniga, 1988, 7-154.
------. *We*. Translated by Clarence Brown. New York: Penguin, 1993.

Films

Cherviakov, Evgenii, dir. *Zakliuchennye* [*The Prisoners*]. 1936.
Ekk, Nikolai, dir. *Putevka v zhizn'* [*Road to Life*]. 1931.
German, Aleksei, dir. *Moi drug Ivan Lapshin* [*My Friend Ivan Lapshin*]. 1984.
Goldosvkaia, Marina, dir. *Vlast' Solovetskaia* [*Solovki Power*]. 1988.
Gusman, Iulii, dir. *Park Sovetskogo perioda* [*Soviet Era Park*]. 2006.
Hartwick, Alan, dir. *Beyond Torture: The Gulag of Pitetsi*. 2007.
Lemberg, Aleksandr, dir. *Belomorkanal* [*The White Sea Canal*]. 1936.
------. *Belomorskoe-Baltiiskii vodnyi put'* [*The Belomor-Baltic Waterway*]. 1932.
------. *Belomorstroi raportuet* [*Belomorstroi Reports*]. 1933.
------. *Port piati morei* [*Port of Five Seas*]. 1932-33.
Mileiko, V., dir. *Kanal imeni Stalina* [*Stalin's Canal*]. 1992.
Shakhverdiev, Tofik, dir. *Stalin s nami?* [*Stalin Is with Us?*]. 1988.
Tarkovskii, Andrei, dir. *Stalker*. 1979.

Newspapers and Periodicals

Karelo-Murmanskii krai.
Krasnaia tabachnitsa.
Perekovka.
Pravda.
SSSR na stroike.
Tridtsat' dnei.
Vokrug sveta.

INDEX

Adamova-Sliozberg, Ol'ga 27
Aleksandrov, Grigorii 110, 141, 175
   Circus 110, 141
   Volga-Volga 175
All-Proletarian Home 92, 181
Alymov, Sergei 24, 83-6, 95, 98, 107, 114-15, 120, 123, 143, 165, 168, 179, 205, 210, 213
   "B. M. S." 85
   "Explosions and Music" 114
   Kiosk of Tenderness 99
   "Love of Two Seas, The" 85
   "Wedding of the Seas, The" 85
Anderson, R. Lanier 9, 208
Antonov, Fedor 36
Argunov, N. 146-7
Aristotle 172
Arkhangel'sk 35, 141
Atiasov, Vasilii 57
Auschwitz 190
Averbakh, Leopol'd L. 165
Azhaev, Vasilii 128
   "Montage of Life, The" 128
Azov Sea 141

Baikal-Amur 128
Bakhtin, Mikhail 154
Baltic Sea 30, 35, 85, 130, 140-1, 170
Bannikova, Marina 100
Barnes, Stephen 20
   Death and Redemption 20
BBK 101, 136, 203
BelBaltLag 36, 78
Beloe lake 130
Belomor 11-20, 27-35, 38-42, 47-8, 59, 79, 83, 101-9, 126, 149-51, 157-8, 163, 173-5, 196-9
   art and theater 33, 48, 87, 109, 117-9, 124, 128-9, 145, 148-9, 187-90
   music 111, 113-5, 124, 143
   narratives 12, 33-4, 56, 71-2, 7?, 85, 90-1, 95, 98-100, 111, 116, 122, 124-5, 135, 137, 143, 165-7, 176, 178-82, 194
   poetry 84-5, 98, 125, 168, 183
   prisoner life 43-4, 68, 73, 78, 80, 84, 89, 92, 96, 99, 145-7, 159, 180
   reforging (*perekovka*) 21, 23, 25, 31, 41, 44, 64, 75, 77-8, 107, 135, 146, 153
   selfhood 32, 53, 127
   see White Sea-Baltic Canal
Belomorkanal, brand 34-5, 83, 166, 168, 176-7, 187, 189-90, 192-5
Belomorkanal, rock group 190-1
   "I Am Not Guilty" 191
   "Letter from Prison" 191
   "Night before Execution" 191
   Song Frame of Mind 191
   "Thief" 191
   "*Zek* in Freedom" 191
Belomorstroi 36, 92, 158
Belov, Petr 176, 184-5, 188-90, 193-4, 196
   Belomorkanal 189
   Rooks Have Arrived, The 189, 194
   White Sea Canal 189
Bentham, Jeremy 79
Berdiaev, Nikolai 171
Berman, Matvei 131
Bessonov, Abram 68
Black Sea 30, 141
Blium, N. A. 41, 78, 88, 109
   Mister Stupid and the Shock-workers of Belbaltlag 78, 88
Bobriki 141
Bogdanov, Aleksei 29
Bolshevism 23, 25, 28-9, 44, 46, 48, 58, 60, 112, 122, 142, 153, 166-7
Braque, Georges 124-5
Bulgakov, Mikhail 159
   Master and Margarita 159
Butler, Judith 159
   Gender Trouble 159
Butyrka prison 101

Index

Caspian Sea 141
Caucasus 11
Central Council of the Society of Proletariat Tourism and Excursion 136
"White Sea-Baltic Canal and the Polar Region" 136
Chekist, The 37
Cheliabinsk 141
Chernyshevskii, Nikolai 24
What Is to Be Done? 24
Cherviakov, Evgenii 120
Prisoners, The 120, 137
Clark, Katerina 43
Soviet Novel, The 43
Communist Party 12, 23, 25, 28, 67, 70, 73, 137, 150, 153, 183
Condee, Nancy 9
Crimea 11
Cultural Revolution 14, 107-8

Dachau 190
Dalinin, Viacheslav 9
Danzas, Iuliia 162
Daughton, J. P. 9
DeBlasio, Alyssa 9
"Declaration of Transrational Language" 98
Dicker-Brandeis, Freidl 47
Dickerman, Leah 135
Dimitriev, Endi 92-3
"Factory of Life, The" 92
Dmitlag 100
DnieproGES 141
Dobson, Miriam 34
Dolgun, Alexander 113
Dostoevsky, Fedor 24, 124, 149
Dubois, W. E. B. 28, 147
Dunaevskii, Issak 110-11, 142
"Song of the Motherland" 110-11
Dvorzhetskii, Vatslav 146, 154-5, 157

Eisenstein, Sergei 137-8, 184
Egypt 40
Epstein, Mikhail 194
Erenburg, Il'ia 159
Trest D. E. 159
Erman, Irina 9

Fedor Dostoevsky 10, 24
Underground Man 149

Firin, Semen 56, 99-100, 131-2
First Congress of Soviet Writers 29, 58, 70
Five-Year Plan 19, 23, 42, 55, 57, 115, 120, 126, 130, 137, 141, 149-50, 166, 182, 190
Florenskii, P. A. 127
Fonvizin, Denis 88
Foucault, Michel 25-6, 207
Freidin, Grisha 9
Frenkel', Naftalii 24, 37, 56
Freud, Sigmund 195
From Crime to Labor 44, 46, 49, 109
Furaeva, Lelia 100

GARF (State Archive of the Russian Federation) 21
Germany 46, 118, 190
Gladkov, Fedor 17, 119
Cement 119
Goethe 172, 181
Faust 32, 181-2
Goffman, Erving 20, 145, 147, 199
Gorcheva, Alla 83
Gor'kii 141
Gorky, Maxim 11-12, 23, 26, 29-31, 52, 54, 56-7, 70, 72, 108, 112, 134, 145, 170
Mother 29
New Life 30
"On How I Learned to Write" 31
Greenleaf, Monika 9
Groys, Boris 96
Guerin, Frances 195
Gusman, Iulii 192
Soviet Park 192

Halfin, Igal 20, 23, 26
Halls, Roger 195
Hellbeck, Jochen 20-1, 26, 206
"History of Factories and Plants" 56-7
History of the Construction of the White Sea-Baltic Canal 31, 38, 52-4, 56-7, 83, 86, 103, 107-8, 112, 126, 150-1, 162, 165, 168, 170-6, 184, 198
Holocaust 33, 48, 188, 190
Hullinger, Edwin Ware 158-9
Reforging of Russia, The 158

Iagoda, Genrikh 37, 100, 131-2

Index

Iansen, D. 115, 117
Il'inichna, Elena 69
Inber, Vera 108, 112, 174-5
Iofan, Boris 150
Isaeva, Lidiia 160
Ivanov, A. K. 58-60
  "Karas'" 58-60
Ivanov, Vsevelod 148-9
Ivanova, Tamara 148-9

Kabanenko, Fillipp 60
Kafka, Franz 126
  "Great Wall of China, The" 126
Karelia 31, 35-7, 54, 58, 62, 93, 130, 139-40, 167, 170, 173, 190, 192, 194
Karelo-Murmanskii krai 100, 145
Kavshchyn, Vladimir 11
Kem' 157
Kharkhordin, Oleg 26
Khilingorsk 141
Khlebnikov, Velimir 98
Kirichenko, Vlasa 143
Kitchner, Iosif 90-1, 93-5, 98, 109
  "Breaking Point" 90
  "Moan of Stones, The" 90-1, 93
Klimova, Olga 9
Klutsis, Gustav 118, 124, 128
Kogan, Lazar' 37, 56, 131
Koldobenko, Mikhail 60, 64-5, 91, 107
  "Bura" 91
  "Filter" 107
Kolyma 27
Komsomol 73, 142
Koshelev, Grigorii 61-2, 64
  "My Path" 61
Kotkin, Stephen 23
Kremkov 114, 116
  "Hymn to Labor Competition" 116
  "Tournament of Labor" 116
Kresty prison 17
Kruchenykh, Aleksei 96, 99
Kupriianov, Andrei 17-18, 86
Kuzbass 168
Kuznetsk 141
Kuznetsov, Vladimir 100
KVO 43

Ladozhskoe lake 130
Lahusen, Thomas 20, 33
Lake Onega 36

Lemberg, Aleksandr 137-8, 140-2, 178
  Belomorstroi Reports 140, 178
  Port of Five Seas 140-1
  White Sea-Baltic Waterway, The 138
Lenin, Vladimir 28, 45, 52, 110-11, 137, 163
Leningrad 17, 141, 146, 183; *see* St. Petersburg
Leonov, Leonid 176
  Soviet River 176
Likhachev, Dmitri 11, 148
Liudi Stalingradskogo Traktornogo 56
Losev, Lev 157-9
  "From a Conversation at the Belomor Construction" 157
Lubianka 120
Lugansk 141
Lunacharskii, Anatolii 29

Magnitogorsk 141
Makarenko, Anton 71-3
  Road to Life, The 71
Malevich, Kasimir 118
Mal'tseva, Alina 183
  "Poem about the Belomorkanal" 183
"Map-guide" 130
Marx, Karl 168, 172
  Capital 172
Marxism 19, 28, 45, 50
Marxism-Leninism 28, 30, 42
Maslov, V. N. 39, 56, 173
Mayakovsky, Vladimir 10, 23-4, 98, 145, 159
  Bedbug 159
Medvezh'egorsk 155, 174
Medvezh'ia Gora 182
Meier, Aleksandr 181-3, 230, 240
  Three Sources 182
  Victim 182
Mel'nikov, G. 63, 107, 110, 114-16, 128
  "From the Baltic to the White" 107, 110, 115
Mirkin, Boris 9
Moiseev, Semen 71, 128
Moldavanka 102-3
Molotov, Viacheslav 36-7
Moscow 11, 13, 34-5, 42, 100-1, 108, 111, 141, 153, 155, 158, 163, 165, 171, 175, 192
Moscow Bureau for the Study of the

Criminal Personality and Crime 45, 48
Moscow's Criminal World 48
Moscow-Volga Canal 44, 46, 52, 100, 128, 168, 170, 175-6, 182, 187
"Music Is Playing in the Moldovanka" 102, 123, 197
My Universities 12

Nalbandian, Dmitri 131-2
Neuberger, Joan 108
New Man 14, 25, 31, 40-1, 52, 57, 70-1, 153, 171
Nietzsche, Friedrich 26-9, 31-2
  Gay Science, The 29
  Thus Spake Zarathustra 26-7, 29
Nikolaev, Mikhail 71
Nizhnii Novgorod 157

Odessa 77, 102-3, 123, 141
OGPU 36-7, 39, 42, 44, 65, 68, 73, 140
Olesha, Iurii 70
  Envy 60
Onezhskoe lake 130
Ostrovskii, Nikolai 60
  How the Steel Was Tempered 60

Palace of the Soviets 141, 150, 163
Panama Canal 55, 115
Panopticon 79, 138, 196
Papazian, Elizabeth 80
Paperno, Irina 20
Perekovka, newspaper 63, 78-80, 82-3, 85-8, 95, 98, 107, 114, 116-7, 125, 153, 155, 174
Peter the Great 35, 121, 175, 178
"Photo-Tourist" 131
Picasso, Pablo 124-5
Pil'niak, Boris 176
  Volga Flows into the Caspian Sea, The 176
Plato's *Republic* 25
Platonov, Andrei 70, 92, 142, 163, 176, 181
  "Epiphan Locks, The" 176
  Foundation Pit, The 70, 92, 142, 163, 181, 197
Podgorskaia, Motia 161
Pogodin, Nikolai 69, 102, 119-23, 137, 143, 147, 154, 162, 198
  Aristocrats, The 41, 69, 102, 119-20, 143, 154, 162, 197

Polevoi, Boris 60
  Story about a Real Man 60
Politburo 36
Polokhin, Mikhail 66-7, 198
Povenets 66, 99, 119
Pravda 151
Prishvin, Mikhail 35, 54, 135, 143, 167
  In the Land of the Unfrightened Birds 54, 135, 143, 167
  "Little Spruce Island" 167
  Tsar's Road, The 35
Pushkin, Aleksandr 26, 77, 124
Pushkinskaia 10 184

Rapoport, Iakov 37, 56, 157, 170-1
Ratushinskaia, Irina 27
Real Man 60
Red Tobacco 190
RGALI (Russian State Archive for Literature and Art) 21, 84
Rodchenko, Aleksandr 32, 118, 124, 128, 132, 134-5, 143
  "Reconstructions of the Artist" 135
Rostov-on-Don 11, 141
Rozanov, Vasilii 26
Ruder, Cynthia 9, 13
RUR 69, 76
Russia 14, 26, 35-8, 48, 84, 89, 127, 141, 166-7, 171
  contemporary 35, 40, 165, 177-8, 190, 193-4
  culture 15, 23-4, 70, 77, 108, 118, 145
  pre-Revolutionary 36-7, 40, 46, 71, 112, 197
Russia Company, The 35

Safran, Gabriella 9
Savel'ev, Mikhail 100
Seigel, Jerrold 26, 53
Senderovich, Sasha 9
Shaginian, Marietta 176
  Hydro-central 176
Shalamov, Varlam 27
Shklovskii, Viktor 12, 31, 41, 145, 174
Shumovskii, Teodor 127
Shuvalov palace 98
Siberia 11, 19, 168
Siniavskii, Andrei 76, 102
Skachko, Praskov'ia 76-7, 147, 160
"Slap in the Face of Public Taste" 124

Sobolev, Iurii 100
Society of Proletariat Tourism and Excursion 136
Solikansk 141
Solovki 11, 24, 30, 62, 155, 162, 176, 185
Solzhenitsyn, Aleksandr 51, 165, 176
  "Archipelago Metastasizes, The" 176
  Gulag Archipelago 165, 176-7
  One Day in the Life of Ivan Denisovich 51
Soviet Union 13-15, 21, 29, 32, 37-8, 44-8, 57, 86, 89, 107, 110-1, 127-8, 134, 141-2, 149-51, 158, 163, 166-7, 186, 190, 197
  ideology 25, 31, 38, 42, 50-1, 60-1, 71, 105, 166, 170
  see USSR
Spielberg, Steven 188
St. Petersburg 17, 24, 98, 108, 146, 175-6, 181, 183-4
Stakhanov, Aleksei 150
Stalin 30, 36, 44, 46-7, 84, 107, 130-4, 143, 145, 151, 160, 170-1, 175-6, 183, 186
Stalin Is With Us 113
Stalingrad 141
Stalinism 14, 16, 19, 21-6, 33, 35, 40, 49, 101, 114, 132, 142-4, 149-51, 157, 164, 177, 185, 188, 196
Stanislavsky 149
Stratanovskii, Sergei 176-8, 181-4, 188-9
  "Waterway" (Gidroarteriia) 178-82
Suez Canal 55, 115
Sukhanovka 120
Sverdlovsk 141

Tashkent, *see* Polokhin
Terent'ev, Igor' 40, 80, 96, 98-101, 109, 116-19, 132, 157
Terent'eva, Tat'iana 100-1
Terezin 33, 47
Thirty Days 78, 198
  "Conversation in Prison" 198
Thomas, James 9
Tolstoy 80, 124
Transsiberian 192
Tret'iakov, Sergei 80
Trotsky, Leon 25, 111, 142, 171-2
  Literature and Revolution 171
Tupikov, Fedor 67-8
Turkestan 168

USSR 17, 45-6, 57, 62, 110, 130, 141; *see* Soviet Union
USSR in Construction 85-6, 118, 123, 128, 132, 134, 141, 143, 168, 187

Vedernikov, Prokofii 167
Vertov, Dziga 128, 138
  Enthusiasm 128
Vitkovskii, Dmitrii 44
Vladivostok 99
Voinov, Vadim 176, 183-8, 196
  Conditioned Reflex 185
  Difficulties of Growing Up, The 186
  Here's Your Shovel 186
  Pharaoh's Profile II, The 186
  Purge, The 185
  Record 186
  Silhouette of a Proletarian 186
  Smoking Break 187
  We Have Constructed 186
  Wounded Elephant in a Family Album 185
Volga River 134
Volkhov 141
Vziaemskii, Orest 64

We Will Unite the Seas! 85-6
White Sea 35-6, 85, 130, 140-1
White Sea-Baltic Canal 13, 19, 24, 50, 55, 60, 62, 70-5, 96, 99-102, 127-8, 130, 137, 151, 155, 166-8, 174, 183, 192-3
  and the arts 70, 78-80, 89-90, 101, 124, 131, 139, 145-6, 157, 159, 176-8, 183, 189
  construction 25, 34-8, 41, 46, 119, 126, 141, 143, 146, 163, 170
  reforging (*perekovka*) 25, 41-3, 53, 58, 72-3, 79, 173
  see Belomor
Widdis, Emma 61
Worker and the Theater, The 117

Zarod, Kazimierz 113
Zdanevich, Ilya 96
Zdanevich, Kirill 96
Zemskov, Viktor N. 37
Zhdanov, Andrei 183
Zhitkov, Iosima Korneevich 67
Zoshchenko, Mikhail 12, 52, 148-9

www.ingramcontent.com/pod-product-compliance
Lightning Source LLC
Chambersburg PA
CBHW071738150426
43191CB00010B/1622